Housing Finance and the Urban Poor

For Jan, Merijn and Peter

Housing Finance and the Urban Poor

Peer Smets

RAWAT PUBLICATIONS
Jaipur and New Delhi

ISBN 81-7033-878-6

Published by
Prem Rawat for Rawat Publications
Satyam Apts., Sector 3, Jawahar Nagar, Jaipur - 302 004 (India)
Phone: 0141 265 1748 / 7006 Fax: 0141 265 1748
E-mail : info@rawatbooks.com
Website: rawatbooks.com

Delhi Office
4858/24, Ansari Road, Daryaganj, New Delhi 110 002
Phone: 011-23263290

Printed at Chaman Enterprises, New Delhi

Contents

List of tables, figures and boxes

List of tables

List of figures

List of boxes

Preface

This book is the result of the research project entitled 'finance of low-income housing and basic facilities in Hyderabad, India' Fieldwork for this project took place in 1993-94 and 1996. To a large extent I was guided through this project by Jan van der Linden, who familiarised me with theoretical and practical insights into the living conditions in Third World Cities. However, I was deeply saddened when he fell seriously ill in 1996. By the end of 1997 he had retired from his academic activities and died on 20th November 1998. Despite his death, he remained a great inspiration for the writing of this book. This is why I have dedicated this book to his memory. The second person to whom this book is devoted to is my wonderful daughter Merijn, who entered this world just a couple of months after Jan died. Death and life still continued to surround this Ph.D. project. In August 2000, Peter Kloos, my original promotor, passed away. It was a strange and sad experience to return from a trip to India and Pakistan, and then attend his funeral within hours after my arrival in the Netherlands. It was less than a month before that we had discussed the progress of my book. Things change so quickly in life. Peter is thus the third person to whom I dedicate this work. Jan's work had been taken over by Ot van den Muijzenberg and after Peter passed away Isa Baud became involved in this Ph.D. project. Both became my promotors and I am extremely grateful for their guidance. Ot and Isa have helped me to bring this book to its conclusion.

The research project, which forms the basis for this book, was financed by the Vrije Universiteit, Amsterdam and the Dutch Ministry of Development Affairs. First of all, I want to stress that this book could only have been written with the co-operation of slum dwellers, slum leaders, and financial agents such as moneylenders, pawnbrokers, and chit fund organisers in the Indian city of Hyderabad. Furthermore, I am indebted to G. Ramalakshmi and M. Ramesh who assisted me in the slum areas in gathering the desired information.

Apart from the fieldwork in the slum areas, I would like to thank all the employees I have interviewed from the Municipal Corporation of

Hyderabad, the Collectorate, the Hyderabad Urban Development Authority, the Andhra Pradesh State Housing Corporation, the Andhra Pradesh Urban Development and Housing Corporation, the Housing Board, the Housing and Urban Development Corporation, the Al-Ameen Islamic Financial & Investment Corporation, the Housing Development Finance Corporation, Canfin Homes Ltd., LIC Housing Finance Ltd., Dewan Housing Finance Development Ltd., GIC Housing Finance Ltd., AB Homes Finance Ltd., Vysya Bank Housing Finance Ltd., Fairgrowth Home Finance Ltd., the National Housing Bank, Abt consultants, SPARC, NSDF, the Federation of Thrift and Credit Associations, and other Indian NGOs involved in habitat improvement schemes.

During my fieldwork in Hyderabad I resided at the campus of the Centre for Economic and Social Studies (CESS), where I was afforded the use of the institute's facilities and could enjoy the beautiful green scenery of the campus which is centrally located in Hyderabad. At CESS many people helped me in different ways and quite a lot of people acquired a special place in my heart. I do not want to mention them all for fear of missing one out. The neighbours and their children were also great. During my stay in Hyderabad, I had moral support through correspondence, phone calls and personal visits (especially Marjan who stayed for four months) that I appreciated a lot.

I could never have got in touch with CESS without the co-operation of the Centre for Asian Studies Amsterdam (CASA). Furthermore, my contact with the Institute for Housing and Urban Development Studies (IHS) in Rotterdam and the Human Settlement Management Institute (HSMI) in New Delhi was extremely helpful in facilitating my fieldwork. I should not forget to mention the Municipal Corporation of Hyderabad, whose employees helped me to familiarise myself with the city and its slum areas and the employees of the agencies dealing with basic facilities in Hyderabad

I am indebted to members of the CASA promotion group under guidance of Jan Breman and Ot van den Muijzenberg, where first drafts of chapters of this thesis have been discussed. In addition, the 'Mutuals Group' that deals with savings and credit arrangements at the Amsterdam School for Social Science Research (Erik Bähre, Aspha Bijnaar, Abdulah Kane, Marcel van der Linden, Hotze Lont, and Abram de Swaan) has offered me a lot of interesting discussions and insights in the operation of financial mutuals in context. Moreover, I am grateful to Ad de Bruijne, Meine Pieter van Dijk, Bob Goudzwaard, Mayke Kaag, Peter Kloos, Dick Kooiman, Jan van der Linden, Paul van Lindert, Philip Quarles van Ufford, D. Narasimha Reddy, Mark Robinson,

Mike Rodell, James Scott, Theo van Tilburg, and several anonymous referees for commenting on earlier versions of the entire book or parts of it. Thanks are also due to Thérèse Onderdenwijngaard, Marlies van der Kroft and Isa Baud for brainstorming on the title of this book and to Paul van Lindert for his enthusiastic support. In addition, I would like to thank Carmen Mensink for designing the cover of the book, Sjoukje Rienks for the lay out and Jo Swabe for improving my English.

Finally, I would like to thank my AIO (Ph.D. candidates) room mates: Alfons van Marrewijk, Daniel Miguez, Kassahun Berhany Alemu, Mayke Kaag, and Frans Kamsteeg. Moreover, I want to stress that I hope that I did not forget to mention specific persons or institutions. If so, my heartfelt apologies.

Finally, it should be mentioned that parts of this book have been earlier appeared in the following publications:

1995 Poor and in need for a house in the city! The government is there to help, but who is really helping who?, *Nagarlok*, 27 (4): 78-92.

1996 *Informal housing finance in Hyderabad, India*. Urban research working papers, no. 40. Amsterdam: Vrije Universiteit.

1996 Community-based finance systems and their potential for urban self-help in a new South Africa, *Development Southern Africa*, 13 (2): 173-187.

1997 Private housing finance in India: reaching down-market? *Habitat International*, 21 (1): 1-15.

1999 Housing finance trapped in a dilemma of perceptions: affordability criteria for the urban poor questioned, *Housing Studies*, 14 (6): 821-838.

1999 (co-authored with R.-J. Baken). Better a 'Hut' on the Ground than a Castle in the Air: Public and Informal Housing Finance for the Urban Poor in Andhra Pradesh, India. In: K. Datta & G.A. Jones (eds), *Housing and Finance in Developing Countries*, London: Routledge.

2001 Self-help housing finance in Hyderabad: exploitation or hope for the improvement of slum housing. In: R.S. Sandhu, S.S. Minhas & J. Sandhu (eds), *Sustainable Human Settlements: The Asian Experience*. Jaipur, New Delhi: Rawat.

Introduction

To improve his living conditions Mohandas decides to leave his village without his wife and children and migrates to Hyderabad. Mohandas needs to earn cash due to a severe drought in his village area, which lasted for three years and led to harvest failures. When he arrives in the city, he visits some former villagers, who have already been settled in the city. Mohandas asks them for help in finding a job and is glad that he can stay with them for the time being. Eager to make his own income as a coolie, Mohandas starts building a dwelling, for which purpose he obtains a plot illegally. However, he lacks money for the construction of even a hut and no bank is willing to provide him a loan, because these institutions do not trust that he can and will repay it and consequently consider issuing a loan to him too risky. Mohandas takes out a loan from someone of his village of origin, but this is far from sufficient to cover the construction costs. This credit is supplemented with finance from a moneylender in Hyderabad, to whom he is introduced by a former village-mate, who has already lived in Hyderabad for five years. After the hut is finished, Mohandas' wife and children come over. A couple of years later when the loans are repaid and no other pressing needs arise, the dwelling is improved. The mud walls are plastered with cement and the roof, made out of leaves, is replaced by corrugated iron sheets. Again he mobilises finance from several sources, this time a financial self-help organisation, a moneylender and his employer.

Millions of similar cases occur in Third World cities. Even though the largest share of urban growth comes from within the city, migration still contributes considerably to the growth of cities (UNCHS 1996). The visibility of poverty in the world's big cities has triggered an ongoing debate about ways of solving or at least ameliorating this socially unaccepted situation. For example, new settlers in Third World Cities need finance to settle. They cannot pay for a dwelling out of their own pockets and are dependent on external financial sources. In practice, urban settlers, especially the poor, mostly have no other option than mobilising external finance outside the banking sector to finance the construction of their dwelling. In addition to difficulties in the mobilisation of sufficient capital for housing loans, the affordability of specific terms and conditions for specific target groups and institutional problems of housing finance institutions are all elements of the discussion. The debate surrounding housing finance has mainly had a policy implementation focus. As a consequence of the policy-oriented debate on housing finance, Ward & Macoloo (1992) have concluded that theory on housing finance is not very well developed and a link between social theory and housing finance is absent. This weakens the policy debate on housing finance, because financial processes are integrally linked to other areas of society, from the macro-institutional level down to that of household interactions. Group lending, for example, has become increasingly popular, consequently requiring insight in issues such as power, trust, and grassroots action. Insight in the theoretical debate could even improve the policy-making process. A mechanistic view frequently adopted, which regards solving the housing problem as basically a matter of availability of money. It is hard to fully substantiate this claim, but Jones and Datta state:

> 'In drawing direct causal link between finance and housing, for example, researchers have not looked at how finance impacts on other financial flows within the household. Research, therefore, has not managed to isolate the loan-effect from extra incomes, reduced expenditures, better overall management, inheritance, remittances, windfalls or other loans. It is equally difficult to know what might have happened had loans not been made available or had a different type of loan be offered.' (1999: 23)

While theoretical insights on housing finance are scarce, empirical research on household strategies to obtain housing finance has also not been conducted on a large scale either.

> 'There has been almost no research on existing processes, with the result that most indicators and definitions related to housing in Asia are derived from First World concepts, and experience has shown that they do not apply to Asian conditions. This constitutes a major problem in developing appropriate indicators and statistics and this, in turn, makes appropriate planning on a large scale difficult.' (Hasan 1997: 15)

This book aims at overcoming some of these shortcomings and contributing to a better understanding of the housing finance market strategies and the strategies of low-income households for obtaining housing finance in Hyderabad, India. India was chosen as the subject of this research due to its ongoing transition from a mainly state-dominated economy towards a neo-liberal one. In such a context, it is generally assumed that the public, private, Non-Governmental Organisation (NGO), and Community-Based Organisation (CBO) sectors serve different segments of the market, but that they should all play a role in the delivery of housing finance to the poor. This kaleidoscope of actors offers the possibility of obtaining comparative insight in the dynamics of demand and supply in the housing finance market for the urban poor.

To obtain an understanding of the Indian housing finance market, I will analyse access to this market and the strategies of the urban poor for financing their shelter in Hyderabad. Hyderabad was selected as a research area, because both public as well as 'formal' private sector housing finance institutions are active in the city. The public sector interventions deal with the provision of housing finance to the poor through slum improvement schemes as part of the urban community development programme. The private housing finance corporations have branch offices in Hyderabad. It appears that due to the enormous population growth of Hyderabad, it is the poor who are especially the last to gain access to the public and 'formal' private sector housing market, and who have to resort to all kinds of alternative housing solutions and related financing patterns. Moreover, Hyderabad is a city where the population mix of Hindus and Muslims affords the possibility of examining the differences and similarities between financing strategies of housing employed by each religious group.

In this book, the core concepts are the housing finance sector, sources of housing finance, housing finance institutions and financial arrangements. The 'housing finance sector' and 'sources of housing finance' encompass all persons and institutions engaged in providing finance used for construction purposes. 'Housing finance institutions' include public and private institutions that provide housing finance. 'Financial arrangements' refer to the terms and conditions of the loans provided and savings kept in custody. Such financial arrangements may be based on principles of incremental building or the construction of a housing unit in one go. These methods of financing will be refered to as incremental and integral financing respectively. It is of crucial importance to distinguish who uses which financing strategy and why. The central research question is thus: 'What are the matches and mismatches between demand for and supply of housing finance for the poor in Hyderabad, India?' In order to gain insight into these dynamics, the research questions focus on the urban poor's demand for and supply of housing finance. The research questions concerning the demand side are:

- How do the urban poor finance their dwellings in Hyderabad, India?
- Why are these specific financing methods employed by the urban poor?
- What are the advantages and disadvantages of these financing strategies?

In addition to gaining insight in the construction and related financing strategies of the urban poor, it is important to explore the possibilities, alternatives and policies concerning housing finance for the poor. In the literature on housing finance, emphasis is generally placed on 'formal' supply and far less attention is paid to 'informal' supply while informal housing finance supply is of great importance for the urban poor. This should be understood in the local socio-cultural context with emphasis on topics such as the activities of political leaders, officials and slum leaders. This leads to the following questions concerning the supply of housing finance to the urban poor:

- What financing methods can be distinguished for the housing of the urban poor?
- To what extent do the various housing finance policies in Hyderabad and their implementation benefit the urban poor?
- Which alternative options for housing finance policies and schemes for the urban poor are advisable?

In this study, urban poor households provide the point of departure. The poor are those who lack 'the necessities for human survival and welfare.' (Wratten 1995: 12) The poor earn small and irregular incomes. However, it should be borne in mind that poverty is a relative concept, which is dependent on place, time and one's reference group (e.g. Mangin 1970: xviii). Consequently, there is no uniform meaning of the concepts defining basic human needs and how they can be recognised. However, concepts of urban poverty should generally go beyond the lack of income and encompass items as substandard housing and basic facilities (e.g. Satterthwaite 1997).

In India, the Government divides the urban poor into the Economically Weaker Sections and Low-Income Groups. At the time the research was conducted, the Economically Weaker Sections encompassed households with an income below Rs. 1,250 per month and the Low-Income Groups covered the income group from Rs. 1,251 to 2,650 per month.[1] When I refer to 'the (urban) poor', Low-Income Groups as well as the Economically Weaker Sections are included, unless a particular subgroup is specifically mentioned. Urban in this context refers to the area under jurisdiction of the Municipal Corporation of Hyderabad.

In Hyderabad, the urban poor often live concentrated in so-called slums, which are generally of an illegal nature, based as they are on squats and illegal subdivisions, where land is illegally plotted and sold. I am aware of the negative meaning attached to the word slum, but I prefer to use it from a perspective developed since the term 'slums of hope' was launched as the opposite of 'slums of despair' (Lloyd 1979; Stokes 1962). Thus, dwellers are seen as having the opportunity of improving their living conditions step by step. Another reason why I use the word slum is because it is widely used in policy circles, which can facilitate the discussion between science and policy. The local government has recognised specific neighbourhoods as slum, which indicates that these areas become part of slum improvement schemes, coordinated by the Municipal Corporation of Hyderabad. Apart from these recognised slums, there are also unrecognised slums spread across the city.

Slum dwellers face problems of access to public and 'formal' private housing finance, if that they ever consider approaching such institutions. One of the reasons is that the housing finance sector is underdeveloped and cannot cope with the increasing demand. Hyderabad, located in the centre of India, is one of the rapidly growing Indian urban agglomerations. In 1990, it had a population of about 4.1 million, and is expected to grow to 8 million by 2005, 9.3 million by 2010 and even more than 10 million by 2015 (UNCHS 1996: 452). Other Indian cities have also increased phenomenally in size within this relatively short period. The Indian urban population is expected to grow from 29% by 2000 to 45% by 2025. This is both an enormous absolute and relative increase; in 1975 only 21% of the Indian population lived in urban settlements. Nonetheless, the annual growth rate of the urban population for the period 1975-2025 has been estimated at just over 3% (UNCHS 1996: 448). Along with the number of urban dwellers, the number of cities has also increased. In 1951, there were 76 'large' cities in India with more than 100,000 inhabitants and five metropolitan cities with more than one million inhabitants. By 1991, these urban centres had increased in number to 296 and 23 respectively (Sarupria 1997: 144-145).

1 One Indian Rupee (Rs.) equals 0.033 US $ (1993-1994).

It is hardly surprising that such enormous urban growth within a short period created specific problems for planning and implementing habitat improvement schemes and urban management in general. Many inhabitants of Hyderabad require finance to invest in housing, but Indian financial institutions are faced with problems with respect to allocating sufficient resources for housing finance. One of the reasons is their underdevelopment and the constraints imposed on this sector by the government (Jones & Datta 1999: 7-8).

The operation of the housing finance market in Hyderabad is not only influenced by India's financial and economic reforms, but also by the competition and co-ordination between the housing finance market and the wider capital markets. In the 1980s, the financial and economic sector was slowly reformed, resulting in a more open economy and increased average growth rates of 5.4% of the gross domestic product. It was only in 1991 that the Indian government became more committed to liberalisation and structural reforms. These reforms were designed to encourage national and international investments in India. International trade and the capital market were partly privatised and liberalised, but public sector reform was postponed. Due to structural adjustments accompanying liberalisation, the poorer sections could not rely any more, if ever at all, on the public safety net, due to the limited means available (Pugh 1994: 390-391). The main focus was on the development of 'formal' financial institutions such as banks and specialised housing finance agencies, which finance only 20% of the housing stock in developing countries such as India. The buyers belong, with few exceptions, to the better-situated middle and upper class. The remaining 80% is financed through the so-called 'informal' financial sector.

The 'informal' financial sector encompasses those financial arrangements, which are made outside the direct control of the Central Bank of India, while the 'formal' financial sector operations are under the direct control of the Central Bank of India.[2] In between these extremes one can find the so-called 'semi-formal' financial sector with non-banking financial institutions, such as licensed moneylenders and

2 I am aware of the fact that the concepts 'informal' and 'formal' are based on inadequate social, economic, political and spatial determinism (see e.g. Hospes 1996: 6). Despite all criticism the concepts have a function of labelling phenomena as long as there is no alternative available. The 'informal' sector has received considerable attention despite the shortcomings of such a concept. The concept 'informal' sector 'has generated new interest and insight which help explain (a) the persistence of underdevelopment in (...) the developing world as well as (b) the emerging signs of change in terms of improving situations in many developing countries.' (Amin 1996: vi)

chit funds (financial self-help organisations), operating under control of the Central Bank of India. It is in the so-called 'informal' financial sector where many urban dwellers, who lack access to public or private housing finance agencies, mobilise the finance required for constructing or improving their dwelling.

Many policymakers are unaware of the housing finance role played by the 'informal' sector (ESCAP 1991: 22-23), while at least 50% of the households in many developing countries, and 80% in India, are dependent on finance from wages, employers, the wider family, friendship networks, and agents in the 'informal' financial sector to help them constructing homes. This suggests that the poor and a large part of middle-income families cannot afford 'formal' housing finance (Pugh 1990; 1994: 385-387). In comparison to the 'formal' housing finance sector, the 'informal' sector is thought to generate twice as much finance (ESCAP 1991: 29).

Baken and Van der Linden (1993) suggest that problems of access and equity play a crucial role in the free market, but are of less importance in the so-called 'informal' sector. Others, such as Boleat (1987: 163, 177), consider the 'informal' financial institutions inefficient, because of their incapability to provide long-term loans. Such long-term availability appears to be of crucial importance for housing loans in general (UNCHS 1989: 4). In the 'informal' housing finance sector interest rates are frequently higher, but the loans have shorter terms. Moreover, good repayment records in the 'informal' sector show that the poor are generally able to repay credit (Cohen 1983: 97).

What does this mean in the Indian context? In 1984, a national housing policy was formulated, which provides strategic plans for institutional reform in line with the UNCHS and World Bank guidelines. In addition, the *Nagar Palika* act was introduced in 1994. This 74th constitutional amendment act has increased the functions and responsibilities of urban local bodies and enables them to mobilise resources and undertake innovative measures to finance commercially sound schemes and projects. Many state governments have amended municipal acts and enabled the privatisation of public services. It is not obligatory for the state governments, however, to transfer powers of taxation to local bodies, which have a very small tax base. The size of the available funds depends on the willingness to allocate a portion of state revenue to the local bodies. An important reform that may have helped in this regard is the bringing of the public bodies to the people through a process of democratic decentralisation (see also Kundu 1996: 202-204).

The availability of housing finance is crucial for coping with India's housing shortage, as recognised by the National Housing and Habitat Policy of 1998 (ADB 1999: 2). In comparison with other developing countries, however, initiatives to improve the Indian housing finance market were rather late (Patel & Burra 1994). In India, emphasis was placed on the development of the entire housing sector, including housing finance along with other elements such as deregulation, regularisation of security of tenure, infrastructure, and target subsidies. Financing is private as well as public. Since the 1970s, the leading 'formal' private agency is the Housing and Development Finance Corporation (HDFC). It has demonstrated the possibilities of deepening and widening the private housing finance sector, including the provision of credit to the poor. The national public sector agency Housing and Urban Development Corporation (HUDCO) nowadays is allowed to raise finance at the open capital markets. However, due to budget restrictions the HUDCO has limited possibilities for investing in the development of housing for the urban poor (GOI 1992: 11-14; Pugh 1994: 390-391).

The development of 'formal' housing finance systems and linkages with grassroots initiatives are a relatively new phenomenon in developing countries such as India (e.g. Arrossi et al. 1994; Patel 1999). In the meantime, more experience had already been obtained through agricultural credit schemes, which were established to increase the production of small and marginal farmers (e.g. Adams & Von Pischke 1994; Bouman & Hospes 1994; Von Pischke, Adams & Donald 1983). Although rural credit schemes provide lessons for urban finance systems, the problems in urban areas occur on a larger scale, in a higher concentration and in more commercial surroundings (Saunders 1981). Insight obtained for dealing with agricultural credit schemes has been used to analyse the dynamics of micro (enterprise) finance, especially for micro entrepreneurs (Adams & Von Pischke 1994), and housing finance. It was only at the end of the 1990s that micro finance was seen as being helpful for dealing with the urban poor. In 1997, the Micro Credit Summit Campaign started with the aim of reaching 100 million of the world's poorest households, especially the women of these households, with credit for self-employment and other financial and business services by the year 2005 (Micro Credit Summit 1997).

Instead of using the term micro credit, I prefer to use the term micro finance, because the concept finance also includes a savings and insurance component. The attention paid to micro finance could encourage the housing finance sector to deal with smaller loans, although in reality many housing finance institutions are hesitant to deal with the poor. It is remarkable that since micro finance has become a popular theme among policymakers and scientists, less attention has been paid to housing finance in general. This is reflected in a declining number of publications. In the meantime, the number of publications on micro finance has grown. These micro finance publications deal with themes such as poverty reduction (e.g. Johnson & Rogaly 1997; Mosley & Hulme 1998; Navajas et al. 2000), replication of successful micro finance systems (e.g. Taub 1998; Todd 1996), institutional perspectives (e.g. Bhatt & Tang 1998), and impact assessment methodologies (Hulme 2000; Johnson 1998). Moreover, the increase of NGOs dealing with micro finance parallels a renewed attention among academics for social capital (e.g. Misztal 1996; Putnam 1993; Seligman 1997; Wilson 1997). '[T]he notion of social capital has provided the World Bank with the analytical capacity to propose its new agenda without having to come to terms in any serious or substantive way with the critical literature of the old consensus' (Fine 1999: 12).

Apart from many similarities, there are also differences between micro finance and housing finance for construction. Firstly, housing loans, compared with micro finance for income generation, are generally larger in size, reflected in a longer repayment period and a higher level of risk. Secondly, agents specialised in housing finance, who want to raise capital on the private market, face problems of a short-term supply, because the housing loans are relatively long. Thirdly, contrary to credit for income-generating activities, the provision of housing finance does not directly lead to an improvement of income which can be used for repayment of the credit. However, 'the greatest benefit may be in terms of savings in the cost of repairs and renovations as housing consolidation takes place.'(Jones & Mitlin 1999: 32)

In reality, the urban poor have remained dependent on self-help housing, whose financing methods are dependent on family savings, employer support and 'informal' sector lenders and financing systems (e.g. Baken & Smets 1999; Mitlin 1997; Patel & Burra 1994). The Government of India recognises the need to gain insight into the dynamics of this 'informal' sector for housing and possible linkages with the 'formal' financial sector. In addition, it promotes the introduction of innovative savings and lending instruments

> 'to integrate the housing finance system into the capital market by enabling access of Housing Finance Institutions to the funds on a competitive basis with other financial institutions and permitting NHB [National Housing Bank] and HUDCO to set up mutual funds for housing, apart from their access to external aid.' (GOI 1992: 12-13)

The fieldwork material upon which this book is based was collected during the period September 1993- September 1994 and in May-April 1996 not only in Hyderabad, but also Mumbai and New Delhi. To gain insight into the demand side of the housing finance market, I focused on the habitat and livelihood strategies of the urban poor. For this purpose, material was gathered in 13 medium-sized low-income neighbourhoods, ranging from 76 to 530 households, with huts, shacks, concrete houses and all kind of other constructions in these slums with no housing schemes. These slums were located within the Municipal Corporation's area and selected in such a way that they were spread across the old city of Hyderabad, the new city of Hyderabad and its twin city of Secunderabad (see Appendix 1). Although I attempted to obtain a random sample, reflecting the percentage of Hindus and Muslims living in Hyderabad, Muslims are slightly overrepresented.

In the slums surveyed, I organised a survey of households by myself. I tried to make it as random as possible by interviewing households, selected by requesting the co-operation of at least one, but preferably more, person(s) who were living along a particular street, where the door faced to. When co-operation was refused the next door was tried until my assistant and I succeeded even if we had had to pass several doors. After completing an interview the next interview was selected five doors along. This resulted in a sample of 15% of the slum dweller households (N = 379). Many dwellers could not remember specific details of their investments in their homes. Such people could only provide an indication of the investments they had made many years ago. Despite this shortcoming, the figures obtained provide an approximation of how and why the poor finance their shelters and why they do it in a particular way. The information gathered through questionnaires was supplemented with information from local leaders, financial agents and informal talks in the streets, at teashops, in community buildings and in the houses of dwellers.

To gain insight into the supply side of the housing finance market in Hyderabad, I examined the operation and maintenance of 'informal' housing finance suppliers, non-banking financial institutions, the public sector, private housing finance corporations, NGOs and CBOs. I conversed with 'informal' financial sector suppliers; friends, neighbours, relatives, moneylenders, pawnbrokers, participants and organisers of chit funds, employers, and colleagues of the interviewed slum dwellers. In addition, employees of non-banking financial institutions (licensed moneylenders, registered chit funds, finance corporations) and non-banking financial co-operatives (salary-earner's co-operative societies and housing finance co-operatives) also provided information about the operation and maintenance of these suppliers of housing finance.

Information about the public sector was gathered by investigating public housing schemes for the Economically Weaker Sections in six slums in Hyderabad. There, similar surveys were carried out, resulting in a 16% sample of the slum dweller households (N = 96), supplemented by discussions with (semi-)government officials and field workers of the Municipal Corporation of Hyderabad, public housing and housing finance agencies in Hyderabad and New Delhi.

For the research on housing finance corporations in the private financial sector, data were gathered by interviewing employees and managers of the Al-Ameen Islamic Financial & Investment Corporation and eight housing finance corporations in Hyderabad (HDFC, Canfin Homes Ltd., LIC housing Finance Ltd., Dewan Housing Finance Development Ltd., GIC Housing Finance Ltd., AB Homes Finance Ltd., Vysya Bank Housing Finance Ltd., Fairgrowth Home Finance Ltd.) and the head office of HDFC in Mumbai. Furthermore, discussions with staff of the National Housing Bank in New Delhi also took place. Finally, a greater understanding of the NGOs' and CBOs' role in the field of housing finance was gained by interviewing employees and members of NGOs and CBOs in Hyderabad, New Delhi and Mumbai. All the oral information gathered has been supplemented by information collected from leaflets, reports and other kinds of unpublished and published literature.

The methods of research employed were semi-structured interviews and informal discussions. Moreover, participant observation was adopted as a method for gathering information in slum areas, with the emphasis on observation. I experienced that participation in a slum area is rather difficult when one does not live in the neighbourhood concerned. I was living outside the slums where the research took place and visited these neighbourhoods at very different times, spending many hours there on an almost daily basis. This provides some insight into the way of life of the slum dwellers. To interview the settlers, I employed a female MPhil student as an assistant and translator, which worked well until she faced 'purity'problems due to her Brahman background. She refused food and drinks offered by slum dwellers and faced identity problems due to being in 'filthy' slums. Some time later, I got in touch with a non-Brahmin male teacher, who was willing to assist me during the rest of the research period. I trained both assistants in interviewing techniques and after the interviews discussions often took place about what had happened.

Before surveying a slum, permission was obtained from the slum leader. Entering slum areas was not always easy, because of screaming or threatening dwellers, who did not trust us at all. Under such circumstances, my research assistant and I tried to gain the trust of the different factions of dwellers by having discussions with all their leaders. In some slums this was not possible due to communal frictions between Hindus and Muslims. These communal frictions are deeply rooted in the history of the Muslim state of Hyderabad, where Muslims suppressed the Hindu population. After incorporation into the Indian Union, the Hindus took revenge on the Muslims. This resulted in ongoing frictions between both communal groups. These communal frictions caused problems for doing fieldwork, especially in the old city, because my research assistants were Hindus and the slum population mainly Muslim. Solutions were sought by making use of an additional Muslim assistant in the specific neighbourhoods concerned. Furthermore, research activities in slums in the old city were hindered, because the government had sent bulldozers to remove new houses constructed near water tanks. This led to unrest among the dwellers and distrust towards the researcher. Despite such frictions, we could gain the trust of the dwellers, enabling the collection of the desired information, which was cross-checked by interviewing several people about the same topic. Despite the difficulties mentioned above, it was advantageous of being a non-caste 'white' person of Dutch origin, which enabled me to get in touch with all kind of different castes without the constraints of purity and pollution.

This book, encompassing the research material, is organised in the following manner. Firstly, the main debates on the urban poor's livelihood strategies, including housing and its financing, are dealt with in theoretical and historic perspective. Chapter two focuses on Hyderabad's history with special attention to its housing finance, land and housing market. The third chapter describes characteristics of the surveyed dwellers of slums where no housing schemes have been implemented. Special attention is paid to the livelihood strategies of the urban poor, including their construction activities and its financing. This all provides us with insight into the demand side of the low-income housing finance market. Furthermore, different sections of the housing finance market are discussed with the focus on the supply side and its underlying logic, which are compared to the livelihood and building strategies including the financing strategies of the urban poor. Chapter four deals with the savings and credit relations of slum dwellers to, for example, friends, neighbours, relatives, employers, moneylenders, pawnbrokers and finance corporations. A discussion of the use of financial self-help organisations as a source of housing finance follows in chapter five. Attention shifts to the public sector in chapter six and the 'formal' private housing finance sector in chapter seven. In both these chapters the focus is on the characteristics of the schemes developed. Apart from the public and private sector, other possibilities of intervention can be distinguished. However, not only partnerships between public and private bodies, but also alliances with NGO and CBOs are possible. These are highlighted in chapter eight. For Hyderabad, these developments are recent, taking place after my fieldwork period. Therefore, I mainly restrict my discussion will be mainly of a theoretical nature and examine more or less similar case studies from other Indian cities. Finally, a conclusion summarises the results and provides a brief view of the future.

1 The urban poor and housing finance in theoretical and historic perspective: the main debates

In order to gain insight into the dynamics of housing finance strategies at the demand and supply side of the housing finance market, this chapter will highlight the main debates concerning housing finance for the urban poor. Firstly, I will begin with the demand side by discussing the concept of household and its related dynamics. In order to secure their livelihood, a poor household employs livelihood strategies, using mainly financial and physical capital as well as human and social capital, distinguished in networks, reciprocal relations, trust and social control. The general notions discussed thus far will be employed to describe different views on housing and its financing strategies. One housing finance school of thought includes the livelihood strategies of the poor, while an economic perspective neglects such strategies completely. Further to this, the supply level of housing finance, where the concepts of affordability, cost recovery, replicability, and the promotion of housing finance in developing countries are discussed. I will focus on the role of different agents in the housing finance sector alone and in partnership; i.e. public sector organisations, 'formal' private entrepreneurs, NGOs, and CBOs. Due to the difficulties of reaching the poor adequately with housing finance, innovative schemes have been developed. These will be discussed in the last section. Here, especially the views of the World Bank are discussed, because the Bank is an important policy trendsetter for the local financing systems.

1.1 Households

In this book, a household will be defined as those persons living under the same roof and eating from the same pot. If such a household, as 'the basic unit of society involved in production, reproduction, consumption and socialization' (Moore 1991: 54), consists of several members there is potential for tasks to be shared within the household. Existing conceptualisations of the household assume different divisions of labour. If a household is seen as a uniform unit, its members have a common set of preferences for allocating their available resources. It is assumed that all resources such as finance, labour and land are pooled and all expenditures are made from a common pool. In economic terms, each household is thus seen as a homogeneous utility-maximising unit having joint utility functions (Becker 1973; 1974a; 1974b).

This Beckerian view of a household is questioned by many, because it does not always coincide with everyday reality and the underlying assumptions have been increasingly challenged (e.g. Fapohunda 1988; Folbre 1994; Haddad et al. 1994: 2-3; Moser 1992; Sen 1983). Firstly, a household should not be treated as a nuclear family (husband, wife and two or three children). Secondly, one should not assume a clearly defined sexual division of labour within the household with the male head of the household working outside the home and his spouse taking care of the household and looking after the children (Moser 1989: 1800; 1992: 53). Thirdly, a household often does not have a single locus of activities, labour and resources (Roberts 1991: 62). Fourthly, strategies employed often differ among households, depending on factors such as the amount and regularity of income, household size, household members' age, changes in migrant lives, conflicting interests within the household (e.g. Mencher 1988: 114; Papanek and Schwede 1988: 79-80; Singh 1978: 81). Finally, the operation and maintenance of a household should also be seen in its own context (Folbre 1994).

Folbre (1994: 25) has provided opportunities to model self-interested decision making and bargaining processes within the household. One of such opportunities is reflected in the view of the household as a collective entity, which allows different household members, dependent on age, gender and life cycle, to have different interests. The urban poor may therefore operate as individuals or in a coalition model within a household (see also e.g. Banck 1980: 239; González de La Rocha 1994; Lenten 1993; Roberts 1991: 63). Such a coalition model can be of a conflictive nature, which Sen (1983) calls 'co-operative conflict'. By employing such a mode, it is possible 'to recognize inequalities, possibly substantial within the household' (Sen 1983: 25). Folbre goes one step further and suggests the model of purposeful choice, which encourages us to see 'how people define and pursue their desires, but avoids any implicit dichotomy between rational and irrational.' (Folbre 1994: 28).

In the nuclear household of husband, wife and children, both parents do not always financially contribute to the household income. Especially in female-headed households the workload rests on the shoulders of women, because apart from reproductive and management tasks within the household a lot of time has to be invested in income-earning activities. Such female-headed households can be distinguished in two types. The first type is the *de jure* female-headed household, where the male is missing due to a divorce or death. The second type is the *de facto* female-headed household where the male is temporarily absent due to, for example, migration (Moser 1989: 1801-1802). A female-headed household is not always financially worse off than a nuclear family or extended family. This may, for example, be due to the income earned by children. There is greater vulnerability for elderly people living alone, or for women with sick and/or old husbands but no earning children (e.g. Mencher 1988: 107).

The economic conditions of vulnerable households are characterised by a shortage of financial income and/or other resources that they own or have command over (Von Benda-Beckman and Von Benda-Beckman 1994: 11). Private means, monetary as well as non-monetary (food, clothes, utensils) are mainly derived from employment or self-employment, possibly including that of other household members, which may be supplemented by gifts or credit. Moreover, remittances can, but do not always, form a substantial part of their household budget (e.g. Kaufman and Lindauer 1984; Keare and Parris 1982: 51). There are gender inequalities in the distribution of goods and money within the household, which makes it difficult for the women to ensure satisfactory levels of care and well-being of all household members (e.g. Folbre 1994). The interests of both older generations and the men in the household are first met, even when women channel a higher percentage of their income into the household than the men (e.g. Moser 1998). In addition, women generally display better ability to save, good recovery records from loans taken out, and positive influence on their husbands' loan repayment behaviour. On the other hand, women will often have a decisive say at times of social or financial stress when men opt to sell their houses (Datta and Jones 1999; Peltenburg 1990; Shah 1990: 108).

1.2 Poverty and livelihood strategies

Poverty is generally defined in terms of a lack of income or consumption, which may harm the health of the people concerned. Here, physical goods such as shelter may be included (e.g. Satterthwaite 1997). In contrast, Rutherford (2000: 1) restricts the description of a poor person to someone who has not much money. However, poverty may also encompass poor health and the habitat status, illiteracy, several types of vulnerability, and humiliation, as well as a lack of coping capabilities and skills (e.g. Chambers 1995; Satterthwaite 1997; Wright 2000: 9). Due to the static value attached to the concepts of poverty and poor, Chambers (1989) suggests the use of the concepts 'vulnerability' and 'vulnerable', which have a more dynamic nature and point to 'insecurity and exposure to risk, shocks and stress.'(ibid.: 1).

Although Rutherford's view of poverty is generally unfashionable among academics and policy makers, I will still use this definition since the main topic of the book is housing finance and the urban poor, who have those little finance. The public sector assistance programmes use the poverty line, which is estimated at Rs. 297 per person per month for Hyderabad.[1] Although the use of such a poverty line is arbitrary (Dandekar et al. 1993) it still provides an indication of existing differences given that poverty is defined by an index in which income, consumption and/or social indicators are combined (Bhattacharya et al. 1991: 273; De Wit 1993: 18). Furthermore, it should be noted that households may sometimes live under the poverty line and at other times with an income above the poverty line. This dynamic is also reflected in the way they deal with their financial means, including savings, credit and gifts.

In order to make ends meet with a low, fluctuating and often irregular income, the poor employ so-called livelihood strategies. These strategies refer 'broadly to the ways in which urban poor households organize their production and consumption activities to guarantee the maintenance of their members' (Chant 1991: 26). The poor generally try to 'reduce risk, increase adaptability, and seek a degree of autonomy, by developing and maintaining wider options, through the ability and willingness of different household members to do different things in different places at different times' (Chambers 1989: 3). Most poor people are able to list their desires and needs in order of priority, where a balance has to be found between short and long-term expenditures and postponement of expenditures (Folbre 1994: 27; Lont 1999; Smets

1 This figure has been reached by indexing the urban poverty line for Andhra Pradesh, which was Rs. 151.28 per person per month for 1987-88 (Minhas et al. 1991: 1674). The inflation rate used as percentage of the consumption price index is 9.1% for 1988 (ADB 1990: 137), 6.5% for 1989 (ADB 1992: 170), 13.6% for 1990, 13.9% in 1991 (ADB 1993: 140), 9.6% in 1992, 7.5% in 1993, and 11% in 1994 (ADB 1995: 141).

1999). These dynamics contradict the culture of poverty theory where the poor are conceptualised as being caught in a web of poverty, resulting in apathy and despair, because they cannot cope with middle-class norms and values (Lewis 1975).

Livelihood strategies[2] differ 'according to the type of household, the stage of the household's domestic cycle, and the external environment' that shape the organisation of time and labour conditions of the household members (González de la Rocha 1994: 15). To cope with expected and unexpected hardships of daily life, people employ strategies in which savings, credit, gifts or insurance(s) can play an important role. Poor people try to minimise their risk of taking out credit, but would prefer to save a lump sum, even when it takes them a lot of efforts (Wright 2000: 137-138). A powerful incentive to encourage people to save and make sacrifices appears to be home-ownership (Boleat 1987: 177). If people save from their budget, they can do so in different ways. Savings can be put aside from the income before consumption or are leftovers after consumption. Moreover, saving can be distinguished in 'saving up', 'saving down' and 'saving through'. 'Saving up' means that one saves over time to enjoy a lump sum in the future. However, when savings are used to repay a loan, one may call this 'saving down'. Finally, 'saving through' refers to a more or less continuous stream of savings, while a lump sum is paid out at some intermediate point in time as done, for example, by insurance companies (Rutherford 2000: 6-8).

Apart from the use of savings, credit can help the poor to overcome a period in which they face a shortage of finance. Chambers (1989: 1) stresses that 'debt makes households more vulnerable', but Lont (1999: 21-22) demonstrates that households have strategies for reducing such a vulnerable situation by taking new debts to repay old ones. When insufficient money is available to repay a loan, many people opt for replacing urgent loans with less urgent and less unpleasant ones. In so doing, a cheaper loan can replace a more expensive one or a loan from a friend or relative can be repaid in time to maintain the relationship.

Montgomery (1996: 293) has attempted to rank livelihood strategies 'by degree of reversibility and the value of the resource commitment', by drawing on Maxwell and Frankenberger and his own research. He distinguishes low-stress, medium-stress and high-stress coping strategies.

---

2 Livelihood strategies can also be traced in the literature under labels such as household strategies, household economic strategies, existence strategies, coping strategies, and survival strategies.

Table 1 Hierarchy of livelihood strategies

Coping with economic stress	Comments
Low-stress coping strategies • Expenditure savings activities (e.g. gathering fuel, fodder, food) • Changes in diet (cheaper foods) and reduced consumption (eating less) • Periodic migration by one or more household members to look for a higher wage income • Calling in small 'informal' debts from kin, friends and neighbours	Primarily effective for dealing with minor shortfalls in income; are relatively low value and reversible; insufficient for meeting major crises and contingencies.
Medium-stress coping strategies • Using up cash savings • Pledging future labour in return for advance wages or loans • Taking cash or kind loans from kin, friends, neighbours, moneylenders and shopkeepers	Likely to help counter sudden crisis and contingencies, but are less reversible and reduce future coping strategy. They may therefore act as 'ratchets' forcing a household further into poverty (especially if an initial crisis is compounded by subsequent shocks)
High-stress coping strategies • Mortgaging or pawning assets (utensils, jewellery, land, etc.) • Sale of non-productive assets (initially small ones, such as household utensils; or larger ones such as housing materials, tin roofing sheets, a hut, etc.) • Sale of working capital at knock-down prices (e.g. petty trading goods to be sold) • Sale of productive assets (small animals, livestock, tools, means of transport, etc.)	Hard to reverse; indicators of severe distress and increased vulnerability to further stress. May constitute 'ratchets' from which a household may be unable to recover

Source: Montgomery (1996: 293); own research.

The urban poor try to secure their livelihood by individual and/or collective action, which can be used alone or in combination with each other. Newberry (in Platteau 1988: 5) calls individual action 'self-insurance'. Collectively preferred ends, such as a savings deposit and credit can be properly met in a financial self-help organisation. However, when people do not want to bear the costs of the collective good and only opt for the benefits, problems with free-riders may occur. In order to cope with free riders, selective incentives of a material, social, or psychological nature can be used. Selective incentives of a material nature provide participants with a lump sum or credit. Social and psychological incentives tend to work better when members interact face-to-face (Hechter 1988: 35-37; Olson 1980: 51, 60). In larger groups face-to-face relations decline. Consequently, legal control mechanisms are increasingly required for the survival of the larger group (Hechter 1988: 105).

Selective incentives can be seen as self-constraint, external constraint, and social pressure to self-constraint. Self-constraint applies when people force themselves to undertake action such as saving individually or within the family. External constraints such as physical violence force people to do, or refrain from doing, certain activities such as paying contributions to a pension or insurance. However, when the members of a group put pressure on each other to enforce self-discipline, one may speak of a social constraint towards self-constraint. In such a situation, the social pressure of the group influences the behaviour of its members (De Swaan 1996: 12; Elias 1990, part 2: 239-260).

Livelihood strategies, however, are not always successful; the poor, compared with the surrounding population, are subject to higher rates of, for example, mortality, accident, illness, permanent injury, abortion, miscarriage, and addiction. However, successfully employed long-term strategies are generally linked to with social mobility (Schminck 1984: 90-91).

In the above, I have defined poverty mainly in terms of finance. It is assumed that those living close to the poverty line employ livelihood strategies, in which social capital plays a crucial role. The concept of social capital will be discussed in the following section.

1.3 Social capital

Livelihood strategies encompass the use of social capital, which is a term used separately from other types of capital such as human, cultural, financial and physical capital (see e.g. Bourdieu 1989: 120-141; Fine 1999; Moser 1998). Van Bastelaer (n.d.: 3) considers the social capital of a society to include 'the institutions, the relationships, the attitudes and values that govern interactions among people and contribute to economic and social development.' It is a combination of structural and cognitive social capital; the sum of institutions that underpin society, including shared values and rules for social conduct that keep society together. The interpretations of social capital differ enormously. Van Bastelaer distinguishes three types. The first interpretation restricts the notion of social capital to a set of horizontal networks between people and related norms that influence the productivity of the community (see Putnam 1993). Secondly, a broader concept of social capital is associated with Coleman (1990), who includes horizontal as well as vertical associations among people, but also other entities such as private enterprises. The third interpretation encompasses the political and social environment, which forms the social structure and enables the development of norms and values. Apart from horizontal and vertical local networks, it also includes institutional structures, such as economic bodies, the state, the political regime, the legal system, and civil and political privileges, including their relationships (see North 1991; Olson 1982).

The use of social capital has been criticised because it is a container concept encompassing too many different features and neglecting its political context (e.g. Fine 1999). On the other hand, social capital has a potential for a multidisciplinary approach in which economic and social sciences may be combined. Moreover, scientists of various disciplines and policymakers 'may once again be able to find a common language (...) that disciplinary provincialisms have largely suppressed over the last one-hundred-and-fifty years' (Woolcock 1998: 188).

Here, the concept of social capital, in line with Coleman's view, will be used in connection with urban poor household members. The access to social capital will influence the individual opportunity of investing different kinds of capital. Moreover, the desire to possess social capital forces the participants in networks to collective action or to obtain individual financial help from others. That is why I restrict my discussion of social capital to the concepts of network, reciprocal relations, trust and social control mechanisms.

For survival, members of urban poor households are dependent upon relations with persons within and outside the household. In a low-income neighbourhood, the urban poor often depend on several social networks for their livelihood strategies and/or improvement of economic status (Baken 1990: 79; Roberts 1991: 61). Such network(s), which often differ between men and women, can extend beyond the border of the neighbourhood even to the settlers' village of origin. Both men and women are involved in community activities, but in different ways. Men are more involved in local politics, generally within the framework of formal political parties. On the other hand, women are more involved in household management and neighbourhood activities dealing with the provision of items of collective consumption (e.g.

Moser 1992: 56; Shah 1990: 108). A social network in a specific neighbourhood can be of a horizontal and/or vertical nature. A horizontal organisation is an organisation of people such as a slum dwellers' federation or neighbourhood association, whose participants have more or less the same value orientations and power status. However, horizontal organisations of slum dwellers can be very problematic due to envy, ineffective leadership, the different ethnic or religious identities of slum dwellers, and the existence of machine politics (De Wit 1993: 26). Failure to organise in a horizontal fashion can be a livelihood strategy to ensure, for example, employment. In other words, organised labour is not always the best guarantee of employment and consequently to income (Olson 1980: 176; Schenk-Sandbergen 1988: 57).

Vertical relations between the leaders[3] and inhabitants of popular neighbourhoods in Hyderabad are often of a patron-client nature. Such a relationship is based on anticipated advantages for both parties involved. A patron expects respect, support, services and/or votes in return for the goods and services he promises and/or delivers to the client(s). Since the patron can influence the allocation of goods and services, he has more advantages in the bargain and transaction; it is he who can fix the exchange price (Ellemers 1969: 433-434). Patrons tend to solve conflicts only to a certain extent, some tensions are maintained. In this way, these leaders render themselves indispensable. The actions to render clients dependent may also have a violent nature. Similar characteristics can be ascribed to brokers, who are intermediaries in a chain of patron-client relationships, where the broker is a patron to his clients lower in the hierarchy and is himself a client of those higher in the chain (e.g. Baken 1990: 77; Burgwal 1993; De Wit 1989: 25; Smets and Hanssen 1996; Van der Linden 1996).

Many financial transactions are based on reciprocal relationships, which indicates 'that a gift or service received creates for the recipients a reciprocal obligation to return a gift or a service of at least comparable value at some future date' (Scott 1976: 167). Reciprocity can be distinguished in terms of generalised reciprocity, balanced reciprocity and negative reciprocity, which is a distinction made by Sahlins for traditional societies, also applicable to urban settings such as Hyderabad. With generalised reciprocity the balance between giver and taker is only restored over a long period of time. Consequently, the expectation of a counter performance within a short period is unlikely. When the

3 The leaders often form a part of an intricate network of interest groups and individual actors. In general, the relation between settler and leader is of a political patronage nature (e.g. Baken 1990: 16; Mitra & Nientied 1989: 26; Van der Linden 1988).

balance between the actors involved is returned to equilibrium within a short period, it is called balanced reciprocity. In comparison to generalised reciprocity, this is a more impersonal and economic-oriented relation. However, the most impersonal economic exchange can be found in negative reciprocity. Here, no attempts are made to balance the input of the actors involved, but the actors aim to extract the best out of the exchange. When a kind of equilibrium is maintained, this is more by accident than design (Sahlins 1974: 193-196).

Trust is essential in balanced and generalised reciprocal relationships. The topic of trust has recently re-attracted academic gained attention (e.g. Fukuyama 1995; Misztal 1996; Seligman 1997; Smets, Wels and Van Loon 1999), but I will restrict myself here to the elaboration of some simple insights. Luhmann (1979: 64) states that 'trust accumulates as a kind of capital which opens up more opportunities for more extensive action but which must be continually used and tended and which commits the user to trustworthy self-presentation.' Trust generally deals with the known and unknown. If people depend completely on the unknown and trust, this can be viewed as blind trust, which provides others with the opportunity for exploitation (Gambetta 1988: 213-235). Still the question arises of how trust comes into existence. A reputation of being trustworthy can be earned or ascribed. 'Earned trust' refers to trust that one has to obtain by showing positively valued behaviour and transactions, which is expected to continue similarly in the future. For 'ascribed trust' nothing has to be proved, because this trust is associated with the status one has, which may be derived from the family background or ethnicity (Knorringa 1999: 70). Once a trustworthy reputation is secured, it can be seen as 'frozen trust' (Wels 2000: 30), but when one has to prove it over and over again in future interaction, it may be viewed as 'process trust' (Knorringa 1995: 38). For the caste-based producer and trader relations in the shoe industry in Agra, India, ascribed trust is considered necessary for earned trust. Moreover, it is not always easy to earn trust, because ascribed distrust could be 'so high and persistant that it does not allow earned trust to come up' (Knorringa 1999: 80).

Trust can also be looked at in another way. Firstly, trust in people is dependent on face-to-face interaction, long-term acquaintance and mutually reliable credentials. Secondly, trust can be seen as reliability in an abstract system such as an institution, where faceless commitments take place (Giddens 1995: 34, 80-83). For the last type of trust, Luhmann (1988) suggests the use of the word confidence instead of trust. In practice, trust and confidence may influence each other. Trust, however, is not always sufficient to guarantee that people will behave as expected. Then, control mechanisms can play an important role in enforcing other people's behaviour. Control can be divided into institutional and social control. Institutional control or control of an organisation, place or system refers to the set-up and enforcement of regulations provided by those institutions to influence people's behaviour and action. Social control refers to

> 'social processes by which the behaviour of individuals or groups are regulated. Since all societies have norms and rules governing conduct (...) all equally have some mechanisms for ensuring conformity to those norms and dealing with deviance.' (Marshall 1994: 485)

In short, networks, reciprocal relations, trust and social control mechanisms, as parts of social capital, play an important role in gaining access to housing finance.

1.4 Housing and its financing strategies

From the 1960s onwards, Abrams (1964; 1966), Mangin (1967) and Turner (1968; 1972; 1976; 1988) have shown that the poor have their own rational, innovative and creative building strategies. Before discussing the financial consequences of such a building strategy, I will focus first on the poor's building strategies. Turner in particular shows that in everyday practice, the poor build and improve their houses in quality and size incrementally. Such incremental building activities, taking place over years and even decades, are dependent on the individual household priorities, the means available and change according to the family cycle, or changes in the life of migrants in the city. Therefore, housing should be considered a process. Housing should not be judged according to its physical appearance, but its users' value has to be the main point of evaluation. In other words, 'what it means' for its users instead of 'what it materially is'. There is a continually changing variety of individual and/or household needs, priorities and possibilities, which helps spread the costs of the construction activities over time. The components required for the construction process should be left up to the individual users, or to decentralised local and small-scale institutions. Large organisations tend to provide standard products and cannot adequately deal with the enormous variety of changing housing needs. This view forwarded by Turner from the late sixties onwards has a liberal flavour, although it is linked with a government's task in providing prescriptive rules and regulations, and infrastructure such as sewage systems and roads. The government also has to ensure access to land, building materials, construction skills and finance (Turner 1968; 1976). Turner sees a huge potential of self-help possibilities for the poor, but the power element in analysing the role of the state is neglected. However, the aspect of power was brought forward through the debate[4] between Turner (e.g. 1968; 1976) and Burgess (1978). By promoting a self-help approach Turner assumes a neutral state, contrary to Burgess, who takes into account the interests and roles of politicians, administrators, and financiers. This elite group often manipulates the urban poor in a financial and political way (cf. Nientied et al. 1982: 15).

Incremental building demands incremental financing, which will be only invested when there is some security of tenure (e.g. Abrams 1966). Investments in incrementally-built housing are dependent on the household member's needs, priorities and possibilities, where equilibrium will be sought between short and long-term possibilities. Turner (1968: 355) illustrates this necessary flexibility with an example:

> '[I]f the inhabitant wants to save money to send his children to school, a poor but cheap house will be better than an expensive one of high material standards that would ruin the family's long-term expectations.'

Apart from the flexibility in expenditures, the housing loan should be relatively small and have a short term of maximum 1.5 year (for an overview of the period associated with short, medium and long-term see Table 2). Moreover, the creditworthiness of the borrower should be based on non-conventional collateral, because mortgageable assets are generally lacking. Incremental building is financed from many 'informal' sources such as 'individual and group savings, windfalls, fabrication of their own building materials, sweat equity, small loans from neighbourhood moneylenders, barter arrangements and community self-help, and remittances from family living abroad' (Ferguson 1999: 189).

During the last decades such self-help has increasingly been taken seriously as a fruitful method by which the urban poor can construct

4 However, this debate is a misnomer since the different views of what 'reality' is and how it must be studied does not separate the various participants, but make them 'discuss different things.' Both theoretical starting points, Marxist against liberal views are internally heterogeneous, which makes it impossible to construct a continuum from Marxist to liberal views (Nientied & Van der Linden 1988: 144-145).

Table 2 Terms of housing loans

Loan-term	
< 1.5 year	Short-term
1.5 – 5 year	Medium-term
> 5 year	Long-term

their shelters. However, emphasis is laid on technological solutions for self-help. The theoretical debate about self help

> 'has remained purely speculative, and at the same time the discussions and disagreements among practitioners – especially organized around the World Bank activities and proposals – have hardly related to the main theoretical and political issues.' (Fiori and Raminez 1992: 30)

In other words, if the incremental building process was taken seriously at world planning level, the poor would be helped to improve their habitat by preserving investments made in their dwellings.

Interpretations about incremental financing differ. Pugh (1994) erroneously claims that the mainstream housing literature (e.g. Mathéy 1992a; Turner 1976), which I will call the self-help school, has misunderstood and misconceived the economics and finance of self-help housing.

> 'Self-help housing without loan finance is a process whereby labour (often non-monetized) and materials are added incrementally for construction and improvement over a period of years. The labour value (monetized and non-monetized) along with the value of the materials can be measured and attributed as saving and investment. In the process, housing standards are often increased over the years. Loan finance enables occupiers to 'bring forward' the higher standards to the 'present time' of building; the loan repayment scheme allows households to adjust and smooth their patterns of consumption, saving (including payment of the principal of the loan) and investment. Overall loan finance for occupiers can be viewed as a partial substitute for saving, replacing some 'self-help' saving.' (Pugh 1994: 388)

Pugh also claims that Turner and Burgess

> 'account self-help only in terms of financial out lays such as interest rate liabilities and loan repayments, ignoring the real economic costs which include the value of time given to the construction and management activities in self help.' (Pugh 1994: 388)

The outcomes of an expansion of the housing finance market may increase the size of the housing sector due to increased savings and investments in housing. In this respect, the poor tend to build their shelter incrementally. Concerning incrementally-built shelter, Malpezzi (1994) argues that:

> 'very few households approach housing other than incrementally, in the sense of paying for their housing in parts, whether rich or poor households in rich or poor countries. What is desirable is to divorce incremental payment from incremental consumption, so that households can consume their desired bundle, or closer to it, sooner. (...) The existence of financial and rental intermediation implies that consumption decisions can be made less dependent on current income and more dependent on long run ('permanent') income, and long-run desired consumption. What is required, then, is the collateral development of housing finance and of private rental markets as the construction market moves downmarket.' (ibid.: 459)

These economic strands of thought on housing finance neglect the livelihood strategies of the poor and show that decisions concerning the construction of a dwelling would be more efficient if financial decisions could be separated from building decisions (production of shelter). This would permit building and consuming now and paying for it later. In other words, a (potential) house-owner, who has taken out an integral housing loan, constructs or buys a house and enjoys its benefits directly or very soon. Paying for it later takes the form of repaying the housing loan in instalments. In the case of tenants, their house is built by others and the rent paid for as long as they are living in the house. Tenants and house-owners start consuming now and generally have to pay for it over a long period of time. Pugh and Malpezzi suggest that it is better to enjoy the benefits of a complete housing unit now, instead of consuming it incrementally and enjoying more or less the same benefits somewhere in the future. This is possible because all income groups pay for their shelter incrementally. To take the argument one step further, one could say, by referring to Renaud (1987: 30), that the methods of financing dictate the mode of construction. Larger loans would lead to building in one go, which avoids the waste of resources. Incremental building often takes place with inferior materials, and for the improvement or extension of the existing structure parts of the shelter frequently have to be demolished. Often only a fraction of the material can be reused. Patel (1999: 159) describes how over twenty years loan repayments for a 60 square meter apartment equal the amounts pavement dwellers in Mumbai pay for repairing their dwelling, especially during the monsoon period. The conclusion is that '[l]ow-income households are, therefore, building expensive but low quality housing.' Here, it is not the direct consumption of a better quality house, but the flexibility in financial management and loan repayment that lead to a consolidated and possibly improved habitat condition over time.

1.5 Affordability, cost recovery and replicability issues in housing finance

Credit has to be repaid, but the major question is how much should be recovered, how and from whom? Several discussions about these issues are found in the housing finance literature. In the 1970s and early 1980s, habitat improvement schemes encompassed mainly sites and services projects and the upgrading of already existing shanty-towns. In order to cope with the costs of these habitat pilot projects, the investments had to be adjusted to the financial capacity of the different income groups. The idea was that the funds used would flow back to a revolving fund and enable the replication of these projects. Initiatives were taken up for the development of cheaper building materials and construction techniques. In many developing countries institutions for the mobilisation of revenues for the housing sector were initiated. The price of land was adjusted by means of cross subsidies and the incorporation of payments for basic facilities and services for which people could not easily pay individually. Moreover, housing units were promoted in which the owner-occupant could rent out a part of his dwelling (Cohen 1983: 91-93; Roy 1987: 91-92; World Bank 1980).

These pilot projects failed to make the housing units affordable for the poor, which damaged the cost recovery of the investment in these schemes and the possibility of replicating the successful ones (ESCAP 1991: 4; Kim 1997: 1598; World Bank 1993a,b). The implementation of these habitat schemes was far too greatly constrained by restrictive building rules and regulations. Moreover, the government subsidies discouraged the adjustment of standards to the different income groups and consequently cost efficiency. As a consequence the units provided were too expensive, which favoured the relatively better off rather than the poor (Cohen 1983: 96). In order to find a way out, attention was paid to, what Burgess, Carmona and Kolstee (1997) call the 'affordability-cost recovery-replicability' formula. Below each element of this formula will be discussed.

Projects ought to be affordable for their beneficiaries. Otherwise they could not repay their loans. The affordable size of a loan was generally determined by taking into account the capital costs required for obtaining credit, its financing terms, the size and regularity of the household income and physical possessions and the propensity to invest in housing. Conventionally it is thought that if the capital costs, financing terms and household income are known, the propensity to consume housing or the willingness to invest in the dwelling will follow automatically (Lee 1990: 64). Hancock (1993: 129), by referring to Bramley, is more specific and states that housing is only affordable for households if, after deduction of the housing costs, rent or repayment of a housing loan, sufficient means are left over to provide for the necessities of life without falling below some poverty standard. A house can be made affordable by means of a subsidy. However, this option is rather limited for Third World cities due to the scale of their housing problems and the shortage of financial means.

Another indicator of the affordability of housing for the poor is the rent-paying capacity as part of the residents' income (e.g. Gupta et al. 1993: 74; Kundu 1993: 38; Rodell 1990: 82-83). A third affordability criteria of housing is the proportion of the income a household is able to invest in shelter. In this respect, the loan amount required depends on the construction costs minus subsidies and the owner's own resources such as down payment, building materials and labour. The size of the monthly instalments can then be calculated by taking into account the loan term and interest rate. The relation between the monthly income and the instalment size shows its affordability (e.g. Lee 1990: 64; Malpezzi 1991; Rodell 1990: 81-82; UNCHS 1990: 44). It is often assumed that when the household's income rises and the basic needs of food and fuel are met, more resources will be spent on shelter. Furthermore, it is thought that investment in shelter requires long-term planning. Dependent on the size of a down payment, the buyer generally has to borrow a large sum, which must be paid back over a long period. Consequently, the income of the buyer anticipated in the future should be taken into serious consideration. In addition to a living space, part of the shelter can also be used to rent out, or to start a shop and/or workplace. Income derived from a shelter can be incorporated into the calculation of its affordability, but including these factors complicates such a calculation greatly (Rodell 1990: 83, 88). In practice, it appears that the size of the income, even with an expected growth in the future, is an inadequate criteria for determining the affordability of shelter (World Bank 1980: 5).

Mortgage lenders started using a housing expenditure-to-income ratio, which assumes how much an average household is able to spend on housing at the maximum of 25-30% of their income. These ratios, which are in fact rule of thumb measures, are used for different purposes such as explaining a typical household expenditure pattern, analysing administrative rules for allocating subsidies, defining housing needs, public policy purposes, predicting the ability of a household to pay rent or to repay a mortgage loan, and selecting households for a rental unit or a mortgage loan. However, these ratios are increasingly criticised, because of the inaccuracy of defining the actual income of a household and predicting the willingness of the beneficiaries to allocate a specific part of their budget to housing. In reality, households can be found which spend both more and less on housing loans than the ratio indicates (Hulchanski 1995: 471-484; Jørgensen 1977: 146).

Even if the affordability criteria fit the poor, the question remains of whether the beneficiary is willing to repay the loan. For this purpose, security (conventional collateral) for the repayment of a loan may be demanded. Down payments are secured by pledging or mortgaging material goods, which can be sold or confiscated in case of default. Such resources for down payment can be items such as crops in the fields, land, savings with a financial self-help organisation, gold, jewellery, and occasionally an automobile or a house. Apart from these material goods, lenders may also ask for a regular and high enough salary from the borrower. When conventional collateral is not available, this can be replaced by non-conventional or social collateral, e.g. knowledge of the borrower's character, savings behaviour, and repayment record. If the (potential) client is considered trustworthy, social control mechanisms, such as peer pressure, must ensure that the borrower repays in time. One of the conditions demanded is that the borrower cannot escape this social control. Creating a common set of perceptions that defaulting on payments is not tolerated and/or the threat of physical violence can encourage the repayment of credit. Such peer pressure can damage the most vulnerable, as illustrated by Montgomery (1996: 290), who provides:

> '... contrasting examples of the extent to which members develop mutual trust, and are prepared to support individuals facing distress. Where such trust and support fail to develop, the result can be institu-

> tionalized suspicion which enhances the perception of risk amongst solidarity group members. Certain forms of repayment discipline imposed on solidarity groups, if not tempered by additional mechanisms to protect individuals, may contradict these social objectives of generating trust and mutual support.'

Lending on the basis of items pledged reduces the risk of non-repayment and the necessity of close contact and surveillance. However, lenders, who generally ask for conventional collateral, also ask for non-conventional collateral or social collateral. Thus, a lender can only serve a small clientele unless he, as Bouman (1989: 70-71) indicates, employs a network of intelligence agents to ensure social control. In that case, one lender can serve a larger circle of borrowers.

The amount, which the poor are willing to pay for improved housing is even a better determinant than the affordability criteria (Jørgensen 1977: 229). It is often thought that the poor do not spend a large enough portion of their income on housing and that this should be increased. The efforts to invest are also dependent on personal status of the owner or tenant, and the options to move out. The underlying assumption is that the activities of the poor are to a large extent determined by the hope of acquiring a decent, permanent dwelling, especially if the location is much appreciated (ESCAP 1991: 21-22). Apart from the personal status, the security of tenure plays a role in the willingness to pay for the habitat (e.g. Mitlin 1997; Van Lindert 1997). Security of tenure does not necessarily mean that a title deed is available, but that the chance of removal from an illegal plot is minimised, for example when some basic facilities are provided by public agencies. Here, *de facto* en *de jure* legalisation have to distinguished. *De facto* legalisation encourages dwellers to pay, while *de jure* legalisation can, paradoxically, jeopardise the willingness to do so as illustrated below.

> 'In countries where informal settlements have a *de facto* tenure security (for whatever reasons), the upgrading and regularisation programmes so aggressively marketed by international agencies have failed except in prime locations. This is because residents see little reason to pay for substandard development (...), or for facilities they have already acquired through years of lobbying or working together, and for *de jure* security, which offers them nothing. In addition, to achieve that *de jure* security, they have to follow backbreaking bureaucratic procedures, cater to corruption, and be viewed with hostility and suspicion by government functionaries.' (Hasan 1997: 38; Italics PS)

In line with the above arguments, Jørgensen (1977: 57) suggests that the 'poor are often willing and able to pay even more for something better, if they could only get it.' However, for such housing finance the terms and conditions are of crucial importance as Jørgensen (1977: 231) suggests: 'If finance was offered respondents would be able not only to pay a higher price for a house but a higher interest rate and to repay the loan over a shorter time than on normal commercial terms.' Despite the history of conceptual, theoretical and methodological errors of the affordability ratios they are still in use. Therefore, I will suggest that it is of crucial importance to focus on the usage of affordability criteria in a specific context (cf. Hulchanski 1995). Alternative methods of measuring the affordability of housing schemes can be employed after the implementation of such schemes by looking at the default rate and/or population turnover in the neighbourhood concerned (Keare and Parris 1982: 47). Affordability can also be judged by encouraging beneficiaries to save a similar amount as the future repayment of the loan instalments. If such savings behaviour over a fixed period of time is satisfactory, it can be expected that the loan is affordable (UNCHS 1996: 384).

The second criteria of the affordability-cost recovery-replicability formula is the cost recovery of habitat schemes. Cost recovery from the beneficiaries is required, because funds for such investment are scarce and insufficient to solve the housing shortage in one go. Cost recovery enables the re-use of the funds in other habitat projects and schemes over a relatively long period of time. The recovery of the investments can take place in one go or in instalments over a period of time. After the delivery of a house it becomes an individual asset, which makes the recovery of investments easier. However, if the costs are not recovered from the beneficiaries, the state has to pay these deficits and indirectly the taxpayers (Roy 1987: 90).

Cost recovery can be of a direct or indirect nature. Direct recoveries refer to the down-payment of hire-purchase or rent. The cost recovery of shelter constructed for renting out is spread over a long period of time, and for houses constructed for direct sale the cost recovery can take place over a short period by a hire purchase system or in a lump sum at once (Roy 1987: 91).

When the income of the poor is taken as starting point for cost recovery, the standards of housing have to be adjusted to their paying capacity. The poor are held responsible for the payment of the full, non-subsidised costs of the units over time. Under such circumstances the income of the poor will be the primary parameter to which architects, engineers and housing specialists have to adjust (Cohen 1983: 93).

The introduction of subsidies can improve the cost recovery of a habitat scheme. Subsidies can be provided directly on the market price or rent of a dwelling including the plot, or indirectly on the interest rate or the building materials, or on all these put together (Jørgensen 1977: 85). The use of subsidised credit or soft loans reveals that access rather than costs are the main problem for the poor. In reality, the relatively better off succeed in obtaining these loans instead of the poor. Moreover, the use of subsides on the credit reduces the chance for replicability due to the costs involved (e.g. Mitlin 1997: 27-28). The World Bank (1993a: 46) also stresses the need to refrain from soft loans because all kinds of subsidies should be of a transparent nature and subject to review. Moreover, subsidies have to be targeted to the poor and not to their houses. Finally, the World Bank stresses that rent control and the construction of subsidised public housing is not advisable to avoid price distortions at the housing market.

Cost recovery is increasingly propagated as the alternative to the use of subsidies. However, the reduction of subsidies affects mainly the lower middle-class groups, because these subsidies often are a substantial part of their income (World Bank 1991: 45). Full cost recovery may not be feasible among the poorest, but some cost recovery must be feasible. The poor do not have access to abundant finance, but they have the desire and skill to build houses. Moreover, they are used to doing it very cheaply. Cost recovery can be improved when the production costs of a housing unit are reduced by making use of specific building materials and technical constructions, but also through by self-help. For example, the superstructure can be left to the individual initiative and designs. This not only reduces the extent of cost recovery, but also enables individuals to satisfy their housing needs and taste (Jørgensen 1977: 57; Roy 1987: 96).

Problems with the affordability, cost recovery of pilot projects, sites and services and slum upgrading projects led to a loss of investments, which made their replication a failure in the 1980s. Then, standards were reduced, densities increased, and labour-intensive employment and community participation introduced, which was not very successful either. Some Indian cities such as Calcutta and Chennai still succeeded in replicating pilot projects. The supply of housing could, however, not cope with a growing demand (World Bank 1991: 26-27). Causes for this shortcoming include, for instance, the following factors. Firstly, too little attention was paid 'to the policy framework for larger-scale and longer-term replicability, including land, housing finance, and municipal finance policies.' Secondly, there were only '[l]imited efforts to strengthen the local institutional framework and the local financial base for shelter (...) investment and maintenance.' Finally, politics generally does not effectively deal with the urban poor's shelter problems (ibid.: 27).

The 'affordability-cost recovery-replicability' formula was then abandoned for several reasons. On account of the structural adjustment programme in the 1980s public expenditures decreased, public budgets declined and subsidies were reduced. As a consequence, investments in slum upgrading projects and sites and services declined. The emphasis came to lie on the provision of public and private housing finance, reducing and targeting subsidies, financial regulatory reform and private sector provision (Buckley 1999; Burgess, Carmona and Kolstee 1997: 113-114). Therefore, training and strengthening of the financial sector had to be promoted. The financial sector was poorly developed and faced problems in mobilising private savings, which has consequently led to urban investments constraints for financing. In combination with inflation and the lack of appropriate mortgage instruments, housing finance institutions often have to face a rapid decapitalisation and failure in financial management. This renders investments in housing dependent on public resources. The reform of the financial sector, including urban-related finance, has to move away from establishing new forms of directed credit and subsidies through public institutions. Instead competition between demand for financing urban investments and other investments in the economy must be encouraged in a so-called level playing field (World Bank 1991: 40-44). In line with the decline of government budgets in the 1980s and a need for a strengthening and development of housing finance institutions, the World Bank's principal housing finance specialist Renaud (e.g. 1984; 1985) published a number of overview papers and monographs in which he argued that housing finance could not be dealt with properly without taking into account reforms of property rights and institutional conditions, which enable private enterprises, households, and financial institutions to operate in the housing finance market.

The Global Strategy for Shelter, adopted by the UN in 1988 and promoted by the World Bank and the UNCHS stressed the development of broad-based housing finance systems as part of the national financial sector. Market-based finance systems were preferred above directed credit systems, because the former would lead to larger volumes of housing finance. Therefore, housing finance institutions had to be allowed to compete in mobilising funds at real interest rates and by offering different financial products (Kim 1997: 1599; World Bank 1993a: 118). Moreover, to reach the poor more adequately, interest subsidies had to be replaced by transparent and targeted direct subsidies.

This move away from soft loans, which benefited non-target groups was also encouraged by structural adjustment programmes aiming to reduce governmental budget deficits (e.g. Kim 1997: 1598).

Structural adjustment programmes were developed by the World Bank in the 1980s with the aim of encouraging sustainable growth, restructuring public budgets and social sector spending, trade liberalisation, privatisation, the deregularisation of markets and global economic integration. The impact of the structural adjustment programmes is that governments now have smaller budgets and had to reduce their expenditures, for habitat improvement schemes also. Faced with the necessity of earning foreign currencies for repaying debts, countries steered credit to investments that were assumed to be more productive than housing, which fits the first strand of thought mentioned above. This was accomplished by declining credit supply to housing finance by the central banks. Although many developing countries cut back on housing loans in the 1980s, they continued to provide housing subsidies to make housing affordable for low-income groups (e.g. Burgess, Carmona and Kolstee 1997: 118; Malpezzi 1990: 987; Peterson, Kingsley and Telgarsky 1991: 30; Pugh 1994; World Bank 1991: 31).

Despite an enormous housing shortage and the need for improving the existing housing stock in developing countries, the housing finance sector remains underdeveloped and priority is generally given to direct investments in the economy. In addition, it appears that many housing finance institutions face losses many times the value of their capital reserves (Boleat 1987). It is extremely difficult to establish housing finance institutions, especially in developing countries with a shortage of capital, which leads to a competition for funds and extra costs to acquire such capital. In addition, housing finance institutions have to face the friction between short and long-term lending (Jones and Datta 1999: 8). These developments demand a shift of focus towards the housing finance policy and its agents in the next section.

1.6 Housing finance policy and its agents

To create an urban economic environment, in which housing finance institutions can develop, the World Bank (1991) propagates an approach of privatisation and deregulation with the aim of improving efficiency and effectiveness of urban management. The Bank also advocates an enabling strategy, including a shift in the role of the government from direct provider of urban services and infrastructure to a facilitators' role, using a policy of privatisation and deregulation (see also De Soto 1989). The enabling strategies have been strongly associated with Turner's ideas since the early 1980s (Mathéy 1992b: 381; Nientied and Van der Linden 1988). Such enabling strategies are expected to support local initiatives through co-production and/or co-management of different actors, which should have a synergetic nature, i.e. the results of joint production and/or management activities are more than the sum of these results of the separate actors (Ostrom 1996). To overcome the cost of compliance, states are expected to have the capability, effectiveness, and credibility to step into useful partnerships with private enterprises, NGOs and CBOS, and incentives in their institutional arrangements. In addition, direct provision by the public sector has to be reduced (e.g. UNCHS 1989; 1990; 1996; World Bank 1991; 1993a).

The rolling back of the state is not a laissez-faire approach, which denies a role of the state completely (Pugh 1997b: iii-iv). The state has to find a new role as enabler, facilitator and deregulator. Moreover, partnerships must be sought with the 'formal' private sector. Such partnerships can take shape in different forms such as contracting out, concessions, leases and licensed competition. Each form demands a different role of the actors involved. Contracting out is accompanied by a high degree of government control and a higher degree of co-ordination skills of the private sector organisation. Concessions and leases provide private enterprises more freedom of choice, but also more financial risks, while the government can still control the system. In licensed competition, demand and supply meet each other at a competitive market, but the government restricts competition with a regulatory framework (Batley 1996). In practice, local governments aim to contract large national and foreign companies, instead of small-scale local enterprises. It is believed that it is easier to employ legal sanctions if large companies do not comply with contracts. Moreover, the government can obtain more prestige from large-scale projects (Post 1999; Rakodi 1993). However, large private companies may not be interested in going downmarket with the delivery of services due to political instability and the idea that it does not generate enough profits, if at all (Post 1999).

It is remarkable that it is expected that the public sector can be modified easily even though it is dominated by vested interests of specific institutions or individuals. For instance, political alliances make their self-interest prevail over public interests (Baken 2000; Pugh 1997b: vi-vii, iv). Moreover, political manipulation can even lead to transfer of public housing finance institutions from one ministry to another within a relative short period of time (Okpala 1994: 1577-1578), or to a bureaucracy with political-machine-like characteristics, which serves specific labour groups or co-opts opponents (see e.g. Klak and Smith 1999; Siembieda and Moreno 1999). This serving of particular interests could be done more easily due to the scarcity of available public means.

Apart from the state, development roles are also ascribed to private sector enterprises, NGOs, individuals and organised persons in society. These actors may play a role in the playing field of urban governance. 'The concept of urban governance refers to the complex set of values, norms, processes and institutions by which cities are managed. Good governance works towards making cities more efficient, equitable, safer and sustainable' (Taylor 1999: 1). Urban governance involves participatory decision making, co-production and co-management in which actors take part such as the state, local governments, economic and social actors, CBOs, and the media (Environment and Urbanization 2000; ibid.). Urban governance has to be decentralised, but little attention is paid to the risks of contested authority and dominance by some sections of society who try to adjust the governance to their own interests (Pugh 1997b: ix-xi).

It was often thought that participation is 'cost effective: with participation, local people do more; projects cost less; and achievements are more sustainable.' (Chambers 1998: xiii-xiv). However, there is a tendency to show too much confidence in participatory methodologies and it is said that the poor lack the capacity to plan for the future (Martinussen 1997: 232). Others (e.g. Baud 2000; Rakodi 1993; Smets 1996b) have argued that the poor could be helped to help themselves, which has to be facilitated and enabled by the government. It is not always clear, however, what is meant by participation, because it depends on the socio-cultural, political, and institutional context (Biggs and Smith 1998; Smets and Sivaramakrishnan 1997).

Participation can be seen in many different ways. In bottom-up participation, the poor define their own needs and priorities. Participation of the poor can also be formulated on their behalf (e.g. Brett 1996; Martinussen 1997: 42). Furthermore, participation can be differentiated as a 'means' or as an 'end'. Participation as a means 'generally becomes a form of mobilization to get things done', while participation as an end is not instrumental at all, but refers to a process approach (Moser 1983: 3).

For a specific form of participation, called 'community participation', it is not always clear how potential beneficiaries and the intervening agency define the community. One may also question whether community participation is only possible in homogeneous communities defined by for example class or caste, or whether a certain level of heterogeneity still allows it. Abbott (1996: 6) says: '[C]ommunity participation has a multiplicity of interpretations and, as a result, is heavily value-laden' He tries to distinguish different forms of community participation by taking the institutional surroundings, such as the role of the state, into account. In this way, he makes use of a continuum of an open and closed state, which offers the possibility of differentiating arenas of empowerment and community development. However, his theoretical explorations are rather abstract (Abbott 1996: 112-129). Despite the multi-interpretability of the concept 'community participation', many habitat improvement schemes still start with the idea that community participation has to be incorporated (e.g. Fiori and Raminez 1992: 38). The promotion of all kind of partnerships and alliances taking place to enable a more efficient and effective urban governance appears to be logical, but Devas (1999: 2) states that

> '[u]rban government and management studies tend to assume that the state is in a position to control what actually happens. Studies of the urban poor and NGOs/CBOs tend to see the state (...) as either irrelevant or oppressive. There has been relatively little which explores what actually takes place between (...) the various actors and interests involved.'

1.7 Innovative housing finance schemes

To enable greater access to housing finance by the poor, the World Bank (1993a: 39-40) propagates '[i]nnovative institutional arrangements (...) such as mutual guarantees and flexible payment schedules', because conventional housing finance does not reach the urban poor adequately, if at all. Conventional housing finance is generally meant for the purchase of a complete housing unit or construction of such a housing unit in one go. It is also characterised by finance with a term of 10-30 years, by mortgage loans with a minimum and regular income requirement, immovable tangible assets and a registered title deed as collateral. Repayment of the loan is generally fixed in equal periodic payments including interest and capital. Such financial terms and conditions require a regular income of a sufficient size, the availability of personal resources for down payments and collateral. Moreover, the loan, generally large in size, seldom covers the complete cost of the housing unit. Institutions, commanding long-term loans of a large size, have to face a high risk of default, which makes many financial institutions refrain from the provision of housing finance (Jørgensen 1977: 48-49; Wegener 1982: 425-432). In addition, the urban poor are difficult to reach due to complex procedures and insufficient financial resources, the inadequacy and sparse coverage of the banking network and the inadequacy of housing standards prescribed by banks for eligibility for lending. The urban poor generally lack a regular and high enough income and any proper security to pledge what makes obtaining mortgage loans rather difficult. Even when the poor can obtain a housing loan, they face problems of access due to cultural, informational and physical barriers. But most of all, the poor are considered high-risk borrowers (e.g. Ferguson 1999:185-187; Jørgensen 1977: 57; Merrett and Russell 1984: 63; Pugh 1994: 386; Wegener 1982: 425-432). This risk is reflected in the high interest rates, which would in theory encourage a much faster repayment of the credit, since there are no savings or investment opportunities with a higher return (Jørgensen 1977: 79).

The World Bank (1993: 39-40) propagates innovative financial schemes and institutional arrangements, but suggests that such innovations should take place within the framework of mortgage finance. The challenge is to determine terms and conditions of housing finance for the poor, under which the lender should be eager to provide the loan and the borrower to accept it. For this purpose, some know-how about the livelihood strategies of the urban poor households is required (Aziz 1997: 3; Baken and Smets 1999), in addition to an understanding of how private sector agencies serve them (Baud 2000: 6). Knowledge of the livelihood strategies can lead to a bottom-up approach that aims at transforming 'informal' financial organisations into regulated financial institutions. On the other hand, top-down policies, as formulated by the central bank, provide guidelines about how formal financial institutions have to deal with poorer sections in society. In practice, bottom-up and top-down policies do not necessarily coincide (Ferguson 1999: 198-199).

As an opportunity for coping with the needs of the poor, community-based financial institutions are promoted. At first sight, it may look as if financial co-operatives would be beneficial for the poor. UNCHS (1984b) suggests that membership of community-based finance institutions is open and voluntary, control is democratic for

5 The cases presented in a special issue of Trialog on community-based housing finance do not indicate that credit at commercial interest rates can serve the poor successfully (Cabannes 1995: 54).

shareholders and members, interest on the share capital may be limited, and equitable distribution of annual surpluses and the education for members takes place. Another strength of community-based housing finance institutions is their ability of mobilising savings among the poor. The credit delivery[5] of community-based housing finance is restricted to short-term loans, while there may be considerable unused funds available. This is mainly due to a lack of opportunities for short-term investments by co-operative members. Instead of such short-term housing loans they are believed, however, to need long-term finance (ESCAP 1991: 30). Despite this preoccupation with long-term housing loans, there are also examples innovative housing finance schemes, which opt for a short-to-medium term loan (see Table 3).

Table 3 Terms of innovative housing loans

Housing loan schemes	Term
Paac, Casa Melhor (Brazil), Pam and revolving funds (Mexico)	< 1 year
Focaup (Senegal), Building Materials Banks (Chile)	about 2 years
Catholic Social Services (Pakistan)	3 years
PMV, Cupocredito (Colombia), SHARE (India)	4 years
UCDO (Thailand), uTshani (South Africa)	15 years

Sources: Arrossi et al. (1994); Cabannes (1995: 56-57); Smets (1996c: 21).

On the basis of an analysis of micro finance systems, which to large extent fit the provision of micro finance for housing, Wright (2000) advocates a combination of savings and credit. Saving encourages the poor to put some money aside and shows their ability and willingness to make regular payments. These savings should not be 'locked in savings', which cannot be withdrawn, but 'voluntary made savings' that are available for withdrawal, usually on demand. Short-term credit should be provided at full cost and on an individual basis (Wright 2000: 136- 143).

Credit always asks for repayment. In order to cope with problems of default, a guarantee fund can be established, but this only copes with the consequences of default. To minimise repayment risks, the lender can look into the borrower's (re)payment history and draw on social control mechanisms rather than on conventional collateral. Social control mechanisms can be seen in a group guarantee mechanism, where the selection of the group members, five to fifteen members, have to be based on self-selection encompassing mutual trust and friendship to enable peer pressure as well as peer support. To enable the operation of peer support, loans are only provided to people, who are well known or a person who is brought in through a reference or guarantor. The working of peer pressure and support can be strengthened by for example 'the 2:2:1 staggered loan disbursement method', where two members have to make all their repayments on time for a period of four weeks before the next two loans will be released. Only when the four borrowers continue repaying their instalments on time, the final loan will be provided. Here, group members, who want to have a loan, pressure the borrowers to pay their instalments in time, unless the loan repayments are temporarily postponed (Mitlin and Satterthwaite 1992: 176; Wright 2000: 132-133, 140).

Without housing finance only small quantities of construction materials of an inferior quality can be bought. Several NGOs providing micro enterprise finance added housing finance to their portfolio, to enable clients to purchase better quality materials (Mitlin 1997). However, Ferguson (1999) argues that a group guarantee system is not so suited for NGOs and lender-based micro finance of housing. These lenders generally operate in different neighbourhoods, where those waiting for loans to be funded and those having to repay loans may not know each other or come into contact with each other. Furthermore, a larger loan and a longer loan term carries the danger of default and 'would impose greater risk on the other members' (ibid.: 192). Moreover, apart from the consolidation of an incrementally-built construction, the organisation of collective action for obtaining basic facilities require some technical assistance, which increases the costs of the schemes (Ferguson 1999: 193).

Apart from the group guarantee system, it is also of crucial importance for the repayment behaviour to consider whose money is used in the scheme. When only the own money of group members, the so-called 'hot money', is involved, people are more committed to repayment. However, if a line of credit or gift from an external agency ('cold money') is used, the discipline for repayment is much less, if at all present (Wright 2000: 137). That is why NGOs and federations of CBOs are asked to act as a guarantor to secure repayment of cold money (see e.g. Arrossi et al. 1994; ESCAP 1991; Mehta 1994; Mitlin 1997; UNCHS 1984a; 1991; 1996). Income-generating strategies can be individually based, but for obtaining credit the groups have to provide social collateral. This needs collective action based on self-interest and not applicable in other schemes (Mitlin 2000: 209).

Innovative housing finance lenders can deal with finance only or combine it with a welfare or social development focus (e.g. Datta and Jones 1999: xvii-xviii). In this respect, Copestake (1996: 25-28) distinguishes a minimalist, a radical and an alternative approach. The minimalist and radical perspectives are based on materialistic and individualistic notions of social welfare, while the alternative approach deals more with moral issues. A minimalist approach, close to neo-liberal thinking, aims at an expansion of enterprises through the provision of a minimum of services. Here, poverty is not regarded as a lack of financial means, but a problem of access to credit and saving deposit facilities. Credit programmes should be adjusted to the needs of the beneficiaries concerning access, credit size, administration and appraisal costs, incentives to enforce repayment, and the like. The ultimate aim is that credit schemes should become self-sustainable in a competitive environment. In this context, credit subsidies are seen as an obstacle in reaching this goal. According to the radical perspective, unequal distribution of and access to finance and other resources causes poverty. Then, providing credit does not help the beneficiaries by improving their income and security. It will more likely lead to indebtedness, a loss of income and dependency. Consequently, subsidies are here only acceptable, if at all, in relation to the wider impact of the programmes. The centralisation of power and the lack of participation here are an important constraint, which could be solved by means of empowerment of the beneficiaries. The alternative approach deals with the relationship between power, material welfare and well being. Resource constraints should be seen in relation to consumption aspirations, which are determined by social norms and individual preferences. Here, credit is seen as an instrument, among other ones, for creating harmonious socio-cultural processes for the management of resources. Projects, which promote this view, will provide credit subsidy on basis of moral commitments (Copestake 1996: 25-28).

Habitat improvement schemes are more successful if different schemes, such as those dealing with income generation, housing and neighbourhood improvement, are integrated in such a way that social, economic and political and environmental problems can be taken into account (Mitlin 2000; Wratten 1995: 29). However, in practice 'single-faceted strategies and programmes are still common.' (Mitlin 2000: 207)

Complications for promoting innovations concern legal constraints, land tenure problems, organisational 'weakness, lack of flexibility, procedural bottlenecks in the administrative organisation and social impediments like the weakness of social networks or the lack of credibility.' (ESCAP 1991: 10). In order to learn from experiences, a search for successful projects or 'best practices'[6] in a specific context has taken been in progress since the 1990s. Best practices are hard to develop and implement, however. Such development models cannot be universally applied and need some adjustment to a specific economic, political and socio-cultural context (e.g. Baken 2000; Desai 1996; De Wit 1993; ESCAP 1991: 4; Holton 1992: 183, 244; Smets 1997b; South Commission 1990: 131-133; Van der Linden 1997). Instead, it would be more realistic to aim at implementing a practice that is better than the previous one in that specific context (e.g. Hulme 2000). Despite the aim for collecting these practices, '[w]ell documented case studies are very scarce, and those that do exist rarely focus on the details of financial management and community organisation.' (Mitlin 1997: 30).

The collection of 'better practices', 'better' policies and a 'better' role for the public, private and other sectors deserves attention. Here, the state has a task to resolve conflicts of interest but acts generally in accordance with the interests of the powerful. In this context, it is not advisable to develop in detail the more feasible policies, but rather to work out 'better' possibilities embedded in the framework of existing power relations. The 'better' economic policies – such as privatisation and deregulation – may jeopardise the interests of the most powerful within and outside the government and will therefore be rejected or, if adopted because of external pressure, prevented from bringing about the intended effects (Martinussen 1997: 272-273). The replication of 'better' practices, with tested methods and systems, carries the danger of being uncritically implemented. These 'better' practices hinder a careful investigation into the needs and opportunities of the target population, including local constraints. This occurs especially when such schemes are promoted by powerful apex funding agencies as currently being promoted by donor agencies (Wright 2000: 109-113).

Finally, it should be noted that innovative housing finance schemes can compete with the 'informal' housing finance sector. Due to such competition the operation of the 'informal' systems cannot only improve their effectiveness, but also be supplanted by successful 'formal' financial institutions when they do not succeed to do so (e.g. Baken

---

6 '**Best practices or sound practices?** Originally introduced by the World Bank, the term *best practices* has gained wide recognition. It is an **inappropriate term**, as we learned from the organizational sciences during the 1960s that in complex organizations there are only *satisfying*, no *optimal* (or *best*) solutions. It is also a **dangerous term** in that it may lead to a search for universal solutions and to careless replication without regard to given circumstances.' (Seibel 1997: 4; Seibel's emphasis)

and Van der Linden 1993: 12; Boleat 1987: 159, 163; Igel and Srinivas 1996). Another critical point is that existing informal financial self-help organisations and agents, which could be of help for strengthening schemes, are often ignored (Nagarajan et al.: 1994: 219; Wright 2000: 114-115).

Conclusion

In this chapter, I have examined the existing debates concerning the main questions of this study. Firstly, the focus is on how the urban poor finance their shelter. According to this self-help perspective, the main debates on household dynamics, poverty concepts and livelihood strategies have been linked to the more specific question of incremental financing strategies for shelter building. Moreover, different views on incremental financing have been discussed. The view of the self-help school stress that incremental financing should be seen in line with livelihood strategies. The other strand of thought, the economist school (e.g. Pugh and Malpezzi), assumes that incremental financing should be seen from the viewpoint of economic efficiency and neglects the livelihood strategies of the urban poor. This book will show which view best fits.

This discussion of different interpretations of incremental financing has enabled me to take a step from the grassroots level to the actual providers of housing finance, who must deal with aspects of affordability, cost recovery and replicability. These terms and conditions, among others, form the basis of the present housing finance policy and the implementing agents. Still, there are serious problems in reaching the poor adequately, a gap that innovative schemes have tried to close. The factors and conditions influencing the effectiveness of their work have been discussed here.

Following this discussion on the analytical frameworks used in the studying the mismatches and matches between supply and demand for housing finance of the urban poor, I will shift this discussion to the context of Hyderabad. Here, I will pay specific attention to its land, housing, and housing finance market.

2 Hyderabad

This chapter briefly describes the history and development of Hyderabad and provides the framework of the housing finance market as described in this book. It appears that the population pressure on the land and housing in Hyderabad city has increased. Moreover, the housing supply lags behind its demand, and many people are housed by means of self-help initiatives. In order to highlight this, the land and housing market as economic entity will be discussed. This will be followed by a short overview of the structure of the Hyderabad housing finance market.

2.1 Hyderabad in historic perspective

The housing finance market as a financial landscape is dependent on its social and historical context. Financial relations often cannot be separated from the structure of social and economic relations in which they operate, and their historic development (Crow 1994). Here, this context is determined by the history of the twin cities of Hyderabad and Secunderabad, which are both located in the Indian state of Andhra Pradesh (see Figure 1). When Hyderabad is mentioned in this book, these twin cities are meant unless I specifically mention that one of them is in focus.

Geographically, the twin cities are located on the Deccan plateau. These urban areas situated between granite rocks formations. The altitude of this semi-arid area is 485-610 metres above sea level. Hyderabad was established in the basin of the Musi river, a tributary of the Krishna, which divides the old and the new city of Hyderabad located south and north of the Musi respectively. Secunderabad is located north of Hyderabad (Afzal Mohammad 1995: 21, 32). The phases of the spatial growth of Hyderabad city are shown in Figure 2. To understand such a spatial growth, I will shift my focus to Hyderbad's history.

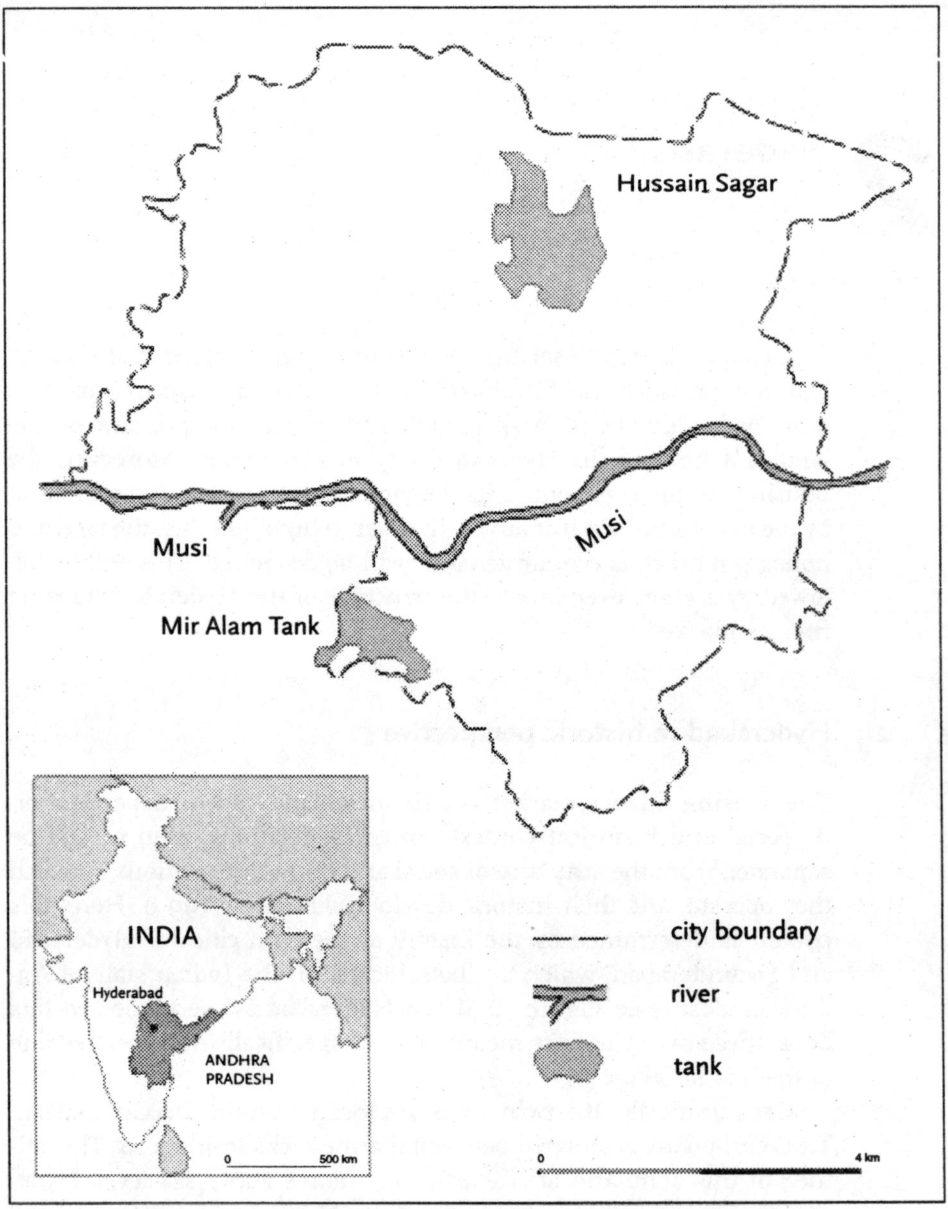

Figure 1 Location map of Hyderabad city

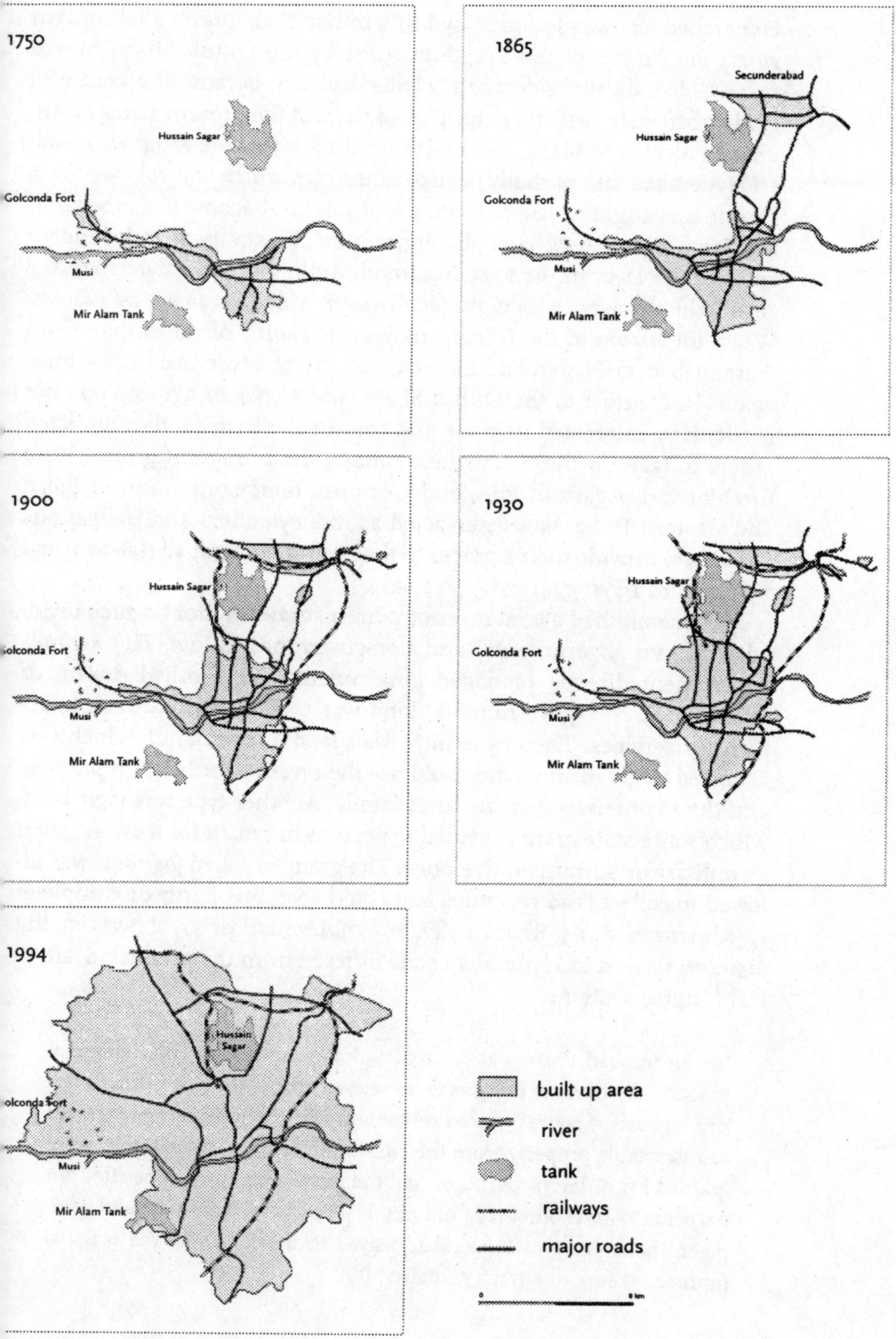

Figure 2 Spatial growth of Hyderabad city

Hyderabad city was founded by Muhammad Quli Qutub Shah in 1591 when the capital of the kingdom ruled by the Qutub Shahs moved from Golconda to Hyderabad. Hyderabad city became the centre of Hyderabad state, which encompassed parts of the present states of Andhra Pradesh and Maharashtra. It was in 1656 that the Mughals invaded Hyderabad and partially destroyed the city, which was followed by a second onslaught in 1686. In 1713 Asaf Jah had become the subedar of the Deccan, but only later did he acquire the status of independent ruler of the Deccan. In 1725 Nizam-ul-Mulk Asaf Jah established the Asaf Jahi dynasty, which provided seven rulers, known as *nizams*. When the *nizam* of the Deccan moved the capital of the empire from Aurangabad to Hyderabad in 1763, the city of Hyderabad grew once again. In contrast to the Qutub Shahs, the Asaf Jahi dynasty was not particularly interested in trade and commerce. Instead, they attracted others to take up these activities. Among these migrant groups were the Marwari, Agarwal, Jain, and Goswami merchants from northern and western India, who later acted as moneylenders and indigenous bankers to provide their services to the state of Hyderabad (Jatkar 1993: 25; Leonard 1971: 574).

The *nizams* had a land revenue administration system, which divided land into governmental and non-governmental lots. The *nizam*'s government directly managed governmental land, called diwani or khalsa land. Non-governmental land was transferred to others in return for services. There was *sarf-e-khas* land (crown land), which was allocated to the *nizam*, who could use the revenue for his own purpose and the maintenance of his royal family. Another type was jagir land, which was a state grant provided to persons in return for services, such as military or administrative ones. The grantee, called *jagirdar*, was allowed to collect land revenues and could keep this partly or completely (Khusro 1958: 1-5; Reddy 1987: 86-87). Leonard (1971) shows that the *jagirdari* system in Hyderabad state differed from the original idealtypical Mughal system.

> 'In Hyderabad there was no real *jagirdari* system, for that essential practice, the transfer of *jagirs* to prevent an official from acquiring a territorial base of power, was so seldom implemented. *Jagirs* were treated as inheritable property from the eighteenth century, though they were granted for different purposes and the grants sometimes specified "in perpetuity" and sometimes did not. If there was a legitimate and competent heir, *jagirs* in Hyderabad stayed in the family of the original grantee.' (Leonard 1971: 577; italics, PS)

The suburbs of Hyderabad city consisted mainly of *jagir* land and land under *sarf-e-khas*. The *nizam* or his *jagir* was the only ones entitled to develop such land. In reality most of the land remained vacant and undeveloped. Furthermore, the *jagir* lands were fragmented, since the *jagirdars* had large families and many descendants, who inherited the land (Afzal Mohammad 1995: 86).

As a result of the subsidiary alliance of the *nizam* with the British East Indian Company in 1798, the cantonment Secunderabad was established north of the Musi. By the end of the 19th century, Secunderabad had become an influential residential and business area. In the mean time, the power of the *nizam* weakened and the political power moved from the old city of Hyderabad to Secunderabad (Bhole 1988: 23-30).

From the 1930s onwards, Hyderabad state was threatened from both above and below. From above, Indian nationalist movements and the British-Indian government aimed for constitutional change and Indian political federation respectively. The influences from below were reflected in regional conferences held to promote the Marathi and Telegu culture and language, which led to an orientation towards neighbouring British provinces. The links between local and all-Indian movements in combination with a weak Deccani nationalism jeopardised Hyderabad state. In order to maintain the independence of Hyderabad state and their interests, the elite claimed the Muslim identity of Hyderabad state (Kooiman 1998: 657-658). After the creation of the Indian Union, Hyderabad state remained outside the union until the police action of September 1948. During this police action, the Indian army marched to replace the *nizam*'s government. In 1949 the *jagardari* system of the *nizams* was dismantled by means of, amongst other things, the introduction of the *jagirdari* abolition regulation. As a result, many rich elite Muslims migrated mainly to Pakistan and an economic depression occurred in Hyderabad state. The lower ranks within the *nizam*'s administration became impoverished after having lost their patronage ties, which were an important source of their income. It was only in 1956 that Hyderabad city – encompassing the area of Secunderabad as well as Hyderabad – became the capital of the newly formed state of Andhra Pradesh. The centralisation of the political and administrative power in Hyderabad city provided the incentive for a new development boost (Bhole 1988: 25, 31; Naidu 1990: 65).

Since the incorporation of Hyderabad city into the Indian Union, employment opportunities increased and diversified. In the pre-independence period of Hyderabad city, enterprises in grain, cloth and utensils were mainly established and controlled by the Marwari community in the old city. From the late 1940s onwards, the Marwari took over the property of Muslims in the Pathergatti-Ricabgunj area. During this period there were frequent riots in the old city, caused by the great influx of Hindus in the old city, which was predominantly, Muslim (Naidu 1990: 11, 21, 66).

During the post-independence period new employment opportunities arose due to public sector planning and investments. Industry developed along the major highways and broad gauge railway lines in the periphery of the city since the 1960s. The growth axis of the industry was concentrated in the north-east periphery along the broad gauge railway line in the Moulali-Nachram-Uppal sector (Bhole 1988: 44-46). This capital-intensive industry mainly invokes chemicals, heavy electrical machinery, and electronics. Examples are Bharat Heavy Electricals (BHEL), Electronics Corporation of India (ECIL), Nuclear Fuel Complex (NFC), Indian Drugs and Pharmaceuticals Ltd. (IDPL), and Hindustan Machine Tools (HMT). Furthermore, Hyderabad attracted a large number of research institutions such as national training institutions, central research complexes and laboratories, defence research, training and service institutions, international research institutes, state research and training complexes. These capital-intensive industries and research institutes indirectly expanded the scope for employment of the urbanites by attracting other enterprises (Sarupria 1997: 150-151), such as Bill Gates' Microsoft and related information technology institutions (Karmali 1998). Despite these new enterprises, some 50-

Table 4 Population growth of Hyderabad (Population size in millions)

	Core city/ Municipal Corporation of Hyderabad area		Urban agglomeration/Hyderabad Urban Development Authority area	
	Population	% increase	Population	% increase
1951	1.026		1.131	
1961	1.119	9	1.249	10
1971	1.607	44	1.796	44
1981	2.142	33	2.546	42
1991	3.043	42	4.344	68

Note:The population for 1951-1981 is adjusted for the jurisdiction which prevailed in 1981, while the population in the urban agglomeration includes 277,484 persons (6.5%) at tributable to new areas added since 1981.

Source: Sarupria (1997: 150).

60% of the urban dwellers are still dependent on the so-called 'informal' sector for making a living (Sarupria 1997: 151).

The growth of the city took place especially in east and north-westerly directions (Bhole 1988: 76). The urban area of Hyderabad includes some suburbs, which have been kept outside the limits of the Municipal Corporation of Hyderabad encompassing Hyderabad and Secunderabad, but have an industrial, military, political and administrative function.

Historically, Hyderabad faced problems in its population size due to, for example, the famine of 1898, the flood of 1908, and cholera and plague epidemics in 1911-21 (Gopi and Markandey 1994: 17-18). Despite these drawbacks for population growth, the core city and the urban agglomeration have significantly grown. For the figures of the second part of last century see Table 4. Gopi and Markandey (1994: 18) explain the increased growth rate of urban agglomeration in the period 1981-1991 as the result of the nine municipalities – Rajendra Nagar, LB Nagar, Uppal, Kapra, Malkajgiri, Alwal, Qutubullapur, Kukatpalli and Seri Lingampalli – inclusion in the urban agglomeration (see Figure 3).

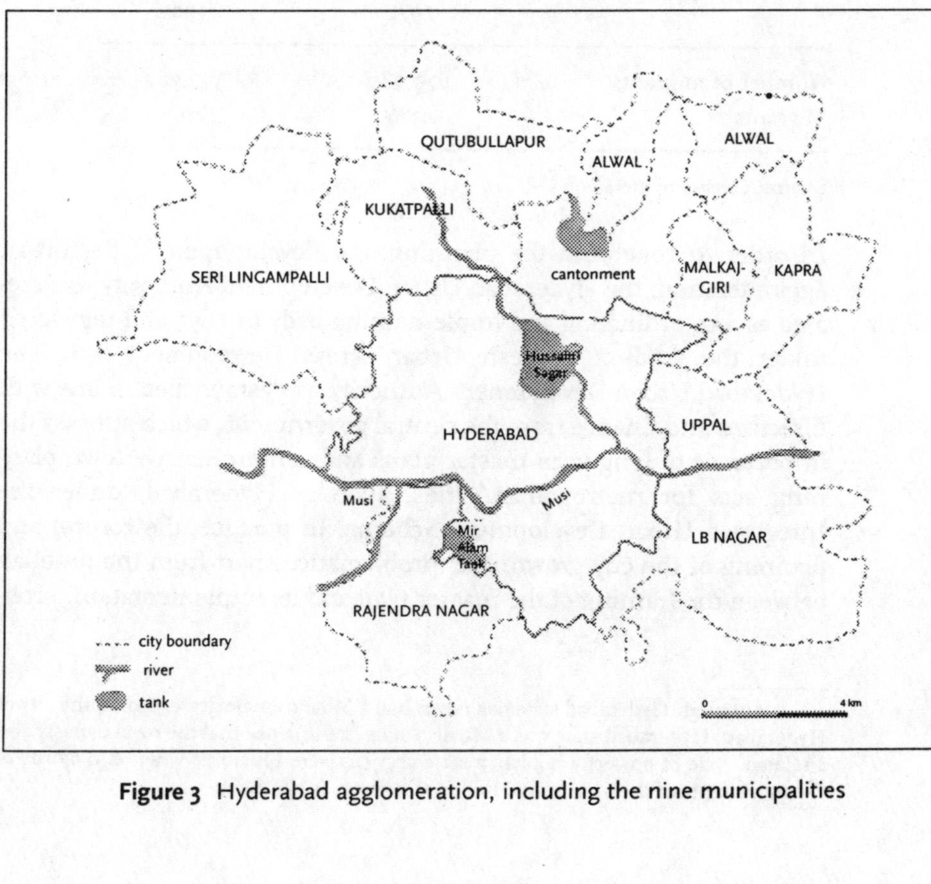

Figure 3 Hyderabad agglomeration, including the nine municipalities

The data in Table 5 illustrates how migrants are a minor part of the population of Hyderabad. Population growth of the core city and the urban agglomeration is mainly due to the internal urban population growth.

The population of the Hyderabad Urban Development Authority area includes a variety of different religious groups (see Table 6). Although Hyderabad has a Muslim image, the majority of the city is composed of Hindus, while Muslims make up only about one third of the urban population.[1] Apart from divisions along religious lines, the urban population can also be divided according the main spoken language, which more or less coincides with the religious groups. The most popular languages spoken by the dwellers in the Hyderabad Urban Development Area are Telegu (51.46% in 1981), which is the official language of Andhra Pradesh, and Urdu (32.74% in 1981) which is predominantly spoken by the Muslims (Gobi and Merchant 1994: 52).

Table 5 Hyderabad (Hyderabad Urban Development Authority area): migrant population (1971, 1981)

	1971	1981
Number of migrants	409,980	507,262
Migrants	23%	20%

Source: Census of India.

In order to cope with the planning and development of the urban agglomeration, the Hyderabad Urban Development Authority was created as a co-ordinating and implementing body in 1975 and registered under the Andhra Pradesh Urban Areas Development Act. The Hyderabad Urban Development Authority was established in line with directives and finance from the central government, which stresses the importance of long-term master plans and comprehensive town-planning acts for metropolitan cities, such as Hyderabad, under the Integrated Urban Development Scheme. In practice, the control and planning of the city growth was problematic. Apart from the time lag between the framing of the master plan and its implementation, prob-

1 Although Hyderabad state has never had a Muslim majority, except in the city of Hyderabad, Hyderabad state was a Muslim state in the sense that the royal dynasty and a related circle of powerful nobles in state services were Muslims, whereas majority of the inhabitants of the state were Hindus (Kooiman 1998: 646).

Table 6 Hyderabad (Hyderabad Urban Development Authority area): population by religious groups (1971, 1981)

	1971 (in %)	1981 (in %)
Hindu	60.76	62.91
Muslims	35.35	33.51
Christians	3.14	2.95
Others (e.g. Parsees, Jains and Sikhs)	0.75	0.63
Total	100	100

Source: Census of India.

lems of control are rooted in the clashes of interest between the Hyderabad Urban Development Authority and politicians in power. Moreover, the development activities of the Hyderabad Urban Development Authority and other agencies in Hyderabad, and the internal authority structure of the Hyderabad Urban Development Authority overlap or are even contradictory in nature. Each agency engaged in the development activities of the metropolis is to a large extent politicised and has its own clients. As a consequence, the Hyderabad Urban Development Authority had to compete and lobby to obtain its executive power (Deb 1997: 160-163).

The Hyderabad Urban Development Authority faced problems in coping with riots due to communal frictions and dilapidated state of sections of the old city, which led to the creation of a state-financed registered society without a statutory basis: the Quli Qutub Shah Urban Development Authority (QQSUDA) in 1981. The expectation was that this development authority would improve the living conditions in the old city. Two years later the QQSUDA was shelved, but was revived again in 1985. However, the implementation of almost all executive jobs of the QQSUDA was carried out by the already existing and well established urban development organisations such as the Municipal Corporation of Hyderabad and the Hyderabad Urban Development Authority. For example, decisions taken by the QQSUDA conflict with the zonal development planning of the Hyderabad Urban Development Authority such as the widening of the Lad Bazar Road, or construction of commercial complexes within the old city. The fragmentation of authority and lack of co-ordination between different government agencies damaged the functioning of the QQSUDA (Deb 1997: 164; Naidu 1990: 147-150).

The operational frictions between the Hyderabad Urban Development Authority and the QQSUDA are also rooted in the communal tensions between Hindus and Muslims[2] in the twin cities of Hyderabad and Secunderabad. Due to riots, urban dwellers moved from the old city to the new areas north of the Musi. In the old city of Hyderabad, Muslim enclaves surrounded by Hindu *mohallas* can be traced. Conflict prone areas are neighbourhoods where the one community is caught up, surrounded and outnumbered by the other or adjoining areas with different communities. When neighbourhoods are located along a procession route,[3] they are more prone to riots. Another conflict occurs when one community invades the neighbourhood of another community, such as the Marwari who bought up properties in the old *mohallas* (Naidu 1990: 31, 140).

Frictions between Muslims and Hindus are stimulated by means of the communalisation of politics in two ways. Firstly, the hegemony of the Congress Party after the incorporation of Hyderabad into the Indian union was established in an aggressive way, as illustrated below:

> 'While Gandhi and Nehru preached non-violence overseas, they had no qualms about their use of tanks and aerial bombing against poorly equipped, fledging forces of Hyderabad. Backed by the military, Congress Party gangs engaged in mass killings, rape and destruction of Muslim property all across the state. When it was all over, the Indian leaders made sure that no record of the atrocities became public knowledge.' (Khalidi 1988: x)

Secondly, as a reaction to the Muslim party *Majlis-e-Ittehad-ul-Muslimin* (MIM), the Hindu party *Jan Sangh* emerged, which gave rise to the creation of Hindu vote banks[4] in the Islamic neighbourhoods. Later on, Muslim as well as Hindu factions fought their way into the Congress Party and the Hindu party *Bharatiya Janata Party* (BJP) was

2 The communal and political differences between Hindus and Muslims only became of great importance when India's independence was approaching. Previously, Muslims and Hindus were not monolitic blocs, but subdivided by sect, caste and language (Kooiman 1998: 646).

3 Muslim processions remained the same in the 1980s while Hindu religious processions were changed and placed under official patronage (Naidu 1990: 128).

4 In a vote bank, clients promised, in exchange for the goods and services offered by the patron, to vote for their patron. during election time.

established as a separate party, which merged with *Jan Sangh*. The afore-mentioned factors stimulated feelings of antipathy between the Muslim and Hindu communities, which is also reflected in the operation of the Hyderabad Urban Development Authority and QQSUDA. The representatives of the political parties, especially the MIM and the BJP, in the QQSUDA transformed all policy issues into political debates, delaying or even paralysing the process of policy formulation and its execution. Moreover, the pre-occupation with party politics consumed most of the time available, which restricted the attention to policy issues (Naidu 1990: 118, 149).

Hyderabad acquired the status of mega city in 1994. This was accompanied by the allocation of a fund of Rs. 9.13 billion for making the metropolitan area more attractive to foreign development authorities by means of extending and improving its infrastructure (Deb 1997: 158).

The population pressure on the available land is still increasing, even after new areas have been incorporated into the urban agglomeration. This population pressure, in combination with private initiatives and public interventions, influences the dynamics of the land market as will be illustrated in the next section.

2.2 The land market

Although old land tenure and revenue systems were abolished after the incorporation of Hyderabad into the Indian Union, the nature of the land market in Hyderabad is to a large extent still determined by agreements made under the *nizam*'s rule. After the incorporation of Hyderabad state in the Indian Union *sarf-e-khas* and *jagir* land was partly confiscated by the government while the remaining land still has a disputed status. An inadequate registration system lies at the basis of many legal disputes. During the 1950s, land prices in the old city have dropped as a result of migration of many elite Muslims out of the old city. During that period their subordinates and servants claimed the land without having official title deeds. Moreover, Hindus obtained the opportunity to invest in land, contributing to pre-existing tensions (Naidu 1990: 27; Nayani 1987: 57).

As a result of the old land rules and regulations, in 1967 the majority of the land in Hyderabad city was privately owned (70%), which restricted public institutions from playing a role in balancing land use planning and urban development over time. It appeared that then 39% of the land within the Municipal Corporation of Hyderabad area was vacant,[5] which declined to 27% in 1981, which is still very substantial. Moreover, the urban development authorities and the Municipal Corporation of Hyderabad could not acquire private lands under the Land Acquisition Act, 1894 due to time-lag problems in the acquisition procedures. Some of these vacant lands are thus used for speculation or illegal subdivision (Nayani 1987: 57). Despite this scarcity, the government of Andhra Pradesh provided large tracts of land at the urban fringe to public industries at very cheap prices and provided the required infrastructure in the mid of the 1960s. They created self-sufficient satellite townships such as Ramachandrapuram, Hayatnagar, Moula-Ali, and Kukatpally (Deb 1997: 161). Moreover, new city centres developed north of the river Musi. Vacant land in the inner parts of the city became scarce and consequently the land prices increased (Reddy 1996: 73).

From the 1970s onwards, petro dollars derived from labour migration of especially Muslims to the Gulf countries were mainly used for lucrative and safe investments in urban land and less in businesses or industries. These investments of petro dollars have led to increases of land prices in the old city (Bhole 1988: 177; CEC 1985: 7). These overseas remittances also enabled families to leave the old city and resettle mainly in the south-eastern part of the old city (Nayani 1987: 59). Apart from overseas remittances pushing up the price of land, the land price also depends on many variables such as the location of the neighbourhood, the location of the plot within the settlement, officially permitted land use and other planning regulations, the level of services, and the illegal trade in land. Consolidation of a low-income neighbourhood, just as legalising a low-income neighbourhood, leads to an increase in land prices. Moreover, the high level of the land prices is also caused by an inadequate urban land ceiling legislation, delays in land acquisition, ineffective bureaucracy, corruption, migration, inflation and (artificially created) scarcity (CEC 1985: 6-8).

In order to acquire private land at low costs for distribution among the weaker sections of society, the Urban Land Ceiling and Regulation Act of 1976 was framed. Since then people are not entitled to hold vacant land of more than 1000 square meters in Hyderabad and all land owned above this ceiling is categorised as surplus land. According to this act, no one can dispose of surplus land without governmental permission, which was intended to reduce the operations of land speculators. However, in reality, this act worked counter-productively: the

5 However, land registered as being vacant often in reality appears to be occupied.

transfer of all urbanised land had to wait for governmental permission, which is very difficult to obtain. In other words, the transfer of land was frozen and the scarcity of land only increased.

In reality, less than 5% of the declared surplus land could be transferred. To a large extent these Hyderabadi lands were allocated to registered co-operative housing societies, resulting in corrupt practices in the bureaucracy and political hierarchy (Bhole 1988: 154; CEC 1985: 7). This surplus land could be sold to registered co-operative societies if such a society had been registered before 1976. Furthermore, no individual society member is allowed to own any land elsewhere in the urban agglomeration. The maximum size of the land, which could be sold to the housing society, is 300 square metres per member. Later on, landholders could transfer this surplus land to registered co-operative societies irrespective of their date of registration or after the commencement of the Urban Land Ceiling and Regulation Act. As a result, co-operative housing societies enabled the registration of surplus land, which they kept idle in order to profit from higher land values in the future. Such practices have also taken place by means of mutual agreements between landholder and co-operative housing societies, possibly helped by middlemen (Bhole 1988: 154-155).

One of the exemptions of the Urban Land Ceiling and Regulation Act concerns *waqf* land, because of its Islamic status. *Waqf* land is land as inheritance, tied up with the Almighty, and dedicated to the public, which may be rented at a cheap rate. The caretaker of the property or the *mutawallih* looks after the property according to the wishes of the original owner. To supervise and control *mutawallihs* and *waqf* land, a *waqf* board is established. For a period of six years, the government nominates the members of the *waqf* board and consequently the *waqf* board has the same political colour as the ruling party. In practice, income made from *waqf* land is partly confiscated by the caretakers and *waqf* land is also illegally sold. Moreover, when *waqf* land is squatted on, the *waqf* board does not have any legal powers to remove squatters from the land as laid down in the Waqf Act 1954, enacted by the Government of India.[6] On the other hand, Hindus have an endowment commission for similar plots of land, which has the executive powers to remove squatters from their land (personal communication with Mohammed Ali Khan, consultant AP Minority Commission).

---

6 However, at a collectors conference of May 1994, it was decided that *waqf* properties in their respective districts should be kept free from encroachment and that collectors should encourage a long term commercial lease of *waqf* land lying idle (GAP 1994b: 5).

All agricultural lands of five acres (about 20,000 square meters) outside the city limits can be subdivided without obtaining the exemption under the Urban Land Ceiling and Regulation Act. This encouraged private land developers to buy land from farmers located around the city and sell it for profit. The act also had an impact on the land delivery system in Hyderabad. The number of illegal subdivisons, previously mainly for low-income groups, has increased substantially, because many landowners with large tracks of land, which could hardly be used legally, saw opportunities for selling smaller plots at profitable prices to all income groups. As a result, vacant land within the Municipal Corporation of Hyderabad area was acquired residential use, which public agencies had been unable to do (Nayani 1987: 58, 62, 68). This trade in land flourished. In 1982, 8000 people were involved in landgrabbing and public as well as private land was sold legally and illegally (CEC 1985: 8). As shown above, the Urban Land Ceiling Act worked counterproductively and pushed up land prices, leading to stagnation in the development of the housing industry. In 1999, the Act was repealed to enable and facilitate the revival of the operation of the housing industry and the provision of housing to the urban poor (Ministry of Urban Affairs & Employment 1999).

Apart from the city and the countryside, there are also illegal settlements in Hyderabad. In the 1960s, illegal subdivisions[7] and squatments were established on the fringes of the old city and in the new city closer to the employment centres. These neighbourhoods are located on hillsides and low-lying marshy land. Land can be subdivided and sold at profitable rates in three ways. Firstly, the landowner subdivides and sells the land himself. Secondly, the landowner appoints colonisers for selling the plots, but he does the subdivision in co-operation with a surveyor. Thirdly, the landlord sells plots to colonisers, who subdivide and sell it (Nayani 1987: 57-58). However, subdivision can also take place without the permission of the landlord, whose land claims may be disputed as illustrated by my fieldwork material.

In 1989, a family member of the seventh *nizam* of Hyderabad left the old city to keep an eye on his mother's property consisting of some

---

7 These illegal subdivisions are considered illegal, because the ownership of property is without adequate title deed and there are irregularities in the procedures concerning the transfer of properties. Moreover, the regulation of subdivisions, the master plan, property tax regulations, the Urban Land (Ceiling and Regulation) Act, 1976, building bye-laws, and the unauthorised tapping of public facilities such as water and electricity supply are contravened (Nayani 1987: 54).

> buildings and *inam* land in Begumpet. This property declined due to government claims but also due to illegal sale by the watchman, who was employed to look after the family's property in the beginning of the 1980s. In the mean time, Aziz Muddin, a former lawyer of the *nizam*, claimed 14,000 square metres of land in the same neighbourhood, which was said to be received in return for services provided. In order to legalise this claim, this lawyer filed a court case and simultaneously gave two men a General Power of Attorney (GPA) in order to sell the land for Rs. 957 per square metre. This case was still pending and could even last for about 30 years, which creates enough time for selling the land illegally. The police, local leaders and politicians backed up these land transactions.

Such unclear title deeds linked with a *hiba* (gift) status encourage claims to be laid on land and illegal trade in land. One of the reasons behind such unclear title deeds is rooted in the inadequate land property registration during the *nizam*'s period. The *nizam* provided land to those loyal and faithful to him. After the partition between India and Pakistan, many of these gift-receivers left for Pakistan and sold their land to locals. Many tracts of their land remained unoccupied until many migrants entered the city. On many plots landlords allowed the dwellers to construct their shelter and charged them rents. However, when the land prices increased, these landlords tried to remove the dwellers from their land for which they required political support to obtain eviction orders (CEC 1985: 13-14). The Hyderabad Municipal Corporation Act 1955 enabled the commissioner of the Municipal Corporation of Hyderabad to repress and control illegal settlements, but the act was ineffective due to its loopholes resulting in stay orders. In spite of removing the illegal structures, the illegal subdivisions obtained at least some basic facilities (Nayani 1987: 64-65).

Despite rules and regulations, land transactions took place with or without any title deed such as a notary agreement or registration. Land transactions took place on a large scale when affluent migrants from the coastal areas of Andhra Pradesh bought land in Hyderabad. New colonies were established even in water tanks and ponds. Speculators and the rich acquired large chunks of land. Local politicians tended to create vote banks by settling migrants on government or individual land, often illegally. As a consequence, slums have increased in number and size for the last 20 years (Narsing Rao 1997: 180). However, the opportunity to establish slums in popular areas, such as the centre of Hyderabad and Secunderabad, has become very small or almost impossible. In these areas the first high rise buildings since the 1970s have been constructed (Bhole 1988: 149-150).

The public agencies dealing with the land market in Hyderabad are faced with difficulties. For example, the housing board was allowed to acquire vacant sites in Hyderabad, but regularly had to face legal disputes, claims of compensation payments or other litigations in connection with the removal of encroachments (Bhole 1988: 138). Moreover, frictions have occurred between the Hyderabad Urban Development Authority and the government of Andhra Pradesh about control of the land within the metropolitan region. It was decided that government land would be transferred to Hyderabad Urban Development Authority in custody and for development purposes. In practice, this transfer was jeopardised by the state Board of Revenue, which was not willing to lose an important source of power. In 1976, the state government

> 'issued an order that till such time as the HUDA [Hyderabad Urban development Authority] makes adequate progress with the preparation of the master and zonal development plans the power of HUDA under Sections 13 and 14 of the Andhra Pradesh Urban Areas (Development) Act, 1975, shall be notified as exercisable by the Municipal Corporation of Hyderabad and the panchyat bodies in their respective areas by delegation under Section 56 of the said Act.' (Deb 1997: 162)

Moreover, the metropolitan development strategy of the Hyderabad Urban Development Authority was also harmed when housing societies and institutions occupied the green belt in between the ring towns and the city. The land acquired under the Urban Land Ceiling and Regulation Act was not allocated to the Hyderabad Urban Development Authority, but to the Board of Revenue and co-operative housing societies (Deb 1997: 162-163). The land registration system was inadequate; land recorded as government land by the Surveys and Land Records department was known as private land owned by *pattidars* (hereditary shareholders in land) by the Board of Revenue (CEC 1985: 7). Nevertheless, it can be said that in Hyderabad enough land for extension of the city is available around the city. Moreover, the problem of squatted land could be solved by sharing the use of the land by the private landowner and the squatters. For example, the landowner could construct a commercial shopping centre on a part of the land, while the dwellers could live on the top of the shopping centre or on the remaining piece of land.

Despite all frictions in the operation of the land market, the government of Andhra Pradesh could provide free *pattas* (land titles) to Economically Weaker Sections households partaking in housing schemes. In practice, *pattas* are also allocated to people who do not officially belong to the Economically Weaker Sections category. The release of *pattas* connected with a housing scheme is also influenced by political leaders. The *tahsildar* (chief revenue officer of a subdivion called *tahsil*) told me:

> '*Pattas* can be cancelled on any ground such as the violation of the building regulations. In practice this only happens in rare cases. We keep our eyes shut. In fact, 75% of the pattas should be cancelled, but only a few are cancelled. Political parties and leaders have here their interest.'

As illustrated above, the land market is characterised by many manipulative actions, which also have an impact on the housing market as will be demonstrated in the next section.

2.3 The housing market

After the formation of the state of Andhra Pradesh, the pressure on the housing market increased and acute housing shortages raised problems in the housing market and especially for the urban poor. Many were dependent on shelter in old neighbourhoods or new established illegal settlements, with unauthorised constructions. In the old city *mohallas* (low-rise, densely packed houses, only accessible through narrow lanes) around palaces and *havelis* (mansions) are popular neighbourhoods for especially the poor. By 1951, the housing density in the old city was already very high and the new migrants, many of whom were rather poor, hardly constructed any new houses. However, houses were subdivided, which caused increased congestion and pressure on amenities such as the sewerage system, piped water, and latrines (Naidu 1990: 20, 91-95). In 1971, 60% of the households in Hyderabad still resided in rented accomodation. In 1981 this percentage was 55.2% (NIUA 1995: 79). In particular, poor urban dwellers sought plots to squat, which until 1962 were mainly around graveyards, which were often *waqf* lands. After 1962, the illegal settlements mushroomed around railway tracks, *nalas* (small channels), wholesale markets, the major hospitals and industrial areas such as Azamabad Industrial area,

Sanathnagar Industrial area and Chandulal Brardari Industrial area (Alam, Alikhan and Bhattacharji 1987: 124).

The housing shortage increased during the 1960s, which was a period of intensive industrial development. Large industries, such as Bharat Heavy Electricals Ltd. and Indian Detonators and Pharmaceuticals Ltd., decided to house their employees in townships around large factories, which were located in the south-east periphery. This was only a partial solution to the housing shortage in Hyderabad. The residential growth in the cantonment in Secunderabad, a military housing area, lagged behind. However, when the cantonment building act was relaxed, co-operative sector housing mushroomed there in the 1970s (Bhole 1988: 7, 48, 57). In the period between 1950 and 1970, co-operatives were stimulated to take part in the housing sector by securing plots for the construction of houses, developing land and helping to obtain finance for their members. The construction activities of the co-operative sector have slowed down since the 1970s and many housing co-operatives appear to lie dormant (Bhole 1988: 152-155). In 1994 there were 789 co-operative housing societies registered in the twin cities, but out of them 259 are dormant or face liquidation. Despite the stringent zoning regulations and building bylaws of the Municipal Corporation of Hyderabad, many multi-storey buildings were constructed across the city. Such high-rise buildings absorb open spaces in the city and replace old buildings (CEC 1985: 3-4). Different occupational groups inhabit housing units in multi-storey buildings in Hyderabad and Secunderabad, mainly belonging to the higher-income groups. Central location and high land value lead to high construction costs and very high rents. Only 3.1% of the residents who live there have an income of less than Rs. 3,000 per month (Reddy 1996: 109, 123).

It was only in the 1960s that the public housing agencies began to take greater interest in housing. Housing agencies and schemes, such as the Andhra Pradesh Housing Board and the Andhra Pradesh Police Housing Corporation (APPHC),[8] were sponsored and subsidised by the government. In addition, the government subsidised industrial housing schemes, and rental housing schemes for state government employees (Bhole 1988: 132-133). Other public actors in housing schemes

8 The APPHC was established in 1971 as a private limited company under the companies act (1956) with the aim of constructing quarters for police employees, who were until that time housed till then in barracks. The government of Andhra Pradesh aimed at accommodating 80% of its police in small tenements by 1990 (Bhole 1988: 143-144).

for the poorer sections in society are for example the Municipal Corporation of Hyderabad, the Andhra Pradesh State Housing Corporation (APSHC) and the Andhra Pradesh Urban Development and Housing Corporation (APUD & HC) and the Hyderabad Urban Development Authority. The role of the private sector in serving the low-income sectors, according to Bhole (1988: 149), appears to be limited.

Table 7 Population, houses and households in Hyderabad (1991)

	Population	Number of households	Number of occupied residential houses
Municipal Corporation of Hyderabad area	3,043,896	515,217	506,354
Hyderabad Urban Development Authority area	4,344,437	784,886	767,675

Source: Census of India 1991.

The ruling political elite made use of the intense pressure on land and increasing land prices by cultivating vote banks. These facts, in combination with the appearance of a large population of poor and underemployed, made it very difficult for the state to provide housing for the poor (Deb 1997: 169).

The major part of the housing stock in Hyderabad is private housing. On account of the measures of the Rent Control Act[9] and the burden of estate duty and housing tax, investments in housing have been made unattractive and unremunerative. Apart from these restrictive regulations, the construction costs have also increased (Bhole 1988: 149, 167).

Despite all kinds of initiatives in the formal housing construction sector, there was still a shortage of housing in 1991 as illustrated by Table 7. This shows that there was almost no difference between the number of occupied houses and households living in the Municipal Corporation of Hyderabad and the Hyderabad Urban Development

9 Changes in the rent control legislation should be accompanied with financial assistance to enable households to consume housing in a more cost-effective, flexible and equitable way. Moreover, fiscal measures had to be introduced to encourage full utilisation of land owned by the middle and upper income households to achieve full utilisation of their land (Mehta and Mehta 1991: 113).

Authority area. In both areas, there was still a group of urban dwellers who have no other option than looking for housing in illegal settlements. In 1981 the urban population of Hyderabad was 2,545,000 with a slum population of 500,000 (19.6%). The estimated slum population of 1991 had increased to 1,112,000 (29.45%) of the total population of 3,707,000 (NIUA 1995: 84). In 1981, these slum dwellers were living in 455 slums in 1981, and 662 slums in 1991. These slums are recognised slums, on basis of the Andhra Pradesh Official Slum Act of 1956. In reality, thought, the number of slums is higher than is given in the official list.

Slum clearance and upgrading programmes for recognised slums were started under the Urban Community Development Department of the Municipal Corporation of Hyderabad. The Urban Community Development Programme started in 1969 with support of UNICEF, which was later replaced by aid from the British Overseas Development Administration (ODA)[10] in 1984 (see e.g. Smets and Sivaramakrishnan 1997). In practice, the incorporation of the neighbourhoods in the urban community development schemes is not always free from politics. There is a lot of lobbying to get a neighbourhood declared as slum, because of the finance dedicated to slum improvement programmes (cf. Naidu 1990: 101). The following example will illustrate this

> 'You can get a blighted area ignored for a century just as you can get all the pucca [concrete] houses in residential area recognized as slum to benefit from urban community development schemes, as urban renewal involves the administration of large amounts of development funds. How, where and in what manner these amounts will be spent is more a matter of political decision making. Next to the Hospital for diseases of Chest and Tuberculosis are 52 *pucca* houses and some double storeyed buildings. Inspite of their condition in 1979, the residents managed to get their area recognized as slum. In 1979, the residents of the area requested the MCH [Municipal Corporation of Hyderabad] to provide water lines. The residents were asked to pay Rs. 45,000/- as betterment charges as per rules of the MCH [Municipal Corporation of Hyderabad]. At this stage the residents approached a politician who decided to contest the 1980 Parliamentary elections. The leader approached the authorities and got the residential area into 'Weaker

10 DFID (Department for Institutional Development) is presently taken up the activities of the formerly ODA.

> Section' category and requested the government to provide water without betterment charges. The UCD [Urban Community Development] was asked to do a survey as a prerequisite for identification of an area as a slum. There were pucca houses in 1979 too but it appears the UCD conducted a midnight survey and could not see *pucca* houses.' (CEC 1985: 14; explanations in between brackets and italics, PS)

Although pressure on the land and housing market was shown to be high, people are still able to construct some form of shelter. For this purpose housing finance is required. How they obtain such housing finance will be the subject of the next section.

2.4 The housing finance market

Institutions and persons operating in the housing finance market deal with savings and/or the provision of credit. The suppliers of these financial services are not always specialised in housing finance, but the borrowers may allocate it for shelter purposes. The formal housing finance sector is controlled by the Central Bank of India, and since 1988 by its subsidiary the National Housing Bank. It encompasses commercial banks, co-operative banks, housing finance institutions, and apex institutions.[11] Contrary to the formal financial sector, the 'informal' sector operates outside direct control of the Central Bank of India and encompasses moneylenders, pawnbrokers, financial self-help organisations, but also friends, neighbours and relatives.

A qualitative and quantitative development of the Indian housing finance sector is in progress. However, the increasing supply of and access to housing finance can lead to a rise in demand for housing. If the housing supply cannot respond proportionately, house prices will increase. An increased housing supply does not automatically lead to a better situation for all. It appears that some elasticity of the supply of housing finance is required in relation to rising demand patterns. As a consequence, housing finance cannot be restricted to the demand side by providing mortgage financing. A housing finance system should also encompass land assembly and development, the provision of in-

11 An apex institution or body is a national, state or city-level body that helps housing finance institutions 'to finance substantial portions of their loan portfolio, by wholesaling funds to them with or without technical assistance or training for the' housing finance institutions (Rosenberg 1998).

frastructure and basic services, financing of housing producers and above all finance for upgrading (Mehta and Mehta 1991: 1111).

In comparison with cities in the so-called developed countries, the formal housing finance market in Hyderabad is not very well developed. The Indian formal sector encompasses budgetary allocations of the central and state governments, but also loans from the open market, from financial and insurance agencies such as the General Insurance Corporation (GIC), the Life Insurance Corporation (LIC), Unit Trust of India (UTI), commercial banks, and provident funds, but also public sector institutions such as the Housing and Urban Development Corporation (HUDCO), the state level housing co-operative societies and private sector housing finance corporations. In addition, housing finance from national insurance and finance companies in combination with central and/or state governmental funds were channelled to the beneficiaries through the Andhra Pradesh Housing Board, and the different state housing corporations such as the Andhra Pradesh State Housing Board (APSHB) and the Andhra Pradesh Urban Development and Housing Corporation (APUD & HC). The formal housing finance institutions mobilise funds from general financial institutions, which leads to complex institutional linkages, of which Figure 4 provides a simplified overview. Despite the continuing importance of the savings performance of households, the housing finance sector encompasses only a small share of the overall financial sector. The small share of the housing finance sector has to be viewed against the background of a well developed financial system in India, which can be compared with that of some upper middle-income developing countries (Mehta and Mehta 1991: 1107). Since the middle of the 1980s, a gradual process of liberalisation of the financial sector has taken place, which started 'with the 1985 Report of the Chakravarty Committee appointed by the Reserve Bank of India' (Buckley et al. 1989). This development was promoted by the establishment of the National Housing Bank as subsidiary of the Reserve Bank of India in 1988 with the aim of supporting the private sector involvement in the housing finance sector.

At the local level, it is important to look at the housing finance of the housing co-operatives in detail. The Andhra Pradesh co-operative Housing Societies Federation Ltd. (Housefed) established in 1966, was effectively functioning since 1970-71 when the Life Insurance Corporation started funding it. Housefed concentrated its activities on the rural areas and the main objective of the federation was the provision of housing finance for the construction of new houses through affiliated co-operative housing societies. The federation encourages the

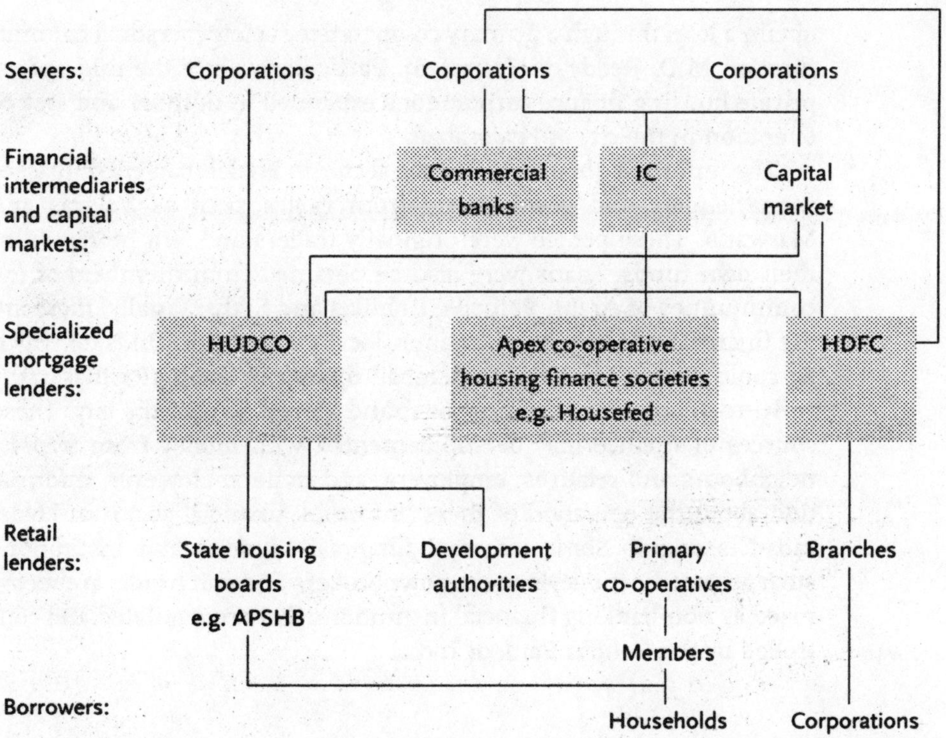

IC = Insurance Corporations
HUDCO = Housing and Urban Development Corporation
HDFC = Housing Development and Finance Corporation
APSHB = Andhra Pradesh State Housing Board

Figure 4 Formal housing finance intermediation.
Source: After Munjee et al. (1990), in Metha and Mehta (1991: 1109).

construction of apartment houses and purchases land and prepares layouts of sites, advances credit for repairs and renewal of old houses, and supplies building materials such as cement and steel to the members of the housing co-operatives (Bhole 1988: 160-161). In the 1970s, Housefed became the major housing finance corporation in the twin cities, with a credit portfolio of 40%. This has since declined to about 10 to 15% in 1993, due to the declining access to public land. In other words, fewer housing loans were provided while sufficient housing finance was available. Housefed offered housing loans to a maximum of Rs. 60,000. Other housing finance corporations were established and even provided loans of up to Rs. 100,000. Housefed provided housing loans for institutional habitat schemes, while individuals could obtain a loan through a primary co-operative society (personal communication M.D. Reddy of Housefed). Particularly since the mid 1980s, private housing finance corporations expanded in number and area of operation in the city of Hyderabad.

The 'informal' (housing) finance sector in Hyderabad encompasses moneylenders and pawnbrokers from castes such as Vaisyas and Marwaris. These people were originally traders and lent money from their own funds. Loans were also be obtained from members of the communities of Arabs, Pathans, Rohillas and Sikhs. Finally, there are the financial self-help organisations, locally called chit funds, of which 25 could be traced in the Hyderabad district in 1969 (Parthasarathy 1983: 101), but which can now be found almost all over the city. These sources of finance may be supplemented with money from friends, neighbours and relatives, employers, and traders. However, information about the operation of these 'informal' financial sector in Hyderabad is scarce. Some informal financial agencies and institutions such as specific moneylenders, pawnbrokers and chit funds, are recognised as non-banking financial institutions that are regulated and controlled by the Central Bank of India.

Conclusion

Housing finance practices are dependent on the operation of the land and housing markets. Both are to a large extent determined by the history of the more than 400 years old city of Hyderabad, which was originally the capital of a kingdom ruled by Muslims. From the establishment of Hyderabad city (1591) onwards, the Qutub Shah and the Asaf Jahi dynasty ruled Hyderabad state. In 1798, the *nizam* allowed the East Indian Company to establish the cantonment Secunderabad north of Hyderabad city. Following India's independence, Hyderabad state was incorporated into the Indian Union by the police action of September 1948. This has led to an impoverishment of the lower ranks within the *nizam*'s administrative system and a migration of rich Muslims to Pakistan. Moreover, the population mix in the twin cities of Hyderabad and Secunderabad (further on Hyderabad) changed from a predominantly Muslim society towards a Hindu dominated one.

From then onwards, public sector institutions face problems in balancing land use planning and development of Hyderabad city due to several reasons. Firstly, the local elite had arrangements with the nizam concerning land tenure and revenue systems, through which land often was transferred to them. Secondly, land ownership disputes have led to many vacant plots. Thirdly, communal frictions and riots between Muslims and Hindus go together with communal frictions within and in between public sector organisations. Fourthly, the spatial development of the city is to a large extent caught up in a system of political manipulations and the creation of vote banks.

Due to an increasing growth of the population of Hyderabad, once it became the capital of the new formed state of Andhra Pradesh in 1956, the pressure on the land and housing market increased and a housing shortage arose. From the 1960s onwards, public agencies became interested in housing. For the development of slum areas, the Urban Community Development Department was created. In order to solve the housing shortage, the government intervened in the land and housing market, but its efforts were counterproductive. Although some poor were lucky and could partake in public housing schemes, others were housed in illegal structures built on squatted or illegally bought land.

All housing, also for the poor, requires finance, but the housing finance market in Hyderabad was not very well developed. Since the middle of the 1980s, a gradual process of liberalisation has taken place. This has created more opportunities for the different providers of housing finance. One should realise that the supply of housing finance can lead to a higher demand for housing and land, which increases its prices. The crucial point is to find a balance between supply and demand, which still keeps the dwellings affordable, especially for the urban poor.

Given that the historic and political-economic field has now been set out in the context of Hyderabad, the focus will shift to the different contemporary segments of its financial market for low-income housing; household strategies, 'informal' housing finance, public and private housing finance and the role of NGOs and CBOs alone or in partnership.

3 Financial strategies of the urban poor

> Erama (35) and her four children (two boys of 12 and 7, and two girls of 9 and 4) live in a hut. She survives by begging while carrying around pictures of several Hindu Gods. Every day she collects Rs. 7-8, which is scarcely enough to buy a daily portion of rice. The hut is built on a piece of land squatted on when Erama's husband was still alive. In April 1994, the hut was partly washed away by the rains, but it was rebuilt with the help of five neighbours, who were willing to do the work for relatively little, just tea, in exchange. Luckily enough she was able to buy some second hand bamboo mats from them to construct temporary walls. These mats cost Rs. 350, which now has to be repaid in a lump sum within a period of two months. For that purpose, she has a cloth in which she puts a few rupees every day. The expectation is that when she has some means again, she will be able to construct mud walls.

The case above illustrates how survival at a subsistence level is rather difficult, especially when unforeseen calamities occur. However, even when the urban poor are relatively better off, they still face the problems of dealing with their small and irregular income. One of the main challenges they face is how to obtain or construct a dwelling. To gain insight into these challenges, I have surveyed 13 slums where no housing schemes are implemented by any external agency. Here, it appears that the dwellers have a specific method of financing their shelters, which is part of their livelihood strategies. In order to understand this, I will discuss characteristics of the livelihood strategies of the urban poor. One of the crucial things the poor need is to be assured of help from others through a so-called network. Furthermore, the methods of sourcing finance and budgeting of expenditures of the poor will be focused on. In addition to this, I will demonstrate how incremental building and its incremental financing fit the livelihood strategies of the urban poor. This will be the basis for the determination of criteria for housing finance, which enable the poor to improve their living conditions in a sustainable fashion.

3.1 The surveyed urban poor

The surveyed households consisted of 48% Hindus, 48% Muslims and 4% Christians and tribals. There is, thus, an overrepresentation of Muslims and other non-Hindus in the sample compared with the entire population of Hyderabad. Furthermore, 53% of the interviewed households live below the poverty line and 47% above it. From the interviewed households a majority of interviewed Muslims had a household income below the poverty line, while a slight majority of the interviewed Hindus have a household income above the poverty line (Table 8).

Table 8 Characteristics of interviewed slum dweller households in Hyderabad

	Hindu		Muslim		Other (Christian, Tribal)		Total	
	abs.	%	abs.	%	abs.	%	abs.	%
Income below poverty line	86	48	104	58	7	47	197	53
Income above poverty line	92	52	76	42	8	53	176	47
Total	178	100	180	100	15	100	373	100

Source: own research (N = 373, missing cases 6; V = 0.10; $\chi^2_{(2)} = 3.4$, $p > 0.05$).

Not all members contribute to obtaining an income for the household. Here, income refers to financial income obtained by any form of activity. The income-earning household members are classified as women only, men only and both sexes. The financial contribution to the household budget appears to be mainly male-dominated, although many women are engaged in income-earning activities (see Table 9). Women are not only involved in productive work, but also have reproductive and management tasks. Consequently, women's workload is often heavier compared to those of men in households.

Although there is no significant relationship in Table 10, it may be useful to note that the percentage of male and female contributors to the household budget is also influenced by their religious practices. Among Hindus, men alone contribute financially to the household income in 55% of the surveyed households and women are the sole contributors in 6% of the surveyed households. A mix of both sexes as financial contributors occurs in 39% of the households. In Muslim

Table 9 Income-earning household members by income

Sex of earners	Income below poverty line		Income above poverty line		Total	
	abs.	%	abs.	%	abs.	%
Men only	105	53	114	65	219	60
Women only	10	5	4	2	14	3
Both sexes	82	42	58	33	140	38
Total	197	100	176	100	373	100

Source: own research (N = 373 households, missing cases 6; V = 0.13; $\chi^2_{(2)} = 5.9$, $p > 0.05$).

households they encompass 62%, 2% and 36% of the surveyed households respectively. For Christians and Tribals, these figures are 47%, 18% and 35% respectively. In other words, men obtain the income of the majority of the surveyed households only or in combination with female household members. It is only a small minority of the surveyed households where female members are the only income earners. Moreover, the percentage of women involved in income-earning activities is the lowest among surveyed Muslim households and the highest among Christians and Tribals, which may give an indication of the Muslim inclination to practice *purdah* (keeping women separate from male strangers by remaining in a special part of the house or by covering their faces and the whole of their bodies to avoid being seen).

Table 10 Income-earning household members by religion

Sex of earners	Hindu		Muslim		Other (Christian, Tribal)		Total	
	abs.	%	abs.	%	abs.	%	abs.	%
Men only	99	55	112	62	8	47	219	58
Women only	10	6	3	2	3	18	16	4
Both sexes	71	39	66	36	6	35	143	38
Total	180	100	181	100	17	100	378	100

Source: Own research (N = 378 households, missing case 1; V = 0.13; $\chi^2_{(4)} = 12.6$, $p < 0.05$)

After having examined at the income level of the interviewed households, the focus will shift to the kind of social network in which household members are involved. These networks are important for acquiring help when needed. This will be illustrated in the next section.

3.2 The importance of a social network

For survival, the urban poor also need relations with persons outside the household. In a low-income neighbourhood, the urban poor are often dependent on more than one social network for their survival and/or improvement of economic status (cf. Baken 1990: 79; Roberts 1991: 61). Being part of a network requires tit-for-tat obligations. In other words, a dweller should be able to invest in such relations to enable help when required The organisation of these networks takes place along caste, religious, gender and neighbourhood lines, but my study reveals that these networks are generally of a vertical nature.

In the surveyed neighbourhoods, the urban poor often have no other option than to enter into a patron-client relationship. When they resist from entering such a relationship, they will be excluded from help from or through the patron in the future. Moreover, the patron can obstruct activities of the non-follower. This can be illustrated by the following example derived from my fieldwork.

> A new settler in Bhavani Nagar bought a hut from one of the old settlers without consulting any of the local slum leaders. The deal was settled and he started improving his shelter. Leaders came and asked for their share of the transaction costs and renovation of the shelter. The new settler refused and wanted to improve his house. One night the leaders came to his house drunk and demolished his door to teach him a lesson. A week later they came back and destroyed the new asbestos roof. They tried to convince the new settler that private initiative would not be tolerated unless they had sanctioned it.

Social networks are important for slum dwellers to gain access to material or non-material help in the event of an emergency. In addition, access to credit is facilitated through the social network. In other words, participation in a social network is a strategy for sourcing and budgeting an issue, which I will discuss in the next section.

3.3 Livelihood; a matter of sourcing and budgeting

Private means for survival, monetary as well as non-monetary (food, clothes, utensils) are mainly derived from employment or self-employment, possibly including that of other household members, which may be supplemented by gifts or credit. In addition, remittances can, but do not always, form a substantial part of the poor's household budget. In Hyderabad, this mainly concerns transfers in kind from relatives to female-headed households and households with unemployed workers. For relatively better-off Muslims, there can be more substantial transfers in money or kind from relatives working in one of the Gulf countries.

The income gained by the urban poor is often low and fluctuates over time. One of the reasons for their low income is underemployment, which is far more severe than unemployment, which the poor cannot afford (cf. Singh 1978: 79, 92). This can be illustrated by an example of a cycle repair shop along the roadside.

> Mohammed goes daily to the roadside early in the morning and squats on the pavement with a cycle pump, some tools, glue and old tyres which can be used for repairing punctured ones. He waits till the first customer comes. During the day he may have a few customers. However, he has to wait till a client comes. This can even take a few hours. During this period it is almost impossible to take up another earning activity. Only when the sun sets, does Mohammed go home. He has to cope with underemployment. If Mohammed was unemployed he could try to improve his income by allocating time for other self-employment or finding a job.

Underemployment reduces the opportunity of working elsewhere, because a lot of the time available is allocated to waiting for customers. Furthermore, women's earnings are often lower than men's due to lower paid jobs. For the same work, women are paid less; for example, for the same casual coolie work women obtain Rs. 25 and men Rs. 40 per day. Households with more earning members can cope better with sudden changes in income due to changes in the labour market for both sexes, changes in weather conditions (e.g. in the rainy period less income can be made by street hawkers), the environment, or changes in the life cycle such as births, marriages or deaths (see also Mencher 1988: 106).

The economic conditions of the urban poor are characterised by a shortage of financial income and/or other resources such as gold, production assets, land and houses (cf. Von Benda-Beckmann and Von Benda-Beckmann 1994: 11). In order to cope with drops of income and unforeseen events, credit is taken out. The poor are in a permanent mode of crisis management; their survival may depend on stopping gaps with one loan by taking out another one. This forces the poor to act according to a short-term framework. In other words, '[g]oing into debt permits the poor to survive ...' (Santos 1979: 122). This differs from the ideas of Moser (1998), who suggests that one should look at what the poor have – income and assets – instead of focusing on what they do not. She proposes an asset vulnerability framework, which includes 'labor, human capital, less familiar productive assets such as housing, and largely invisible intangible assets such as household relations and social capital.' (Moser 1998: 1). Since housing requires relatively large sums, a combination of asset and finance management generally takes place.

3.3.1 Credit and debt

Apart from asset management, the urban poor also take out loans, which leads to indebtedness. Here, indebtedness only indicates that the loan taken out is not yet repaid. To what extent are the interviewed slum dwellers indebted? It appears that 59% of the interviewed households are indebted. To be more specific, 57% of the households, living below the poverty line appear to be indebted, and for those living above the poverty line the figure is 61% (see Table 11). Majumdar (1983: 141-142) reports for Delhi that 53% of the slum dwellers are indebted. For Bombay slum dwellers an indebtedness percentage of 73% is given by Desai and Pillai (1972: 141). Schenk-Sandbergen (1988: 27-31), who conducted a survey among household servants of the Kudumbi caste in Alleppey, Kerala (1979), reveals that out of the 61 households interviewed 82% were indebted. The figures for Amritsar, however, indicate that only 31% out of the 300 respondents report having taken out a loan in the last five years before the interview took place (Sandhu 1988: 71). These figures show that the percentages found in different urban areas differ, but that credit still plays an important role in the budgeting pattern of the urban poor, as it does in the surveyed slums in Hyderabad. It may be suggested that the wealthier can more easily obtain credit, because they, in comparison with those with an income the poverty line, are considered a lower risk as far as the repayment of the loan is concerned.

Table 11 Indebtedness of interviewed slum dweller households in Hyderabad

Indebtedness	Income below poverty line		Income above poverty line		Total	
	abs.	%	abs.	%	abs.	%
Yes	105	57	104	61	209	59
No	79	43	66	39	145	41
Total	184	100	170	100	354	100

Source: Own research (N = 354, missing cases 25; V = 0.04; $\chi^2_{(1)} = 0.6$, $p > 0.05$).

Credit can be taken out for many purposes, of which Table 12 provides an overview. The items are listed in order of declining score. It is noteworthy that shelter as the only purpose of indebtedness accounts for about one third of the indebted households. It appears that there are more debts for the purpose of shelter, dowry, and trade/business among those households living above the poverty line. However, the poor borrowed for medicines and food, which is probably due to their malnutrition and more unhealthy living conditions, as well as their need to borrow even for relatively small expenses. The data suggest that those living below the poverty line are less frequently indebted for shelter in combination with other purposes than those with an income above the poverty line.

Those indebted for three or more purposes are not indebted for shelter. The purposes of being indebted are not specified here, because the combinations are of a complete different nature.

What does this all mean for the topic of housing finance? Of the interviewed households 45% are indebted for housing purposes with those living above the poverty line as a majority. In other words, being indebted for housing is significant among the interviewed slum dwellers in Hyderabad, of which the more relatively better off are indebted for shelter purposes. The figures for the Hyderabadi sample are high compared with those for slums in Amritsar, for which Sandhu (1988: 72) reports that 10% of the credit taken out by slum dwellers was used for shelter purposes.

Many slum dwellers require continuous credit to satisfy their needs. However, if enough means are available people can choose between investments with a short or long-term perspective. To be able to invest in migration to, for example, Gulf countries or the education of

Table 12 Purpose of debts of interviewed slum dweller households in Hyderabad

Purpose of debt	Income below poverty line		Income above poverty line		Total	
	abs.	%	abs.	%	abs.	%
One purpose						
Shelter	35	31	32	35	67	33
Dowry	17	15	18	20	35	17
Trade/business	10	9	9	10	19	9
Medicines	10	9	3	3	13	6
Food	8	7	5	5	13	6
Other	1	1	2	2	3	1
Subtotal	81	71	69	75	150	73
Two purposes						
Shelter/dowry	5	4	4	4	9	4
Medicines/food	6	5	1	1	7	3
Shelter/business	1	1	4	4	5	2
Shelter/electricity	3	3	1	1	4	2
Shelter/ medicines	2	2	2	2	4	2
Shelter/ceremony	0	0	3	3	3	1
Other	13	11	4	4	17	8
Subtotal	30	26	19	21	49	24
Three or more purposes	3	3	4	4	7	3
Total	114	100	92	100	206	100

Source: Own research (N = 206, missing cases 29; for the associations between one or more purposes and income below versus above the poverty line: V= 0.04; $\chi^2_{(1)}$ = 0.4, p > 0.05).

children, short-term needs have to be met to a certain extent. However, during the survey, no debts were reported as outstanding for those purposes. Those dependent on livelihood strategies tried to avoid debts as much as possible. Moreover, if they do become indebted they opt to keep their period of indebtedness as short as possible in order to be able to cope with other necessities such as food, the education of their children, travel to the work place and medicines.

3.3.2 Expenditures

Among other factors, relations between the household members according to age and gender determine the distribution of the resources available within the household. De Wit (1993: 22) describes it as follows: 'Men's and women's access to and control of resources differ systematically and there is a profound distinction between male and female needs and interests.' Men tend to allocate part of the household income for personal expenditure while women's priority is primarily the household budget (cf. Wilson 1991: 31).

Table 13 Expenditure priorities of interviewed slum dweller households in Hyderabad

	Items of priority	Total
Priority 1	food (85%), rent (9%), other* (6%)	100%
Priority 2	clothing (29%), food (13%), rent (13%), education (12%), loan repayment (7%), medical care (5%), other* (21%)	100%
Priority 3	clothing (20%), medical care (18%), education (12%), loan repayment (9%), rent (7%), other* (34%)	100%
Priority 4	medical care (18%), clothing (13%), education (11%), networking (9%), loan repayment (7%), saving (6%), personal expenses (5%), other* (31%)	100%
Priority 5	medical care (12%), saving (10%), networking (8%), **own shelter (8%)**, clothing (7%), education (6%), loan repayment (6%), other* (43%)	100%

Source: Own research (N = 230, missing cases 14).
* Other includes all items with a score of less than 5%.

Expenditures can fluctuate widely on a daily basis. The most substantial portion of the resources available to the urban poor is used for food. A lump sum may be required for the repayment of credit, the purchase of domestic animals and articles, dowries, marriage expenses, business and domestic purposes, including medical care and the entertainment of visitors. Furthermore, religious festivals such as Diwali, Eid-Ul-Fitr and Christmas require large amounts. Due to a shortage of means, urban poor households need to establish priorities. Table 13 shows the expected expenditure priorities of slum dwellers in Hyderabad. It should be noted that the number of households included in this is lower than the total surveyed households, because this item was added to the questionnaire at a later stage of the fieldwork. From that moment onwards the dwellers were asked to provide a list of items in order of expenditure priority. The expenditure priorities reflect the expected behaviour of the dwellers, but in reality it may differ. Nevertheless, the lists of items of priority will provide an indication of the intention concerning the spending behaviour of the dwellers. Before discussing all items of priority in detail, I want to mention that owned shelter is not mentioned as an important priority and only as fifth priority by 8% of the dwellers.

The first priority concerns only two items, food and rent of shelter, while the second priority refers to six items. Slum dwellers gave as the third priority five items and as fourth and fifth priority seven each. This shows that there is more uniformity in the items mentioned when the priority is classified higher. In other words, the diversity of priorities mentioned increases when the priority is considered less urgent.

Food is required to feed the household members. The choice of food as first and second priority does not tell us if food is equally distributed among the household members. In many Hindu and Muslim households, guests and men get the best food followed by the children. Women are last in the queue, which generally means that they are often less well fed among all household members.

Economising on food and living in an unhealthy environment renders slum dwellers more vulnerable to illness. Consequently, the use of medical care including medicines has a high priority; second priority for 5%, third and fourth priority for 18% each and fifth priority for 12% of the households interviewed.

Clothing is important for slum dwellers, because they want to look neatly dressed to encourage prestige and respect from others. Clothing is given the second priority by 29% of the households, the third priority by 20% of the households, the fourth priority by 13% of the households and the fifth priority by 7% of the households. It can be concluded that clothing is a relatively important priority among slum dwellers in Hyderabad.

Education refers to the education of the children, including school fees, books, uniforms and travel expenses to and from school. It scores 12% as second and third priority, 11% as fourth priority and 8% as fifth priority. Education can be seen as an important priority among the slum dwellers in Hyderabad, but it does not have the first priority.

The costs for networking refers to visiting and receiving people such as relatives and friends. In order to spread risks and keep social networks alive, personal contact is required. This implies that the poor need the resources to secure their survival, even through offering tea to guests or sharing a cup of tea at a teashop. The urban poor have to entertain guests to maintain networks for help in the event of distress. However, one may expect that an urban poor household, which has little to eat, cannot afford to entertain guests. Networking is reported as fourth and fifth priority by 9% and 8% of the households interviewed respectively. Costs involved include travel expenses or special food, drinks and/or gifts offered to guests.

The repayment of credit, for whatever purpose taken out, has priority among slum dwellers; as second and fourth priority 7% each, as third priority 9% and as fifth priority 6% of the households interviewed. Repayment of a loan is considered important to ensure future access to finance and other possible means of help. However, loan instalments cannot always be paid on time due to a shortage of available means, but the figures reveal that the poor are willing to repay credit.

Savings are mentioned as a fourth priority (6%) and fifth priority (10%). This conflicts with the frequent claim that slum dwellers are unable to save. However, Majumdar (1983: 140) reports for his Delhi sample that only 24% of the slum dwellers are saving. It can be argued that all households wish to save, but the poorer the household the more difficult it is to put money aside (Lall 1988: 11; Sandhu 1988: 68). Saving can be of great importance, because depending on the form of saving, it can create the opportunity to keep some resources out of the reach of relatives who may claim them for whatever purpose. Women can and some do allocate part of their earnings to a financial self-help organisation to be sure that this money will not be consumed directly (cf. Smets 1992: 59-60). If the poor, mainly women, save, they often separate their savings, even when it is only Rs. 1 a day, from their budget. These savings can be kept in the dwelling, with the employer, relatives or a financial self-help organisation. Some people reported that they buried the larger amounts in their hut to protect their savings from theft. When savings are in kind (a TV-set, radio, gold, vessels, etcetera) they can be sold or pledged in times of need. The practice of saving among the urban poor contrasts with the traditional notion of the savings capacity of the poor, whereby it is assumed that 'savings are residual funds left over from consumption during any given period' (Von Pischke et al. 1983: 10). The poor, however, tend to save while consuming in the meantime, or put savings, in kind or money, aside before consumption takes place. They generally do not wait for leftovers after consumption has taken place. In reality there are no leftovers after consumption needs have been met.

Personal expenditure on items such as cigarettes, alcohol, a cup of tea, and visits to the cinema have a relatively low priority as only 5% of the interviewees, who were predominantly men, reported it as a fourth priority. Women tend to feel responsible primarily for the household expenditures rather than incorporating personal expenses in their expenditure top five.

My data indicate that investments in their own shelter is not the most important priority for the slum dwellers. Shelter only scores as fifth priority in 8% of the households. On the other hand, rent paid by tenants scores high; 9% as first priority, 13% as second priority and 7% as third priority.

In order to illustrate the description of the expenditure priorities, an example of the spending behaviour of a low-income household will be given. It concerns a household where husband and wife form a coalition model. They are eager to take decisions concerning their expenditures by mutual agreement. In this household, the following expenditure priorities were traced.

1 food
2 education of the children
3 medical expenses
4 clothes
5 offering tea and biscuits to guests (networking)

If the resources available are not sufficient to meet the projected needs, the household's budget can be supplemented with additional financial or non-financial income by means of, for example, labour, gifts and/or credit. When a loan is taken out, its repayment has a high priority. Repayment of loans is important to ensure credit in the future and to avoid harassment by the lender. Its implication is that the other priorities will be considered less important. It should be noted that the priority items are not as rigid as they may seem. Although the opportunities for economising on each item are rather limited, it is necessary in order to be able to cope with other expenditures. In order to meet the other needs, the poor opt for a short period of indebtedness. For the time being other priorities will be postponed until the debt is repaid. A temporary shortage of means to invest in fostering relations for survival lead to the poorest of the poor being socially handicapped. In reality, even these households allocate a part of their budget to receive or visit persons of their social network to ensure help in the future (see also Bhattacharya et al. 1991: 377; De Wit 1993).

The problems of the household budget management become more problematic if one of the household members, often the men, does not feel responsible for it and prioritises his personal expenditures, of which some illustrations follow. A female dweller told me:

> 'My husband is a guide for lorry drivers in the city. I do not know how much income he gets. I get Rs. 200 a month from him. He drinks too much. So I have to wash up utensils at houses nearby. They pay me Rs. 200 a month. Furthermore, I have to do my housework and look after my four children. I face a lot of problems.'

A lock mechanic blamed himself for his selfish behaviour. He said:

> 'I was living with my wife and children in a *pucca* [concrete] house. For some time I did not have any income. 'I was wandering around and not working. I insisted on selling the family house, because I had many debts. My father refused. Five years ago I sold the house for Rs. 21,500. In fact I made my father to sell the house. I got Rs. 11,000 and my father the remaining amount. Before that I used to clear my debts with new loans. I got worried, so I did not work any more. I have even taken three cycles on rent and not returned them. I was indebted to these three shops for Rs. 2,000. I was also indebted for Rs. 3,000 due to gambling and consuming liquor. When the house was sold, my father in law gave me a small plot. My father in law said that I could better make a house here. I invested Rs. 6,000 in the new shelter. I even lost this hut because I continued drinking and playing cards. Now we have a new house and I have promised to change my selfish behaviour.'

Men can also escape their responsibilities in the household by means of bigamy, desertion and/or oral or physical abuse (cf. Noponen 1991: 234). In this situation, women have to take care of household budgeting and allocate their budget almost completely to the most basic household needs. Furthermore, they often feel responsible for the repayment of loans, while it is often their spouses who have agreed to the credit terms and conditions. Consequently, these women have to balance household budgets to repay the loans outstanding (Moser 1992: 62).

Urban poor households may even aim to increase their income by anticipating benefits, which can be gained through government or non-government support schemes. A Hindu street hawker said:

> 'I want to convert to Christianity. We are told that Christians help the poor a lot. That is why we want to convert. In Hinduism, people do not take care of each other. In Christianity, it is different. When I was in their hospital they took care of me very well. They even arranged free blood for me during the night.'

Government welfare schemes are often only intended for the economically weaker sections of Indian society, from which Christians are normally excluded. In order to gain access to certain government schemes, a Christian from Kerala who migrated to Hyderabad changed his name into a Hindu one, because it sounds better. He told me:

> 'When I had changed my name in Narayana, I was even able to get a ration card and take part in governmental schemes for Scheduled Castes. I could even take out a loan for starting a mobile canteen. For this bank loan I needed a guarantor. I went to the Municipal Corporation office and paid a servant to get a signature from his superior. I did not know him. I just went in and asked somebody to get it signed. When I got the loan I used it for my house.'

As shown above, the urban poor can manipulate government and non-government organisations to allocate the benefits of so-called welfare schemes in their own favour. Others may apply for business or crop loans and use them for other purposes they need money for. They even buy the machines if the allocation of the loan is going to be checked. After the inspection has taken place they sell the machines and use the money for their perceived needs, such as the repair of the roof of their house. These initiatives can be seen as a form of everyday resistance. This is 'a stratagem deployed by a weaker party in thwarting the claim of an institutional or class opponent who dominates the public exercise of power' (Scott 1993: 24). Such acts of resistance challenge the norms and values of the so-called do-gooders, and can be better understood when we know more about the spending behaviour of urban poor households.

Budgeting by poor urban households is problematic due to the limited means available and conflicting interests within the household. These influence the kind of shelter the urban poor prefer and can afford. That is why it is important to look into the meaning that shelter has for the slum dwellers, which will be examined in the next section.

3.4 Shelter and its meaning for slum dwellers

Slum dwellers can live in rented or their own shelter. Table 14 shows that 62% of the sample taken are owner-occupiers and 38% are tenants. There is no significant difference in this respect between households living below and above the poverty line. Here, it appears that the size of income cannot be considered to be a good indicator for being a tenant or owner-occupier.

Table 14 Tenants and owner-occupiers

	Income below poverty line		Income above poverty line		Total	
	abs.	%	abs.	%	abs.	%
Owner-occupiers	121	62	109	62	230	62
Tenants	74	38	67	38	141	38
Total	195	100	176	100	371	100

Source: Own research (N = 371, missing cases 8; V = 0.00; $\chi^2_{(1)} = 0.0$, $p > 0.05$).

The shelter in which people live can be of a different kind. The type of shelter, as well as items of daily use such as bowls, plates and clothes reflects the nature of poverty quite well (Bhattacharya et al. 1991: 374). Moreover, shelter quality is of greater importance for women, because they are more tied to the home than men due to the combination of their productive, reproductive and management tasks within the household. It also includes the physical well-being of family members for whom women have a care responsibility. In Hyderabad, the physical quality of shelter can be divided into *kaccha, semi kaccha* or *pucca*. *Kaccha* constructions have walls made of mud, corrugated iron, cloth or wood and a thatched roof of leaves, grass, plastic, or any kind of waste material. Shelter of a *semi-kaccha* nature consists partly or completely of concrete or cement plastered walls with asbestos or iron sheets, or country tiles on the roof. *Pucca* refers to concrete or brick masonry buildings with a concrete roof. *Kaccha* shelter is especially for the poorest, while *semi-kaccha* and *pucca* buildings in slum areas are for the relatively better off.

Table 15 shows that the majority of the tenants interviewed (87%) and owner-occupants (80%) are living in *semi-kaccha* houses. It seems that *kaccha* houses are mostly inhabited by owner-occupiers, because such a shelter is a starting point for the poor when they begin to construct shelter in an incremental fashion.

Table 15 House types of tenants and owner-occupiers

	Tenants		Owner occupants		Total	
House type	abs.	%	abs.	%	abs.	%
Kaccha	10	7	39	17	49	13
Semi-kaccha	123	87	186	80	309	83
Pucca	8	6	8	3	16	4
Total	141	100	233	100	374	100

Source: Own research (N = 374, missing cases 5; V= 0.15; $\chi^2_{(2)}$ = 8.0, $p < 0.05$).

Tenants and owner-occupiers have their own reasons for living in rented or their own shelter. Most tenants often have to pay a fixed sum of money on a monthly basis. Others do not pay rent, but have to offer services instead such as looking after somebody's children. There were only a few cases where the tenant had provided credit to the house owner:

> The borrower was able to obtain a housing loan of Rs. 2,000 from a person in the neighbourhood. The agreement made was that the loan should be repaid in a lump sum and that the lender could live in a room in the constructed house without paying rent until the loan was repaid.

Renting becomes relatively accessible for the poor when the house owner is flexible in collecting the rent. However, the poor generally do not prefer to rent shelter due to the long-term financial obligation and a long-term deduction of their income, which reduces the opportunity of meeting other needs. This can be illustrated by the following quotations; a street hawker said:

> 'The first six years in this *basti* [slum] I was renting. I wanted to have my own house. I was not able to pay rent.'

Another slum dweller stated:

> 'We could not afford to pay rent because I did a job on a temporary basis.'

Tenants also have to face other kinds of insecurity. The owners of the dwelling they rent can evict them. This occurs when the owner of the dwelling needs the rented rooms for his own family. When the tenants have to leave the neighbourhood it can lead to a loss of their social network. Moreover, tenants cannot use the house as security, because they do not own it. This is reflected in the general non-acceptance of tenants as participants in a financial self-help organisation. Moreover, due to water scarcity in Hyderabad access to water from neighbourhood taps is often denied to tenants. House owners have first access, which places the tenants last in the queue. These tenants often have to go home without any or without sufficient water or have to collect water from a local bore well, the water from which is often polluted, or from other neighbourhoods. Furthermore, when these dwellers collect water from houses with a private connection they are often asked to pay a fixed amount for each bucket, or a monthly fee.

In contrast, privately-owned shelter can have different functions. Firstly, a private-owned urban dwelling can serve as a substitute for the status derived from the possession of items such as cattle and tools, and/or ancestry symbols (Alcock et al. 1963: 85). Secondly, the house can also have a specific cultural function. A house for an extended Muslim family practising *purda* requires for instance separate space for the female members of the family. New couples of the semi-nomadic tribe Mandula[1] settled in Hyderabad leave their parental home and start a separate nuclear unit. Such cultural needs define the type of house preferred. Thirdly, the house can serve as an additional source of income by renting out a part of the house. Moreover, if the house is built in an illegal settlement tax can be avoided. Fourthly, have one's own house offers the possibility of cultivating crops or keeping some chickens or goats, running a small shop, or using the house as a work place. Fifthly, it can serve as collateral for obtaining access to a financial self-help organisation or credit from, for example, money-lenders, pawnbrokers, relatives, friends, and neighbours (see e.g. Bähre and Smets 1999; Smets 2000). This can also be illustrated by the words of a slum dweller in Karachi.

1 The status of the Mandulas is disputed. They are classified as backward class, but they see themselves as a semi-nomadic tribe.

> 'Everybody around us knows that I have spent Rs. 3000,- on this house. So my neighbours know that I would not run away, and when my wife had to be admitted in the hospital, I could borrow from my neighbours.' (Van der Linden 1983: 73).

The social security function of the dwelling is especially important for the poor when traditional means of security, local networks based on kinship, are eroded and access to institutionalised security is absent (Caminos et al. 1968: vii). The security derived from an owned dwelling is minimised if the shelter concerned is under long-term financial obligations such as in many housing schemes.

It may be concluded that an owned dwelling is preferred by most dwellers, because it offers a source of socio-economic security. Moreover, investments in construction and maintenance can take place when means are available and conflicts with other priorities of expenditure can be minimised as far as possible. The limited means available force the poor to build their house bit by bit. Table 16 shows that 63% of the interviewed households have built their shelter in one step, while 37% constructed it in more incremental steps. This does not necessarily mean that the shelter built in one step is a ready-made unit of good quality. It is often a stage in the process of incremental building. Shelter built in one step is generally of a kaccha or semi-kaccha nature, which can be extended or improved over time, as illustrated below:

> In 1982, a coolie called Mathu (27) married a 17-year-old girl. He built a hut on an illegal acquired plot, which was completely demolished by government employees afterwards. In the mean time, their first son has been born. Mathu and his wife joined forces and rebuilt the hut. A few months later, the hut was demolished again, but now some repair was sufficient. In 1984, a daughter was born and two years later a new hut had to be made due to its dilapidated nature. In two days new *kaccha* shelter was made with walls build up of a mixture of bricks and mud. The roof was covered with plastic sheets. Another daughter and son were born in 1988 and 1990. Then, the small hut proved to be really too small for all household members. One wall was demolished and a *semi-kaccha* extension was constructed. This extension was roofed with second-hand asbestos sheets. In 1994, the eldest son turned 12 and was able to join his father at his job of loading and unloading lorries. Their aim was to save money for improvement of the *kaccha* part of the house.

Table 16 Incremental building

Number of steps in 1993/1994	abs.	%
1	141	63
2	61	27
3	14	6
4	5	2
5	3	1
Total	224	100

Source: Own research (N = 224, missing cases 7).

Incrementally-built shelter is more prone to requiring repair than ready-made shelter. Such repairs do not directly lead to a better habitat situation compared with the housing condition at the moment of the most recent incremental building step. In the other words, the repairs referred to relate to the maintenance of the dwelling; most particularly with protection against natural forces. It appears that the major repairs concern the roof and walls (see Table 17). The roof is especially important in view of the monsoon rains. The costs for roof repair can vary from nothing up to Rs. 6,000. The costs involved are low when the settler can acquire some waste material in the city, but they increase when the construction wood is rotten and labour has to be employed. Due to bad construction and/or rain, walls, especially those without cement plaster are prone to collapse. The costs involved for repairing a partly or completely collapsed wall vary from Rs. 100 to 3,000.

Table 17 Most recent repair on house

	abs.	%
Roof	42	64
Wall, door	19	29
Floor	2	3
Other	3	5
Total	66	100

Source: Own research (N = 66, missing cases 17).

Incrementally-built shelter may lead to additional costs due to pulling down and rebuilding parts of the house in another incremental building step. Moreover, incrementally-built shelters are prone to repair. For the building activities, finance is required, which I will discuss in the next section.

3.5 Shelter in slums and its financing

For the construction of shelter, even in illegal settlements, monetary and non-monetary means are required. Financial means can be used to invest in land, building materials, tools, and construction skills. The money required for construction can be reduced by partly or completely self-constructing the shelter. Another option is to collect waste material somewhere in the city, which James Scott (personal communication) describes as 'urban hunting and gathering'.

The first item required for constructing a house is a piece of land. Table 18 indicates that 28% of the interviewees have a piece of land of less than 25 square meters, 40% a plot of 25-50 square metres and 32% land with a size of more than 50 square meters.

Table 18 Land size

Size land in square meters	abs.	%
Less than 25	67	28
25-50	98	40
More than 50	78	32
Total	243	100

Source: Own research (N = 243, missing cases 9).

The question now remains of how these dwellers obtained their plot? Land in Hyderabadi slums can be obtained in different ways (see Table 19). This sample concerns more households (242) than the total number of house owners-cum-occupiers interviewed (230). Since some tenants had already bought some land for construction purposes in the future, they are also included. The dwellers generally aim to occupy a plot near their workplace. In the sample, the majority (65%) had bought a plot of land, while 21% have squatted, but squatting is not always free from costs. The squatters often have to pay some 'protection money'

(Rs. 60 to 2,000) to the slum leaders. Apart from buying or squatting, land can be rented (10%). If the land is rented it concerns illegal practices or land under the sway of waqf boards. Moreover, land without legal title deed can also be acquired as a dowry or just as a gift (5%).

Table 19 Characteristics of illegally obtaining land in slums

	abs.	%
Squatted	51	21
Bought	157	65
Rented	23	10
Gift, dowry	11	5
Total	242	100

Source: Own research (N = 242, missing cases 10).

In order to obtain land for construction, finance is often required, but the amount may differ substantially according to the location and the kind of land (For an overview of the amounts paid related to the different interviewed income groups see Table 20). The sample includes people who have bought a plot illegally and squatters who had to pay after settling to be permitted to stay. There is no significant relationship between the income level and the amount paid for the land.

Table 20 Money paid for land

	Income below poverty line		Income above poverty line		Total	
Price land	abs.	%	abs.	%	abs.	%
< Rs. 500	31	34	25	33	56	34
Rs. 500-1,000	9	10	5	7	14	8
Rs. 1,000-5,000	20	22	12	16	32	19
Rs. 5,000-10,000	12	13	21	28	33	20
> Rs. 10,000	18	20	12	16	30	18
Total	90	100	75	100	165	100

Source: Own research (N = 165, missing cases 3; V= 0.19; $\chi^2_{(4)} = 6.2$, $p > 0.05$).

Among the surveyed households, about one third have paid less than Rs. 500. A higher percentage of households with an income below the poverty line had to pay prices for a plot up to Rs. 5,000, and those with an income above the poverty line pay in the range Rs. 5,000-10,000. However, the payment of even more than Rs. 10,000 for a plot may be explained by the fact that these households, especially those living under the poverty line) had a higher income in the past or had received some gifts from, for example, relatives.

Dwellers may pay for their plot in lump sum or in instalments. More or less half of the surveyed households paid for their land with a lump sum and the other half in instalments (Table 21). A majority of the poor had to pay with a lump sum for the land and the households living above the poverty line score higher in payments by instalment. However, there is no significant difference between income levels and the method of payment for land. However, payment in instalments is generally accepted only when the paying behaviour of the client is well known to the seller of the land. The seller of the land minimises the risk of non-payment by receiving a lump sum payment.

Table 21 Form of payment for land

	Income below poverty line		Income above poverty line		Total	
	abs.	%	abs.	%	abs.	%
Lump sum	43	57	30	47	73	52
Instalments	33	43	34	53	67	48
Total	76	100	64	100	140	100

Source: Own research (N = 140, missing cases 28; V = 0.10; $\chi^2_{(1)} = 1.3$, $p > 0.05$).

If some kind of security of tenure, legally or illegally, has been achieved the settlers are eager to invest more in the improvement of their shelter. Building materials or tools, which are not possessed, can be acquired by gift, exchange, purchase (by cash or on credit), or theft. Construction materials such as bricks can be gathered in bits when they are found or can be bought for a relatively cheap price when financial means are available. The reuse of bricks is rather difficult due to their bad quality; they easily fall apart. If the financial means available are limited, building materials, new or second hand, can be bought bit by bit and stored until enough material is available for the desired construction. Bricks, which are temporarily stored in the open air, are often whitewashed to guard against theft, which is not always successful.

Once land has been obtained, construction activities can take place. For this purpose second hand or new building materials have to be bought. A minority of 9% of the interviewed slum dweller households only bought second hand building materials for the construction or improvement of their shelter. Another 38% report having bought a mix of second hand and new building materials, while 53% bought only new materials. It appears that many slum dwellers are dependent on buying new materials partly or completely, because second hand ones are not always available. Finally, it should be mentioned that many house buyers are not included in the sample because they were not involved in construction activities (see Table 22).

Table 22 Building materials bought

	abs.	%
New	93	53
Second hand	15	9
New and second hand	66	38
Total	174	100

Source: Own research (N = 174, missing cases 57).

The building materials bought by the slum dwellers were mainly paid for with a lump sum (90%). Payments for building materials in instalments concerns only 4% and a mix of both options 6% of the sample (see Table 23). With regard to the compulsory direct payment for delivered goods a trader in building materials told me: 'I am a businessman, so I have to maintain these rules strictly.' Another trader said: 'How can I believe people if I give things on credit. They have to pay me before delivery.' Payment arrangements can be more flexible if a shopkeeper or trader knows his client personally. However, a down payment, the size of which is dependent on the amount of goods purchased, is often required. The possibility of paying in instalments is only offered to known persons, who are also often regular customers. The credibility of a client is judged by taking into account, for example, his place of residence, the legal or illegal possession of a plot, and his employment.

When the trader or shopkeeper does not know a client personally, a well-known person has to introduce him/her to enable him/her to pay for the building materials in instalments. When the building materials can be paid for in instalments, outstanding debts, which are reported to be maximum Rs. 6,000, have to be cleared within a period of five days up to one month

For these payment arrangements a written agreement may be required, although its legal value is almost or completely nil. The repayment of the credit provided is mainly enforced by means of social control – manipulation of the values and norms – but also the use of physical violence. In general, interest will not be charged, but there are examples of interest rates of up to 10% per month. Moreover, the repayment schedule is fixed and only in exceptional cases are traders and shopkeepers lax in collecting outstanding debts. One shopkeeper said:

> 'In the case of default we can only ask them to repay. By stressing their behaviour too much we may lose customers. It is better to keep customers and they may bring new ones in. If such a defaulter introduces new customers, these will never get things on credit.'

It should be noted that the price of building materials is often higher when the trader or shopkeeper offers the opportunity of paying in instalments.

Table 23 Payment of building materials

	abs.	%
Lump sum	165	90
Instalments	8	4
Mix	10	6
Total	183	100

Source: Own research (N = 183, missing cases 48).

Once land and building materials are available construction of the shelter can commence. For this purpose, construction skills are required. These can be learned on an exchange basis, but in addition to different kinds of mutual self-help, the poor often have to employ construction labour (see Table 24). It seems that the minority of the surveyed dwellers (15%) constructed their shelter by themselves or by means of an unpaid exchange labour. The majority (85%) had to employ labour for all the work or in addition to self-help activities. Some dwellers said that it was cheaper for them to employ construction labour rather than be involved in the construction activities themselves. The salary they can earn in one day is often higher than what they have to pay a labourer. The costs of male construction labour is Rs. 40 per day and for a woman even less, while several rickshaw pullers reported a daily income of Rs. 50 to 60. Labour can be paid per hour or day. However, the most popular option is contract labour, because it is believed to speed up the construction activities. Moreover, the price is fixed, so how much has to be spent is known in advance.

Table 24 Type of labour used for construction

	abs.	%
One type of labour		
Self-help	30	15
Contract labour	27	13
Wage labour	21	10
More types of labour		
Self-help and contract labour	23	11
Self-help and wage labour	98	49
Self-help with contract and wage labour	2	1
Total	201	100

Source: Own research (N = 201, missing cases 30).

In the above, it has been shown that different elements of the building activities require financial or non-monetary sources. I will now illustrate how these financing strategies can be transformed in so-called housing finance criteria, which fit the urban poor's livelihood strategies in a sustainable way.

Conclusion

The central question was whether there are significant differences between poor and less poor households. There are only gradual differences within the surveyed group with the exception for Table 9 and 14.

Still some indications can be given. The surveyed slum dweller households encompass almost 50% Hindus and almost 50% Muslims. Of these households, a slight majority of Hindu households are relatively financially better off, while the majority of the Muslims live below the poverty line. Although the household income is gathered mainly by the men, many women of all communities also contribute, whereas only a small percentage of women are the sole earners. The percentage of women, involved in income-earning activities, appear to be the smallest among Muslims, probably giving an indication of their inclination to practice *purdah*. Apart from income-generation strategies, loans are often required as a necessity for survival. The majority of the surveyed slum dweller households are indebted, with a slightly greater percentage among those living above the poverty line. For housing purposes, 45% of the surveyed households are indebted, with those living above the poverty line as a majority. Investments in shelter are not considered among the most important priorities among the slum dwellers, even though privately-owned shelter is important to them. It opens possibilities of improving their status, income and access to sources of credit. To construct shelter one requires land, building materials and construction skills. Land can be squatted upon, illegally bought, rented or obtained as a gift. When the plot is bought, more or less equal numbers of people have to pay it in instalments or lump sum. Of those living above the poverty line, a majority of the surveyed households could pay for with a lump sum. Once land has been obtained one requires construction materials. These building materials are bought new by 53%, second hand by 9%, and a mix of both by 38% of the surveyed households. Building materials had to be paid for mainly by a lump sum. Apart from building materials, labour was required, for which the majority uses a combination of self-help and wage labour. It may be suggested that one requires a certain level of income to be considered trustworthy enough to repay a loan. The surveyed dwellers try to construct shelter and obtain housing finance, while not harming their livelihood strategies for which a social network is of crucial importance. A half-built house or even a hut can be beneficial to the poor's livelihood strategy. The poor prefer shelter, under financial obligations on relatively short or at most medium term. Consequently, renting shelter is not preferred, because it requires a regular payment of rent over a long period, which reduces the household budget for the period that rent has to be paid. The same argument is applicable for shelter for which long-term credit is taken out. This conflicts with the notions as expressed by the economist school discussed in chapter one, but coincides the ideas of the self-help school.

4 Slum dwellers, savings, gifts and their external credit relations for shelter

Rasheed and Zaidia have five children (four girls and one boy). Rasheed works as a rickshaw puller. Due to health problems, he earns only Rs. 600 per month. Zaidia runs a petty shop. Her monthly income is some Rs 200. In 1988, they were forced to vacate their rented unit in one of the slums in Hyderabad. They decided to buy a piece of land without title deed in a nearby slum area. The costs of the plot were Rs. 6,000. In order to cover these expenses Rasheed participated in an auction chit fund prior to their move. In this way, he obtained Rs. 4,000. In addition, an interest-free loan of Rs. 2,000 was procured from Zaidia's brother. This loan was repaid within one year.

After they had moved, they constructed a simple one-room dwelling, using scrap and new building materials. For this purpose, four labourers were employed for two days. Part of the work was done by the household members themselves. The total cost of their new house was Rs. 4,900. In order to generate money for construction purposes Zaidia's golden ornaments were sold for Rs. 1,000. Furthermore, Rasheed participated in two auction chit funds and was allocated a total sum of Rs. 2,000. Again, Zaidia's brother was asked for financial aid. He gave them an interest-free loan of Rs. 1,000. Nonetheless, the funds mobilised were insufficient. Ultimately, Rasheed decided to sell his cycle rickshaw. He only received Rs. 900 for it. From that time onwards he had to rent a cycle rickshaw to make a living. In 1992, they decided to add a boundary wall and a toilet to the dwelling. New materials were used and two construction labourers employed for a period of five days. The total sum required was Rs. 3,000. Zaidia participated in a lottery chit fund. She had to pay a monthly contribution of Rs. 150 for a period of 20 months. After drawing lots one of the monthly funds was allocated to her.

Rasheed and Zaidia have financed their dwelling by making use of different sources of finance, savings as well as credit, over a period of time. For each source of finance specific savings, gift and credit arrangements are used. This chapter will shed some light on these savings, gift and credit arrangements by providing an overview of the sources of housing finance employed by interviewed slum dwellers in Hyderabad. Following this overview, the focus will shift to the issue of credit relations. It appears that to gain access to a loan, social networks are of crucial importance. Finally, I will examine the credit relations, which most appropriately fit the livelihood strategies of the urban poor.

4.1 Sources of housing finance

In this section, I will provide an overview of the popular sources of housing finance among slum dwellers in Hyderabad. It seems that the surveyed slum dwellers use only one source or a mix of financial sources for different stages of the construction process. Table 25 illustrates that not all dwellers entered the second phase of the construction process and even fewer of them have advanced a step pass three, four or five. Many dwellers wait for the opportunity to move on to the next stage of their construction process. Furthermore, it is noteworthy that the majority of the surveyed dweller households use only one source of housing finance, followed by a declining percentage when an increasing number of financial sources are used in combination.

Table 25 Number of sources of housing finance used by interviewed slum dweller households in Hyderabad

Financial sources	Incremental building					
	Step 1		Step 2		Step 3-5	
	abs.	%	abs.	%	abs.	%
1 source	101	53	46	65	16	59
2 sources	58	30	18	25	10	37
3 sources	29	15	7	10	1	4
4 and more sources	4	2	0	0	0	0
Total	192	100	71	100	27	100

Source: Own research (N = 192, missing cases 39; V = 0.11; $\chi^2_{(6)} = 7.60$ $p > 0.05$).

This overview does not provide insight into specific financial sources (single sources are specified in Table 26). Here, the financial sources used as single source by interviewed slum dwellers in Hyderabad for the construction or improvement of their shelter are each ranked in order of priority. The main sources of funding are savings, friends, relatives and neighbours, chit funds (financial self-help organisations), moneylenders and pawnbrokers. The other sources mentioned are each only used by fewer than 10% of the interviewed dweller households.

Table 26 Sources of housing finance used as single source by interviewed slum dweller households in Hyderabad

Financial sources	Incremental building					
	Step 1		Step 2		Step 3-5	
	abs.	%	abs.	%	abs.	%
Savings	26	26	20	43	12	75
Friends, relatives and neighbours	27	27	5	11	2	13
Chit fund	21	21	5	11	1	6
Moneylender, pawnbroker	12	12	11	24	0	0
Employer	7	7	3	7	1	6
Retirement benefit, life insurance	5	5	0	0	0	0
Finance corporation	2	2	2	4	0	0
Gift, dowry	1	1	0	0	0	0
Total	101	100	46	100	16	100

Source: Own research (N = 192, missing cases 39).

By comparing the single financial sources used by interviewed slum dwellers in Hyderabad for the different steps in the construction process, it appears that the use of personal savings becomes increasingly important when it comes to later stages of the building process. It may be suggested that these later stages of the building process are less urgent and can therefore be saved for more easily. On the other hand, the use of chit funds, in which saving as well as credit provision can be combined, declines from the second step onwards. The sample for step three to five is too small to draw any firm conclusions. The use of finance derived from friends, relatives and neighbours for step one declines enormously for steps two, and three to five. It may be argued that friends, relatives and neighbours feel more obliged to provide a loan for the first stage of the building process, since it is considered to be more urgent than later phases of the building process. The popularity of moneylenders and pawnbrokers for the second step of the building process is remarkable. This may indicate that these lenders look to secure the loan by keeping an eye on the borrower, whose behaviour can more easily monitored if he/she has more or less fixed residence.

Table 27 Sources of housing finance used for incremental building by interviewed slum dweller households in Hyderabad

	Used alone or in combination with other financial sources				
	only source	+1 source	+2 sources	+3 or more sources	Total
Savings	58	56	20	4	138
Friends, relatives and neighbours	34	29	23	4	90
Moneylender, pawnbroker	23	29	23	5	80
Chit fund	27	28	19	3	77
Employer	11	13	9	2	35
Retirement benefit, life insurance	5	3	1	0	9
Colleagues	0	5	3	0	8
Finance corporation	4	1	1	0	6
Credit co-operative	0	3	2	0	5
Gift, dowry	1	0	0	0	1
Customer	0	1	0	0	1
Bank loan	0	0	1	0	1
Other*	0	4	9	0	13

Source: Own research (N= 192, missing cases 39).

* Other includes unidentified financial sources, but the number of financial sources was mentioned by the interviewed slum dwellers.

When multiple financial sources are taken into account as illustrated in Table 27, it appears that savings, friends, relatives and neighbours, moneylenders and pawnbrokers, chit funds, and employers are the most popular sources of finance for construction purposes undertaken by slum dwellers. Furthermore, it is remarkable that dwellers use finance from colleagues, a credit co-operative, a customer or a bank only in combination with another financial source. It may be suggested that for these sources trust relations are required, which are strengthened when people partake in different networks, that may provide a loan. Bank loans are rather exceptional, since the bank does not trust the poor as clientele, considering them too risky. In the single case observed it was a close relative employed at a local bank office who was able to arrange the bank loan.

As shown above, there is a huge kaleidoscope of sources, which people use to finance their construction activities. The poor opt for those sources they are able to mobilise in the specific stage in their family cycle and migrant life. Nonetheless, some tendencies can be traced in the mobilised sources. The interviewed slum dwellers finance their shelter predominantly from drawing on savings and/or informal credit. There appears to be a shift from credit obtained from closely related people for the first stage of the building process towards the use of savings and more impersonal transactions for the later stages.

4.2 Savings, gifts and credit relations of slum dwellers

Following a discussion of the popularity of different sources of housing finance, my focus will shift to the characteristics of specific way of saving, gifts and credit relations. I will focus on them in line with their order of popularity as financial source for construction, resulting in the following sequence: savings, friends, relatives and neighbours, moneylenders and pawnbrokers, chit funds, employers, retirement benefit and life insurance, colleagues, finance corporations, credit co-operatives, and gifts and dowries. Credit derived from customers or banks will not be discussed here, because they only concern two households. During my fieldwork, I could not obtain details about the relationship between the borrower and his customer at his shop. All financial sources mentioned above are used singly or in combination.

4.2.1 Savings

When the poor save they have a tendency to deduct savings from their income before consumption actually takes place. In so doing, the consumption of savings can be postponed until the desired moment. This contradicts the general notion that savings are what remains after consumption. In other words, savings are left over when financial income is spent on goods and services. Saving can take place in kind (such as Zaidia's golden ornaments and Rasheed's rickshaw) or financially, but in Table 25 and 26 only financial savings are included. Saving does not necessarily lead to shelter improvement. Such investments in shelter are dependent on factors such as 'the sense of uncertainty about the future – jobs, income, increasing costs ...', which forces 'low-income people to sit on their savings rather than risk them' (Benjamin et al. 1985: 92-93).

If the urban poor want to save, a relatively safe place for depositing these savings is required. A relatively safe place means a place where savings cannot be stolen, or withdrawn too easily for one's own use or to meet the demands of relatives. People solve this problem by, for example, burying the money in heir hut, depositing it in storage pots or with 'money guards'. These money guards are paid to keep the money in custody and trusted not to steal these savings. This trustworthiness is earned. It has to be proved over and over again (process trust), and is accompanied by social control to maintain the mutual obligations of the balanced reciprocal relationship between borrower and lender. Others use their savings to buy building materials such as bricks and store them until sufficient materials have been gathered for the desired construction.

4.2.2 Friends, neighbours and relatives

Loans provided by friends, neighbours and relatives tend to be relatively small and have open-ended terms, which may lead to partial or complete gifts over time. Furthermore, these loans may be interest free and often require non-conventional collateral. Credit arrangements between friends, neighbours and relatives are often considered personal, non-commercial arrangements, but charging interest is often considered normal in Hyderabad. This contradicts the notion that loans from friends and relatives are interest-free, as Malliswari (1988: 155) discovered in Hyderabad. The credit relations are usually of a generalised reciprocal nature. It is expected that the loans provided will be repaid, though the instalments may have a flexible nature. Non-repayment can cause frictions in the relationship between a lender and borrower, especially when the loan is used for the consumption of liquor, which reduces the speed or even likelihood of repayment. The loan repayment is mainly based on social control; the borrower is encouraged to repay the loan on the terms and conditions agreed.

The size of the loan may vary between Rs. 50 and Rs. 30,000 and interest rates can mount up to 12% per month. The characteristics of the credit terms and relations with friends, neighbours and relatives are dependent on the closeness of the relationship. If the relationship is more intimate, financial matters will be treated as mutual help.

> 'A friend is not supposed to charge interest. Otherwise what does friendship mean?'

> 'We told our relatives that we were willing to pay interest but they do not agree. We have helped them before when their daughters were married. We did not charge interest then.'

In an emergency interest is often charged. Moreover, interest can be charged when the friend, neighbour or relative concerned acts as an intermediary between a lender and borrower. In such a situation charging interest is considered normal since the broker also has to pay interest.

When the relationship between the lender and borrower is not so close, the financial arrangements are more commercial in nature. This can be illustrated by the following quote:

> 'I consider the lender my friend because he has already lived here for a long time. I regard him as a friend in all matters, except financial ones.'

The making of profit often plays an important role in financial transactions. Some people do not appreciate it if friends and relatives charge interest, but they are forced to accept it since they are in urgent need of money. Others willingly accept that friends or relatives charge with interest. They explain it as follows:

> 'This is not making use of our need, but between helping us in a time of need. In such a situation I do not mind paying an interest rate of 10 to 15% per month. However, friends may refuse to provide a loan when they cannot avoid asking for interest. In such a way, damage to the relationship can be avoided.'

The research in Hyderabad reveals that Muslims, in contrast to Hindus, tend to consider relations with friends, neighbours and close relatives more as interlocked relations, in which no distinction should be made between personal and financial matters. The interlocked nature of relations is also be influenced by the Islamic 'tabu' of charging interest on credit. Furthermore, it should be noted that the concept of friend is often regarded as the basis of structured relations between non-kin. Friendship covers a range of 'relatively casual, depending on the shared activity or setting (...), to deep and enduring relations of mutual support' (Marshall 1994: 189). In Hyderabad, people define the concept of friend as people who help them. Consequently, a moneylender may be viewed as a friend, since he helps in times of financial need. However, when it concerns repayment, the borrower's view of the lender may change. One borrower discovered that he had to repay Rs. 5,400 for a loan of Rs. 4,000, which equals an interest rate of 8% per month. He said furiously: 'This friend is not a friend any more. He has become an enemy.' For the sake of clarity, I should mention that moneylenders are therefore not included in the cluster 'friends, neighbours and relatives.'

In sum, the concepts 'friends', 'neighbours', and 'relatives' are of a heterogeneous nature; the relationship with these people is determined by the norms and values of the society. Loans from friends, neighbours and relatives are of a more generalised reciprocal nature, but a balanced reciprocal one may also be possible. The type of reciprocity is also determined by the closeness of the relation between lender and borrower. Credit from friends, neighbours and relatives is characterised by a continuum from purely commercial transactions to disguised gifts. The trust underlying the relationship between borrower and lender differs. For relatives, it is often of an ascribed nature due to their blood ties, while the trust between friends and neighbours have to be earned. When one obtains trust from a friend or neighbour, it becomes frozen trust. These relationships are maintained by means of self- and social control.

4.2.3 Moneylenders and pawnbrokers

Moneylenders have often been associated with usury or viewed as loan sharks, charging exorbitant high interest rates and bleeding the poor dry. Moreover, they are even seen as getting in the way of economic development, since they may imprison people in a cycle of permanent indebtedness. The borrower's survival is dependent on his capacity to fulfil his repayment obligations in money, labour and/or services to the creditor (Bouman 1990: 170; Schrader 1991a: 1; 1992: 69). The stereotype of the usurious nature of moneylenders also appears in the teachings of most religions. Although different interpretations exist, indications of the rejection of over-high interest rates or even interest at all cannot only be found in Hinduism and Buddhism, but also in the

Qur'an, Bible and Talmud. In contrast to profit made from trade, charging interest is often viewed as usury. However, it is often not clear what is meant by usury and on what kind of costs-benefit analyses these judgements are based (Bouman 1990: 159). However, a growing group of scientists rightly ascribe a legitimate economic function to moneylenders. Seen as financial entrepreneurs, moneylenders bring together material and non-material resources in new and profitable combinations, whereby resources are combined in such a way that financial services can be provided (e.g. Harriss 1981: 5-6; Schrader 1992; Bouman 1990; Hill 1989; Bottomley 1983; McLeod 1994: 86).

In general, the operational features of moneylenders are characterised by relative accessibility, convenient 'opening hours', quick processing, flexible collateral, high interest rates, excellent monitoring systems and often-good recovery records (e.g. Hilhorst and Oppenoorth 1992: 48; Sundaram 1988: 25). Moneylenders provide their clientele with predominantly small loans for a short period, which can even be for a day or a week. The clientele consists mainly of people who are excluded from the financial services of banks and credit unions. In Hyderabad, the loan size for shelter improvement or construction varies from Rs. 200 to 30,000. The loan term varies from six months to four years and the maximum interest rate reported is as high as 20% per month. The loan repayment programme available is rather flexible, but in most cases the interest should be remunerated even when the loan instalment itself cannot be paid.

Moneylenders form a heterogeneous group. A distinction between types of moneylenders can be made by looking at the type of relation existing between borrower and lender and the type of collateral used. A moneylender, who lends while taking physical possession of the collateral, is called a pawnbroker. Such a relation is of a more economic, rather than personal nature. Another distinction can be made on the basis of legal registration. There are unregistered and unlicensed moneylenders. These are also those who are registered and operate as non-banking financial institutions, which are regulated by the Central Bank of India.

In Hyderabad, pawnbrokers can only sell or auction pledged goods, independent of their value, when the agreed term of repayment has expired. Here, the value of the pledged items can be larger than the outstanding loan, but the money generated from the sale of the pledged object is the pawnbroker's[1] (Reddy 1992). To cover himself, the pawn-

1 Outside the Telengana area in Andhra Pradesh a pawnbroker can sell the pledged items when the agreed term of repayment is over, but the value of the pledged good has

broker sends three notices by registered post. If the defaulter does not reply, he can sell the pledged goods.

Licensed moneylenders in particular face police and income tax department inspections. Moneylenders accuse the police of harassing their business several times a year. They often send someone posing as a customer to the moneylender shop to pledge or sell an item, which appears to be stolen. Shortly afterwards, the police will come by and arrest the lender, because the police consider the receiver as bad as the thief. The case may be settled by bribing the police. One pawnbroker reported that each time it costs him 3-4 grams of gold. Another lender told me that he had to pay a bribe of Rs. 2,000 and 10 gram of gold to the police to get his employee released. When I commented that this was a huge amount he replied with the words:

> 'This is India! What can I do? When I do not pay the police, my boy will be kept for three months at the police station.'

Another pawnbroker also had problems with the police. Two years ago the police brought a man to the pawnbroker shop. This man said that he had bought ear tops (a kind of jewellery) at this shop, which appeared to be stolen. The police demand Rs. 500 to settle the case, otherwise the pawnbroker would be carted off to the police station.

To cope with this police harassment and the official rules and regulations, moneylenders and pawnbrokers, mainly Marwadis, founded an association in 1966. Although the emergence of the Andhra Pradesh Bankers and Pawnbrokers Association was expected to lead to a decline of these practices, ironically they actually increased. The association also intermediates in conflicts between customers and moneylenders. Moreover, the association applies for the yearly renewal of the moneylending licenses on behalf of its members.

All members of the Andhra Pradesh Bankers and Pawnbrokers Association are provided with a court of conduct, which provide guidelines for practising moneylenders (see Box 1).

Moneylenders can conduct their activities either part or full-time. The majority of the moneylenders are part-timers, engaging in additional income-earning activities as traders, shopkeepers, landlords, professionals, government officials and military functions (Schrader 1992: 77; Von Pischke et al. 1983: 227-229). Furthermore, slum lead-

---

to be taken into account. Here, a pawnbroker can only sell the pledged item when the outstanding loan, including its interest, exceeds the market value of the pledged good.

BOX 1 Court of conduct

1 Those who do moneylending business should get a license.
In Hyderabad this will be given by the collector and in the districts by the Mandal Revenue Officer or Revenue Divisional Officer.
2 In your business you have to do it with humanity and justice.
This means that moneylenders should not charge higher interest rates when the need of the borrower is high or that he should be flexible in accepting collateral when the loan is urgent and the desired collateral is available.
3 Not resorting to unethical practices to make first money.
4 Not purchasing/pawning stolen goods deliberately with knowledge.
A moneylender can know this when a person is coming all the time with the same articles. Such goods are probably stolen.
5 If any new person comes to the moneylender then do not take that person directly. They should take the surety of an old customer.
6 An E-form (kind of receipt) should be given to the customer, which consists of particulars of the article, those are weight of the article and present value of the article.
7 The accounts should be maintained properly and the government rules and regulations should be followed strictly.
8 Income tax and other taxes should be paid to the government regularly.
9 If the moneylender takes stolen goods deliberately, his membership will be cancelled.
10 The association will not help the persons who violate these principles.

ers can lend to their followers. Indebtedness of followers renders them dependent on the leader. In such a situation the credit relation tends to be of a negative reciprocal nature. The credit offered by slum leaders can be very functional for them, since it can create a group of followers can thus be created. The control of these followers in the urban space is more problematic than in villages, which makes the lenders hesitant of providing credit for a long period. In practice, the loan term is kept short to medium with a maximum term of six years.

Some full-time moneylenders in India are called indigenous style bankers,[2] who provide almost complete banking services to different client groups such as members of princely families or craftsmen. These moneylenders have a high level of organisation and self-regulation

2 Legally speaking, these people cannot be called bankers; nowadays they are classified as non-banking financial institutions.

BOX 2 Money lending rules

The commodities shown overleaf are pledged subject to the following terms, conditions and stipulations.

1 That my postal address given overleaf is correct.
2 That I will inform the Pawnee, forthwith of any change in my address.
3 That the maximum period available for redemption is 11 months from the date of the pledge as agreed to between the parties.
4 My monthly income is Rs. ....
5 That I am bound to preserve the token issued to me by the pawnee in respect of the said commodities.
6 That I understand that the said commodities listed overleaf will not be returned to me unless I produce the said token.
7 That in case the token is lost I am entitled to the issue of another token on submission of a letter sent on payment of sum of Rs. 2/-.
8 That on expiry of the afore said period of redemption, the pawnee is at liberty to sell/auction the said commodities and I shall cease to have any claim what so ever over the same.
9 That I am bound to give 24 hours prior notice to the Pawnee for release of the said commodities after paying all amounts due to the pawnee towards amount borrowed and interest accrued thereon, together with legal/miscellaneous expenses incurred if any.
10 That in case the said commodities listed overleaf are lost for any reason what so-ever I shall be entitled to receive only the sums specified against item No. 7(3) overleaf towards their value.
11 That the commodities listed overleaf are my own and no other person has got any right to the same.
12 That I hereby undertake to abide by the aforesaid terms and conditions and stipulations.

Signature of the pawner

NOTE: Business hours from 9 a.m. to 7 p.m.
Sunday, Jain Festival and Amavasya Days Shop is Strictly Closed.
Schedule (F) Money Lenders Rules.

RECEIPT
(As provided in Sect. 8 of the Act and referred to rule 26)
Paid Rs. ..... and redeemed the articles mentioned in the Receipt overleaf.

Signature of the pawner MoDate .... Signature

through local and regional associations. They are organised along the lines of particular ethnic communities and castes such as Muslims, Marwaris and Jains.

Many full-time moneylenders-cum-pawnbrokers in Hyderabad have a shop which is characterised as follows. The moneylender annex pawnbroker sits on a kind of platform behind his counter with two pairs of scales. Items pledged are exhibited in a glass showcase. The larger pledged, such as brass pots, are displayed along the wall at the back of the office. In front of the counter, chairs are put on a lower level, so when customers sit the lender looks down on them. The office hours are from 9.00 a.m. to 7.00 p.m. and the shop is closed on Sunday.

Pawnbrokers tend to charge lower interest rates, because they can recover the debt in the event of default, since the items pledged can be sold. In other words, credit risks and the recovery costs are low or even negligible. Moreover, the interest rates are dependent on the item pledged. Lower interest rates are charged for jewels pledged compared with, for example, brass pots. The interest rates as reported by the moneylenders are 1-5% per month. Malliswari (1988: 98) reports rates of as much as 10% per month for working capital at the fruit and vegetable wholesale markets in Secunderabad. These rates are higher than the legally permitted rate of 12.5% p.a. for secured loans against goods pledged and 18% p.a. for loans, without conventional collateral. On the back of the token, rules and regulations are listed, Box 2 provides an example of this. Such a token is always written in English, which increases the dependency of poor clients on others. A few lenders added a single Telegu sentence stating that the interest should be paid quarterly. The moneylenders are supposed to record the interest rate charged on the token, though this is often not done. When I asked a moneylender why he did not note down the interest rate on the token, he laughed and said that it is not a point that can be discussed. 'Do not ask me that question'. Clients who complain are told that they can take or leave it. Another pawnbroker explained that it is better not to note down the interest rate, because the income tax department considers the legal maximum rate to be unrealistic and may therefore charge the interest rate noted down.

Pawnbrokers in Hyderabad claimed that 25 to 70% of the market value of the item pledged can be provided as a loan. These figures differ from Malliswari (1988: 96) who reports rates of 50 to 75%. In general, pawnbrokers do not bother about the purpose of the loan, because it is secured by the items pledged. Many different kinds of article can be pawned: gold, ornaments, vessels, radios, TV-sets, clocks, sewing machines, and tiffin boxes. In general, a higher percentage of the value of the item pledged can be obtained as a loan if it is gold or silver. In practice, the maximum loans are Rs. 7,000 to 10,000. To prevent receiving stolen goods, the lender should already know the borrower. Unfamiliar clients have to be introduced by a known person.

Some borrowers decide not to repay the loan, because the debt outstanding including its interest is larger than what the pawned item would cost in a shop or at the market. If the loan is not repaid within a period of about one or two years, the items pledged may be exhibited and sold in the moneylender annex pawnbroker shop. One pawnbroker reported that the loan term for pledged gold and silver can be much longer. However, if the loan is not repaid within one year, interest on interest will be charged.

A moneylender/pawnbroker observed that there is a remarkable difference between men and women, when they approach him for a loan. He prefers to lend to women, because they are better repayers. He remarks about his customers:

> 'When gents come they say *namaskar* [local greeting] and are very friendly in order to get a loan. However, when they come to repay the loan they just throw the money in front of me and ask for the article pledged. They want to show that they are there. Compared with this, ladies stay calm.'

Another lender remarks:

> 'I prefer to do business with ladies. Half of my male clients came for a loan to meet their gambling or drinking habits. Women come for a loan for the hospital, food or school fees. Moreover, ladies do repay the loans better than men do. Ladies come in groups and there are always some known persons in the group. New persons should be brought by a known person.'

In addition to the licensed moneylenders and pawnbrokers discussed above, there are also non-licensed moneylenders, who often operate on a part-time basis. Some moneylenders wait at home for customers to approach them, while others visit their clientele on their doorsteps. To obtain the loans provided, different kinds of documents can be pledged, such as a *patta* certificate (a title deed), slum certificate, and life insurance papers, but also a house on squatted or illegally bought land. Furthermore, borrowers may be asked to sign blank papers, which can be used to make loan agreements afterwards. Such an agreement made without the borrower's participation often leads to extremely exploitative situations. This may be illustrated by the following example:

> In one *basti* [slum] the local leaders made a deal with a moneylender, called Sardarji. He was permitted to lend money in the neighbourhood concerned. The lenders were often asked to sign a blank paper. If Sardarji did not know the lender, one of the leaders would be asked to guarantee the loan. Sardarji visits the neighbourhood daily and collects the loan repayments and provides loans to the slum dwellers. Loans are given at an interest rate of 10 to 20% per month. These loans should be repaid in daily instalments and for a delay of payment a penalty of Rs. 10 or more may be charged. All the financial transactions are recorded in his notebook.

Written loan agreements, often without legal backing, can also lead to the loss of the house the borrower is living in, as this example shows:

> A coconut seller has a part-time business as moneylender. He has given a loan of Rs. 5,000 against an interest rate of 3% per month. On paper it was written down that the loan should be repaid within one year. If the loan is not repaid in time, the house, which was mortgaged, could be confiscated. The local slum leader sanctioned this agreement.

In brief, there are unscrupulous moneylenders in Hyderabad, but most transactions concern relatively small amounts, which have high transaction costs. The interest rates are not always exploitative, though they give an indication of the transaction costs involved. The relationship between borrower and lender is of balanced reciprocal nature, where mutual trust has to be earned, and proved consistently again. Such process trust anticipates expected behaviour guided by a mixture of social and self-control on the part of the borrower as well as the lender.

4.2.4 Chit funds

Chit funds are used by large sections of the Indian population for a great variety of purposes. There are both registered chit fund operators and unregistered (informal) ones. The chit funds combine savings as well as credit. For a detailed discussion of these financial self-help organisations, see the next chapter.

4.2.5 Employers

Employers can provide a loan, with or without interest, to their employees. The maximum interest rate reported is 10% per month. The repayment period is 1 to 6 years. The purpose of the loan is often decided by the borrower, but can be monitored by the employer. This credit provision is a relatively safe arrangement for the lenders, because the instalments of the credit repayment will be deducted from the salary. This can be viewed as an advance of the wage payment. Such a balanced reciprocal relationship, based on earned trust and social and self-control mechanism, can be problematic if the employee stops working for the lender. In such a situation, the borrower often has to repay the outstanding debt in a lump sum. This can become problematic if the employee has fallen ill, which can be illustrated by the following case of a woman, who said:

> 'I took out a loan of Rs. 200. I repaid the loan by a daily deduction of Rs. 5 from my daily wage of Rs. 20. Three days after I had taken out the loan I fell ill and could not repay the loan any more. My employer said that I could only come back if I repay the outstanding debt completely.'

Employers may also be eager to provide a loan to their employees to keep them dependent. As a result, the poor have to continue working for the lender, which can lead to bonded labour. A small entrepreneur dealing with the preparation of and trade in *pooris* (a kind of snack) said that he wanted to release credit to his employees to ensure that they keep working for him.

4.2.6 Retirement benefit, life insurance

In particular, those with regular employment, especially government employees and military, may invest a part of their income in insurance schemes, such as a life insurance or retirement benefit scheme. These schemes pay out a lump sum when the beneficiary reaches the age of retirement. This lump sum, alone or in combination with other sources, enables the construction of a new house for which the interviewed persons have wanted for a long time. The relationship between the client and the insurance agency is of a generalised reciprocal nature, based on earned trust, which has taken on of a frozen nature.

4.2.7 Colleagues

Credit from colleagues is only used in combination with other sources. Finance received from colleagues has virtually the same characteristics as friends, neighbours and relatives, but is only obtained in combination with other sources. Here, it may be safely concluded that once one has mobilised some finance, colleagues will be more eager to provide credit. Colleagues provide credit in the range of Rs. 500 to 10,000, against an interest rate of 3-10% per month, and in exceptional cases with even no interest at all. The repayment of the loans is of a rather flexible nature. When the borrower is not capable of paying a sum this month, he/she can postpone it until a later date. One of the borrowers contended: due to the opportunity to repay the loans in flexible instalments, this lender is like a friend.'

4.2.8 Finance corporations

Finance corporations are recognised as non-banking financial institutions in India. These corporations provide credit, and mobilise savings through, for example, shares, current savings, and recurring and term deposits. Payments have to be made in cash and chequebooks are not accepted. Withdrawals are often allowed, which demand the self-discipline of clients to save (Ghate et al. 1992: 29; Nayar 1992: 200-202).

The relationship between a finance corporation and client is of a balanced reciprocal nature, based on earned trust in combination with a mix of self-, social and institutional control. The loan repayment should take place in instalments within a prescribed period. Due to the impersonal nature of the relationship a material kind of surety is asked for such as a ration card or title deed, though even a car or house may be required. These material sureties are supplemented by personal acquaintance with the borrower. A new member is only accepted if he/she is introduced and guaranteed by a client.

In order to apply for a loan, an application form has to be completed. Such a form costs Rs. 20. When the credit is awarded, the interest is often deducted at source. The interest rate is 3 to 5% per month and the loan size varies from Rs. 6,000 to 30,000. The repayment schedule is fixed and takes place on a daily basis. In practice these loans are repaid within a period of three to four months. Loans are often given for a specific purpose, such as business or for specific consumption goods. However, the borrowers may also use such loans for the construction or improvement of their shelter. A male slum dweller reported that he had used a business loan of Rs. 1,000 for the construction of a toilet and bathroom.

4.2.9 Credit co-operatives

Credit co-operatives are registered institutions, which may be established among employees of the same company or among a group of people of a more mixed occupational background. In both cases, the co-operative members employ wage labour and payment of savings, if at all, and loan instalments takes place monthly. Moreover, participation in a credit co-operative requires the active involvement of the members, at least during the yearly board meeting. As a consequence, a credit co-operative is only accessible to a small group of slum dwellers. The loans obtained vary from Rs. 5,000 to 42,000 against an interest rate 1.2 to 2% per month. The loans should be repaid in fixed monthly instalments over a period of term of 26 to 80 months. When the co-operative is organised by an employer, the repayments are deducted from the member's salaries, and under other circumstances guarantors are required. The relation between the co-operative and its members is characterised by balanced reciprocity, earned trust and confidence, and a mix of institutional and social control.

4.3.10 Gift, dowry

Relatives in particular can provide monetary gifts in order that dwellings may be constructed. Here, gifts are provided as gift from the beginning onwards and do not include loans from relatives, which may be transformed into gifts over time. Another way that gifts provide for housing is the dowry, which encompasses finance that can be used for construction purposes or a complete dwelling. During my fieldwork, I even came across huts that were given as dowry to the settlers. The relationships between giver and receiver are based on generalised reciprocity, social control and ascribed trust.

4.3 Networking as a necessity for access to credit

In comparison to banks, access of the urban poor to the financial services, as described in this chapter, is much easier. However, access to credit is here also dependent on the surety factor. In general, the lender wants to be certain that the loan will be repaid. For this purpose physical collateral can be demanded, but there is little legal obligation for this. Consequently, social factors play an important role. A lender is only willing to provide a loan if he considers the applicant to be creditworthy. Therefore, the lender should possess some knowledge of the borrower's character.

A network is important for getting in touch with potential lenders or with people who can establish contacts with lenders. Networks can differ for household members according to their age and sex. A person's place of work can also determine the size of his network. When the living space and the workplace are combined, such as traders with a shop adjoining his dwelling, the network is smaller than when the home and workplace are in different neighbourhoods.

Networks can stretch from the village of origin to a slum on the other side of the city. Large networks can be traced among moneylenders, who use agents, intermediaries or brokers to ascertain borrowers' creditworthiness, and maintain personal contact with them. This can result in a chain with a powerful moneylender in the city to small-scale lenders and merchants in rural areas, who themselves issue loans to, for example, farmers (Hilhorst and Oppenoorth 1992: 48). There are also rural lenders, who maintain credit relations with borrowers in urban areas such as in Hyderabad, where several slum dwellers obtained a loan from a moneylender in their place of origin and agents are sent to the city to collect the instalments. It is also possible for a network to be limited to one neighbourhood. Recent migrants often have to rely on the networks in their place of origin, but while seeking financial help in the city they need to be introduced by well-known clients of a lender. If the creditworthiness of such borrowers is still considered dubious, the lender can ask new clients to show their identity card, reveal their place of residence and/or to prove their level of income.

Networks are often characterised by a web of interlocked relations of a varied nature. Most relations between a moneylender – with the exception of pawnbrokers and finance corporations – and a borrower are characterised by interlocked transactions, whereby social relations enhance control by one party over the other. By making use of a client's social dependency, a moneylender may enforce the credit repayment. This is especially easy if the moneylender is also a landowner, shopkeeper or retailer (see also e.g. Breman 1980: 16, 21; Hilhorst and Oppenoorth 1992: 49; Schmidt and Kropp 1987). Lenders may insist that borrowers buy supplies from them or sell their produce to them. These lenders may charge unfair prices or prevent the borrowers from buying and selling at 'normal' market rates. Moreover, they can even force the borrowers into a position of bonded labour. An employer can also keep the credit provided to an employee small to keep the option open of getting rid of him within a relatively short period (Schenk-Sandbergen 1988: 53). Long-term credit is not always easily provided in an urban context, since the urban space where the lender and borrower live is too large. Although through networks people can be traced in an urban context, defaulters can more easily abscond; this is one reason why credit relations are kept to the relatively short or medium term. A term of more than six years will therefore be avoided.

4.4 Finance for the urban poor's shelter

Finance can be divided into savings, gifts, insurance and credit components. In general, the Indian financial agents discussed in this chapter, apart from the finance corporations and chit funds, do not offer any opportunity to deposit savings. In Hyderabad, the interest rates per month charged for credit varies; friends, neighbours and relatives either do not ask for interest at all or demand a rate of up to 12%, moneylenders charge 1.5 to 20%, employers up to 10%, colleagues 3 to 10%, finance corporations 3 to 5% and credit co-operatives 1.2 to 2%. The maximum rates charged seem very high, but they do not form the main obstacle in obtaining access to credit. The interest rate charged for a loan can be compared with the profit made on selling certain goods. Bouman (1990: 159) describes it as follows:

> 'One easily accepts that sugar in the neighbourhood shop is priced more expensively than in the supermarket. The careless shopper who has just bought a bicycle or radio for $200 at one shop and, on the way home, comes across another where the same item is priced at $100 in a sales campaign, may curse himself for his stupidity of not having obtained prior information on other opportunities. But most probably he will not return to the first shopkeeper to accuse him of exploiting the innocent.'

Informal lending is often seen as usurious, but when one takes into account the full costs and benefits of lending, the profit margin is much smaller (Bouman 1990: 22). In general, lenders tend to charge high interest rates if high transaction costs are involved due to small-sized credit and default risks (McLeod 1994: 86; Timberg and Aiyar 1984; Von Pischke et al. 1983: 8). Moreover, the interest rate charged by moneylenders is dependent on each specific transaction and its inherent risks. De Wit (1991: 10) describes this situation with regard to the moneylender law: 'the lower the creditworthiness, the higher the interest charged'. This indicates that the poorest households have to pay the highest interest rates for hand loans, which can mount up to 10% per day. The interest rate may also increase substantially due to the urgency of demand, general capital availability, little or no access to formal sources of finance (Malliswari 1988: 180) and the monopoly of the lenders (Hilhorst and Oppenoorth 1992: 49). However, the monopoly profit is low in comparison with opportunity costs, transaction costs and risk premium (Singh 1983). Others state that the interest rates are often determined in competitive markets (Timberg and Aiyar 1984: 51).

It can be said that the accessibility of credit on terms the borrower can manage is of greater importance for the poor than a low interest rate. Credit, which fits the urban poor's livelihood strategies, is characterised by the use of unconventional collateral, a non-predetermined purpose of the loan, a relatively small sum, a short or medium term, and a flexible repayment schedule. Table 28 provides an overview of the characteristics of credit obtained for shelter by slum dwellers. Here the sources of finance are listed in order of accessibility by putting the most accessible first and the least accessible last.

It appears that financial agents – apart from finance corporations, credit co-operatives, and employers – are relatively accessible to the urban poor. In all situations, some personal knowledge of the borrower is required to ensure loan repayment. Finance corporations are the least accessible since they operate from an office, which is often not located in or near the neighbourhood where the poor live or work. Credit co-operatives are located at the place of work or nearby. Pawnbrokers are more accessible given that they operate in and around the slums and have a more shop-like nature. The most accessible sources of finance are friends, neighbours and relatives.

To prove the borrower's creditworthiness, finance corporations mainly demand conventional collateral. One or two guarantors can be used to guarantee the borrower's creditworthiness. Friends, neighbours and relatives do not ask for conventional collateral, but will assess the borrower's creditworthiness on the basis of his social and personal characteristics. Moneylenders and credit co-operatives make use of a mixture of conventional and social collateral. Conventional collateral can be a life insurance policy, jewellery, ornaments or utensils, but also less commonly land or shelter (cf. Gupta et al. 1993: 61). The poor, who often face problems with raising conventional collateral, can be helped more adequately if they are able to obtain credit on the basis of non-conventional credit.

Finance corporations determine the purpose of the loan. The other financial agents do not determine the purpose for which the loan will be used. This does not mean that they do not keep an eye on the expenditure of the loan. If a loan is, for example, used for liquor or gambling the chance that the loan will be repaid diminishes.

Table 28 Credit characteristics concerning shelter

	Accessibility	Collateral	Purpose loan	Loan amount	Term	Repayment schedule
Friends, neighbours and relatives	Relatively accessible	Social	Open, but monitored	Rs. 50 - 30,000	3 months - 11 years or open	Often flexible
Moneylenders and pawnbrokers	Relatively accessible	Mainly social but for pawnbrokers conventional	Open	Rs. 200 - 30,000	1/2 - 4 years	Flexible
Employers	Restricted access	Employment	Open, but often monitored	Up to Rs. 20,000	1 - 6 years	Often fixed
Colleagues	Restricted access	Employment	Open, but often monitored	Rs. 500- 10,000	Open, but exact term is n.a.	Flexible
Finance corporations	Not very accessible	Mainly conventional	Fixed	Rs. 6,000 - 30,000	3 - 4 months	Often fixed
Credit co-operatives	Not very accessible	Social and conventional	Open	Rs. 5,000 - 42,000	26-80 months	Fixed

Source: Own research.

The loan sizes are relatively small, but can rise to an amount of Rs. 42,000. The poor may obtain small loans from all agents except from finance corporations, where loans of a minimum of Rs. 6,000 are provided. It appears that friends, neighbours and moneylenders can provide small loans. The housing loan term varies from 35 days to 6 years. Credit provided on the basis of non-conventional collateral has a short or medium term.

The repayment schedule is fixed with employers and finance corporations. Moneylenders, friends, neighbours and relatives often make use of flexible repayment schedules.

The sample among slum dwellers in Hyderabad suggests that, in contrast to credit from employers and finance corporations, the characteristics of credit from friends, neighbours, relatives, colleagues, and moneylenders fit the poor's livelihood strategies better. In other words, the terms and conditions of credit for shelter from friends, neighbours, relatives, colleagues and moneylenders suit the poor's affordability criteria.

Conclusion

Finance, used for construction purposes, encompasses savings, gifts and credit. Apart from savings as a very important source, gifts are popular. Most sources are loans, for which specific credit relations are required. Credit relations, which may encompass more than financial issues only, are generally balanced reciprocal relations, but among friends, relatives, neighbours and colleagues general reciprocal relations can be found. In order to maintain the relationship, mutual trust is required. Most lenders and borrowers have to earn trust, which has to be proved continuously; this is called process trust. Among relatives, trust is ascribed due to the blood ties. For finance corporations trust is related to their registration by the Central Bank of India.

Slum dwellers, who generally require credit, lack physical collateral, which can be (partly) compensated by muscle power and/or social control on the lender's part. Most credit relations discussed in this chapter require the existence of personal contacts between the borrower and lender. To get in touch with lenders and to demonstrate a person's creditworthiness, networking is of crucial importance.

Apart from credit co-operatives and financial corporations, the other financial sources are of an informal sector nature. Classifying informal lenders is difficult, because they are of a heterogeneous nature. However, one can trace a continuum from purely commercial relations at one end and purely social relations at the other end. Informal credit providers can be divided into personal lenders, commercial lenders and financial self-help organisations. Personal lenders encompass friends, neighbours, relatives, colleagues and employers, which are characterised by personal, flexible lending arrangements between lender and borrower. Moneylenders and pawnbrokers can be classified as commercial lenders, who offer credit in a business-like fashion. Financial self-help organisations encompass chit funds, where people are organised in groups with a financial purpose. This will elaborated upon in the next chapter.

Credit taken out for improvement or construction of shelter in Hyderabad does not always completely fit the poor's livelihood strategies. Despite all its shortcomings it may be suggested that credit provided for shelter by friends, neighbours, relatives, colleagues and moneylenders is most fitting with the poor's livelihood strategies. Remarkably these sources of housing loans are also the most frequently used by slum dwellers in Hyderabad.

5 Collective action: finance through chit funds

Kamlala and his wife Najaja work on an occasional basis as construction labourers. Together they earn a monthly income of around Rs. 800. Along with their three children, they live in a house made of brick walls with asbestos cement sheets on the roof. The house was constructed in 1992, for which they needed Rs. 9,000; Rs. 3,000 was required to pay a stonecutter to prepare a housing plot and Rs. 6,000 for construction costs. These funds were mobilised through participation in two chit funds. Najaja participates in these chit funds in a neighbourhood four kilometres away from their place that they now live. The chit fund organiser is the wife of Kamlala's cousin. It was possible to participate in these chit funds, because a relative organised them. In the first chit fund, sixteen participants paid a monthly contribution of Rs. 312,50 for a period of 16 months. The total monthly contributions are Rs. 5,000, for which members compete by offering the biggest discount for the fund. The highest bidder receives the fund. Najaja succeeded in obtaining the fund (Rs. 3,000) during her sixth month of participation. The remaining amount Rs. 2,000 was divided among all participants. This month each member received Rs. 125 in return. In other words, during this month the contribution was only Rs.187.50 (Rs. 312.50 minus Rs. 125). After completion of this chit fund cycle, a new cycle was begun in which Najaja again participated. In this new chit fund, she again managed to obtain Rs. 3,000, but this time during the first month. After having received the fund, she had to pay still 15 monthly contributions to this chit fund cycle. Kamlala and Najaja then approached the chit fund organiser for a loan of Rs. 3,000. The chit fund organiser agreed, demanding repayment through participation in a new chit fund cycle.

As illustrated by the above example, chit funds can be used as a source of housing finance. They are financial self-help organisations, which can be used exclusively or in combination with other sources. In order to gain some insight into the dynamics of chit funds in Hyderabad as a source of housing finance I will look into their origin and the different types of organisation, by using examples from Hyderabad for illustrative purposes. These financial self-help organisations are forms of what in the social sciences is known as 'collective action'. For this reason, I will use the concept of collective action to explain how people joined and work together. Moreover, the potential of different types of chit funds as a means of self-help for the poorest will be explored. I will demonstrate that collective action is not always beneficial to all income groups.

5.1 Chit funds introduced

In a chit fund, people pool money to meet their need to deposit their savings in a relatively safe place and to gain access to a lump sum; credit or savings. This finance can be used for many different purposes such as medicines, school fees, cycle repair, a wedding, and shelter. The Hyderabad sample reveals that 26% of the slum dwellers use chit fund finance for housing purposes (N = 290).

The way in which the finance is allocated to participants can take place in a democratic or authoritarian fashion. In a democratic chit fund, the allocation of the fund is in hands of the chit fund participants, while in the authoritarian chit fund it is the organiser who makes the decisions. In other words, in a democratic chit fund the collective is responsible for dealing with the risk of default. In an authoritarian chit fund, this is the responsibility of the organiser(s). Apart from allocation mechanism, chit funds can have different organisational set ups, which will be discussed in the next sections, but first I will focus on the origin of chit funds.

The origin of chit funds in Hyderabad probably arose from grain banks, in which grain is stored for hard times, for unexpected guests or expenses (Radhakrishnan et al. 1975: 5). One of the older chit fund organisers said:

> 'Two and half decades ago from now my family migrated to Hyderabad city from a village of nearby district for our survival. A few families also have migrated like us from our village as well as surrounding villages. We were all living in huts in a neighbourhood of a slum namely 'Addagutta' near Secunderabad. We all belong to the same caste (scheduled caste, Madiga). Our respective husbands were rickshaw pullers. At that time we used to play 'Rice chit', 'Mirchi chit' as well as 'Onion chit'. This provides evidence to argue that there existed commodity chits

> among the migrants in early stages of their life styles in the city.' (Radhakrishna and Galab 1997: 10-11)

Other explanations for the origin of such financial self-help organisations can be found in non-monetary mutual aid arrangements, such as joint labour or production among peasants and urban craftsmen. Moreover, financial self-help organisations have also evolved from the need for financial assistance. For certain social events, such as funerals and weddings collective funds have been created. In other cases, such funds have been created for times of insecurity and emergency, or for the improvement of the living conditions of a certain group of members by, for example, laying a water pipe. An individual in need of cash may start an association by asking friends and neighbours to join and lend him money. He/she will repay it by means of invitations to gatherings, for which the borrower pays for the drinks and food (Schrader 1991b: 2). These financial self-help organisations provide security or insurance, but also have an economic and socialising function (Bouman 1994: 375).

In the next three sections, I will provide an overview of three main organisational types of chit funds; the rotating savings and credit association, the savings association, and the accumulating savings and credit association.

5.2 Rotating savings and credit associations

The chit fund as rotating savings and credit association is the most popular type in Hyderabad. Radhakrishna and Galab (1997) give an indication of this popularity by showing that out of their slum samples of 52 chit funds, 51 are rotating savings and credit associations. Two examples of this chit fund type are provided below.

> Twelve Mutaraj caste members visit the house of Elemanda daily to pay their contribution to the chit fund. The contribution of Rs. 15 is noted down by Elemanda, or his wife Yanaki. After twenty days all participants gather in front of the house of the organiser and a lucky draw takes place. A child of less than seven years draws the winning chit out of a steel box. The winner obtains the collected fund of Rs. 3,600 minus a commission of Rs. 150, which has to be paid to the chit fund organiser. This ritual is repeated until all members have received their share once, which takes about eight months.

The second example, which is of a more complex nature, follows.

> Virasjay has lived in a slum for twelve years and has become the general secretary of the neighbourhood committee. Moreover, he organises four auction chit funds, each with sixteen members. In two chit funds, members each pay Rs. 312.50 per month and in the other two Rs. 625 each. The participants trust him as a good manager of the chit funds. They expect that their contributions will be safe and that their share will be paid in time. On the 10th day of each month, all participants of each chit fund meet at his house to deposit their contributions and allocate the fund by means of bidding. Once the bidding activities are over, tea is sometimes offered to the participants. In return for his organisation and management activities, Virasjay charges commission which provides him an income of Rs. 1,000 per month.

Among policy-makers and scientists, chit funds as employed in the case study above, are generally known as rotating credit associations (RCAs) or rotating savings and credit associations (ROSCAs). I prefer the term ROSCA, because it encompasses the saving as well as the credit component of the associations. In fact, a ROSCA consists of a group of participants who make regular contributions to a fund that is given, in whole or in part, to each member in turn.[1] The first collector receives an interest free loan from all other participants. The last in line is saving money, while he/she extends credit to his fellow members. The other members alternate between net debtor and net creditor positions. They save until they receive the fund and then start paying back into it. In short, a ROSCA is an intermediary between savers and borrowers (Bouman 1978: 36-37; Von Pischke 1992: 329). The simplest form of the operation of a ROSCA can be illustrated with an example.

> Suppose there are twelve participants, each of who contributes Rs. 100 monthly. Each one in turn will receive Rs. 1,200 at every monthly meeting. The persons who will receive the fund are chosen by, for example, drawing lots. After twelve months everyone will have received Rs.

1 If the fund is given in part to one of the members, the remaining amount may be used to establish an emergency fund. Among the Bamilèkè in Cameroon, such funds are created for mutual aid in case of death or illness. From this fund no loans will be given, except for the purchase of medicines (Soen and de Comarmond 1972: 1172). In the Indonesian town of Telehu, funds are created to provide loans or grants to members in the event of sickness or death, and for religious purposes. In some cases these services are also accessible for non-members (Hospes 1992b: 233).

1,200 and the cycle is closed. If they want the participants may decide to start a new cycle possibly with new members and regulations.

In this example, it is assumed that all members will pay their contributions to the kitty, even after they have received the fund. Furthermore, no deductions are made to compensate the organiser for his responsibilities. More elaborate ROSCAs may include bookkeeping, issuing of receipts, written rules and regulations and contracts (cf. Kuper and Kaplan 1975: 180-181).

In addition to the drawing of lots, the order of rotation may be decided by auction, seniority, negotiation, consensus, bribery or the decision of the organiser (see e.g. Ardener 1964; Bouman 1978: 38; Nayar 1986; Smets 1992: 13-23). The lottery and auction system will be discussed more extensively below.

In a lottery ROSCA, the order of rotation is decided by drawing lots at every meeting or for the complete sequence at the beginning of the cycle. A lottery system may be introduced to avoid nepotism and corruption while allocating the fund (Soen and De Comarmond 1972: 1174). Suppose all twelve participants pay each Rs. 100 into the common fund, which is distributed to each member in turn. Each member receives Rs. 1,200, but at different times (see Table 29).

In this example, the organiser refrains from taking part of the pot or admission fees. An organiser who is paid for organising and managing a ROSCA normally gains financially. He/she can obtain a fixed share of the fund each month or the first draw during the ROSCA cycle. If there are unsolved default cases, he/she has to make up the deficit. The organiser has to bear the losses, which makes it necessary to have a stock on funds, which may legitimise the organiser benefiting from the first draw (cf. Schrader 1991b: 13).

Not all participants in a lottery ROSCA gain financially. I shall illustrate this by making a cash flow analysis according to the present value model for the first and last recipient of the fund. This model is an organising framework, according to which investments can be modelled to market values. The underlying assumption is that a Rupee today is worth more than one Rupee tomorrow, due to inflation and interest rates[2] (Malpezzi 1991: 210-211). The first recipient of the fund of

2 The used formula for the calculations of the net present value is
$V_i = P_j \cdot 1/R_{j-i}$
V_i = present value at moment i
P_j = payment at moment j
Rj-i = interest rate charged for the period j-i

Table 29 Financial transactions in a lottery ROSCA

	Months												
	1	**2**	**3**	**4**	**5**	**6**	**7**	**8**	**9**	**10**	**11**	**12**	**Total**
Contribution	100	100	100	100	100	100	100	100	100	100	100	100	100
Present value of contribution*	100	99	98	97	97	96	95	94	93	92	92	91	1144
Fund received	1200	1200	1200	1200	1200	1200	1200	1200	1200	1200	1200	1200	–
Present value of fund received*	1200	1190	1179	1169	1159	1149	1139	1129	1119	1110	1100	1091	–

Source: own research

*The inflated interest rate used is 11% p.a.

a lottery ROSCA is in fact repaying the lump sum received for the rest of the ROSCA cycle. The present value is calculated for the total of contributions as well as the fund received in the first month (V_1) against an inflated interest rate of 11% p.a. Here, the first month is taken as point of reference.

$V_{1,\text{ fund received}}$	+ 1200
$V_{1,\text{ contributions}}$	- 1144
	+ 56

The same is done for the person, who receives the pooled savings during the last meeting.

$V_{1,\text{ fund received}}$	+ 1091
$V_{1,\text{ contributions}}$	- 1144
	- 53

The person, who receives the fund at the beginning of the cycle in effect does better, from a financial point of view, than the person who obtains it at the end. The participants need luck in obtaining financial profit from their ROSCA participation.

The auction system sometimes used for determining the order of rotation is the Dutch auction system. In this system, the auctioneers reduce the pooled savings until a bottom price for obtaining the kitty has been reached. The person, who offers the highest discount, obtains the fund and the remaining amount, called the auction amount, is commonly distributed equally among all participants. Here, no minimum auction amount is required. At the beginning of the cycle more people will compete for the fund, which increases the auction amount (Radhakrishnan et al. 1975: 6-7). Table 30 provides an overview of the financial transactions and a cash flow analysis for the first and last recipient of the fund by calculating the relevant present values. It should be noted that the auction amount as mentioned in this Table is equal to the interest that the recipient of the fund has to pay.

The first recipient of the fund has to pay a high price for the money desired. The total amount of contributions exceeds the financial gains during the cycle.

Table 30 Financial transactions in an auction ROSCA

	Months												
	1	2	3	4	5	6	7	8	9	10	11	12	Total
Contributions	100	100	100	100	100	100	100	100	100	100	100	100	1200
Present value contributions*	100	99	98	97	97	96	95	94	93	92	92	91	1444
Collected in fund	1200	1200	1200	1200	1200	1200	1200	1200	1200	1200	1200	1200	–
Auction amount	600	600	500	400	400	300	400	300	200	200	100	0	–
Fund received by winner	600	600	700	800	800	900	800	900	1000	1000	1100	1200	–
Present value fund received*	600	595	688	779	773	862	759	847	933	925	1008	1091	–
Dividend received by each person	50	50	42	33	33	25	33	25	17	17	8	0	333
Present value dividend received*	50	50	41	32	32	24	31	24	16	16	7	0	323

Source : own research

* The inflated interest rate used is 11% p.a.

$V_{1,\ fund\ received}$	+ 600
$V_{1,\ dividend\ received}$	+ 323
$V_{1,\ contributions}$	- 1144
	- 221

For the last recipient of the fund it is completely different. He has no other competitors bidding for the fund. Thus the maximum profit is gained.[3] From a cash flow analysis, one can see that profit has been made.

$V_{1,\ fund\ received}$	+ 1091
$V_{1,\ dividend\ received}$	+ 323
$V_{1,\ contributions}$	- 1144
	+ 270

If the market value exceeds the costs of a specific investment and if people know that they will obtain a negative rate of return on their investments, they are not willing to invest unless other opportunities are unknown or inaccessible (Malpezzi 1991: 211). In a lottery ROSCA, the participants depend on the factor of luck while in the auction ROSCA they have to pay a high price for getting the fund at the beginning of the cycle. For some people, participation is very profitable, for others less so. Nevertheless, participation in a ROSCA seems to be a popular option among many people and even among employees of financial institutions in many countries. Adams (1992: 13-14) illustrates this as follows:

> 'It is surprising how often ROSCAs are found among employees of 'formal' financial intermediaries: in the National Credit Union Federation in Chocabamba, Bolivia; people working for the Development Finance Corporations in both Belize and St. Kitts/Nevis; numerous employees of commercial banks and central banks in Belize, Papua New Guinea, Bolivia, the Dominican Republic, and the Philippines; and in 1987 there was even a ROSCA operating among employees of the International Monetary Fund in Washington, D.C., all of whom had doctoral degrees in economics and finance!'

3 To cope with this inequality, a minimum auction amount for every meeting can be introduced.

IMF staff members have access to the 'formal' financial sector and can probably opt for a more efficient use of their money. Their participation in a ROSCA illustrates that the choice of participation is not always based on expected maximum profit. However, the social ambience of a ROSCA can be a decisive factor in the choice to participate (cf. Von Pischke 1992: 333). In other ROSCAs, people can be encouraged to participate due to the gambling element of a lottery ROSCA. Others may opt for establishing multi-functional relations with other participants or organisers to secure help, in addition to those of a financial kind, in the future. One should take into consideration that other factors may be decisive for participation in these ROSCAs, such as limited or no access to other financial institutions, but also socio-cultural, religious and gender factors.

In general, socio-cultural activities can function as a kind of glue to keep people together in a ROSCA. Here the glue is instrumental to the operation of the ROSCA concerned. The ROSCA participants generally meet during the allocation of the fund. During such occasions, tea may be offered to participants on account of the ROSCA members or the organiser. However, Radhakrishna and Galab (1997: 11) found that in Hyderabad

> 'none of the chit groups were meant for socializing. No refreshments were served, nor do all members always meet after an executed first meeting.'

Common activities for ROSCA participants such as parties, dinners, and celebrating festivals were reported not present during the 1960s in Hyderabad (Anderson 1966: 335), which is rather different from for example the Indian city of Sangli in the 1990s, where they are abundantly available (Smets 1992).

A striking example of religious influences can be found in Islam, which provides Muslims with guidelines for not charging and receiving interest (see e.g. Shaghil 1989; Smets 1992: 49-54).

Women may decide to join a ROSCA with other women because they dislike being overruled by men in a ROSCA. Other women use a ROSCA to keep savings out of the hands of their husbands or family members, who may claim them for their own purpose such as the consumption of alcohol. Soen and De Comarmond (1972: 1172) describe that among the Bamilèkè, women are not allowed to participate in a ROSCA, although they may represent their husbands when they cannot attend a meeting.

ROSCAs have a flexible nature and can adapt themselves to a changing environment. ROSCAs often have 'informal' individually-based procedures and contain effective mechanisms that regulate membership eligibility, credit rating and repayment (Bouman 1978: 37-39; Nayar 1986: 54). However, the successful operation of a specific ROSCA requires mutual trust among its participants. The members, who have not yet received the fund, have to trust that the participants, who have already received the fund, will keep paying their contributions until the end of the cycle. Therefore, the norms and values of the participants in a ROSCA should be roughly compatible, which may be influenced by their age, gender, religions, caste, socio-cultural and socio-economic background. If the ROSCA organiser can ensure that the members meet their obligations towards the ROSCA and its participants, the importance of participants' value orientations being of a more or less homogeneous nature decreases (Smets 1992: 63-68).

In addition to a more or less shared set of norms and values among members of a specific ROSCA, the cycle of a ROSCA should not be too long[4] to ensure observability and social control within the ROSCA concerned. In Hyderabad, the most popular length of a cycle is approximately 1.5-2 year, while in Sangli it is about a year (Smets 1992: 63-68). In a ROSCA, people defaulting and people harmed by others' default, know each other personally, which turns such incidents into personal affairs and possibly into big quarrels (Van der Harst 1974: 69).

Social control seems to be a formidable barrier against fraud and defaulting. This is easier in a small ROSCA, because a small ROSCA ensures members' knowledge of each others' personality (Bouman 1978: 37-38).

In general, the compulsory payment of the contribution to a ROSCA enables people to have access to a lump sum. Furthermore, membership of a ROSCA may be considered a guarantee for loans from, for example, relatives or friends (cf. Van der Harst 1974: 73).

---

4 However, there are ROSCAs reported with annual subscriptions and a cycle of twenty years and more, such as the Japanese kou (Izumida 1992: 170) and the Nepalese *dhikuti* (Seibel and Shrestha 1988: 186). A ROSCA with, for example, 20 members who pay yearly contributions to the association creates possibilities for long-term credit (Von Pischke 1992: 332). However, this long term creates problems if a large number of participants drop out. For example, it is estimated according to Wesselink that about 40% of the participants drop out from savings and credit schemes in Uganda due to AIDS (1992: 13).

5.3 Savings associations

In 1960, 227 members of the semi-nomadic tribe Mandula settled in Hyderabad. Nine years later they started a chit fund, called 'Sangam Chittie'. Each member was asked to pay 50 paise per month each to repay the loan of Rs. 5,000, which was taken out for the construction of a community hall. After three years, the loan was repaid and the payments continued. In 1972, the monthly contribution had become Rs. 1. This money was pooled in a common fund for community purposes such as the construction of a temple. In 1986, the common fund had grown and could offer Rs. 25,000 for the construction of the temple. For additional finance, Rs. 25 was collected from each house.

As described above, people can join a chit fund with the intention of saving for a common purpose such as the construction of a community hall and temple. In a savings association, for which I introduced the term SAVA earlier, people make regular contributions of a fixed or variable size to a common fund, from which no credit will be provided. The fund created accumulates for a predetermined period, after which deposits are returned to all participants (Adams 1992: 13; Schrieder and Cuevas 1992: 46). However, there are also savings associations, whose cycle will not be terminated. Here the pooled savings will accumulate in a fund that will be used for emergency cases, and/or for the improvement of public facilities, or another defined purpose. For the duration of the cycle, the fund is kept by the treasurer at his home and/or put in a savings account at a bank (Schrieder and Cuevas 1992: 46).

Joining a SAVA can be made attractive to participants by introducing a prize, which can be won by all members. In such a SAVA one or more people can win a prize, which can be a specific sum of money or a good such as a scooter, house or refrigerator. This lottery system differs from a lottery, where there are winners and people who will lose their complete input. In such a SAVA all participants win a prize, but their input differs. This can be illustrated with an example of a SAVA in which participants can win an apartment among other prizes. However, one should bear in mind that the target group of this SAVA does not include the poor.

The 650 participants in the lottery SAVA are supposed to deposit Rs. 500 per month to a common fund. The duration of the scheme is 20 months. Every month a lucky draw takes place. Only the people who have paid their monthly payment before the 15th of the month are

> allowed to participate in the lottery. The winner of the lottery gets a prize and does not need to pay any further. In addition to the monthly prize allocated, ceiling fans, scooters, mopeds, TV sets, and refrigerators can be won. In the 19th month, the sole prize is a single-bedroom flat.

The SAVA type described above is also known as a share game or prize chit. Such an association may be considered a prize ROSCA. However, following Schrader (1991b: 8), I do not think it is accurate to call such an association a ROSCA. A ROSCA is characterised by a corresponding number of participants and draws, whereby the savings and credit positions of participants rotate. On the other hand, in a SAVA the number of participants is much greater than the number of draws. Consequently, there is no relation between the large number of participants and the life span of the association. As soon as people receive their prize, they drop out of the scheme. There are therefore no saving and credit positions that rotate among all participants. I shall therefore call such an association a lottery SAVA.

The organiser/foreman in a lottery SAVA controls a large sum of money, which accumulates during the sequence of the cycle. At the end of the cycle, the organiser has to pay out to the non-winners. Providing a certain percentage of interest and/or a present can enlarge the amount of savings. Participation in a SAVA makes saving compulsory for all its participants until they have won the prize. In this way, there can be no problem with defaulters, because players who drop out do not affect other participants in the SAVA. Another incentive for the members to pay their savings on time is exclusion from the prize draw if the payment of their contribution has been delayed (Schrader 1991b: 9; Smets 1992: 17-20).

Depending on the organisational set-up of a lottery SAVA and its operation, the organiser can make a profit out of such a scheme. Profit can be gained by putting the total contributions minus the expenditures for the prizes into a savings account or through using it as working capital (see e.g. Nayar 1973: 17-20).

Shopkeepers or land developers can also use these schemes as a marketing mechanism. In this way, shopkeepers can increase their sales and get access to relatively cheap working capital (cf. Smets 1992: 19). Land developers also make use of these schemes to sell plots and use the lottery mechanism to attract clients. An example follows:

> In one of the suburbs of the twin city of Hyderabad-Secunderabad a scheme was organised to sell serviced plots of 250 square yards, which

> are only allocated after the required sum has been completely paid. A plot costs Rs. 22,500 - 25,500, which can be paid in a lump sum or in instalments. Furthermore, an additional membership fee of Rs. 200 is required. For a period of fifty months 2,000 applicants are grouped together in a scheme with prizes worth Rs. 5,000,000. There is a monthly lucky draw for allocating to the prize winners a free plot, colour television and washing machine. Every sixth months, the prizes consist of a motor-cycle, refrigerator, a video recorder, and ten times Rs. 1,000. Moreover, annually a car, a golden ornament worth Rs. 50,000, a video recorder and 20 consolation prizes of Rs. 1,000 each are provided. Furthermore, there is a mega draw for a car worth Rs. 350,000, gold ornaments (Rs. 100,000), a four-door refrigerator and thirty prizes of Rs. 1,000 each.

The incentives of possibly winning a prize and still obtaining the desired item can encourage the participation of rational actors enormously.

5.4 Accumulating savings and credit associations

> From 12.00 a.m. onwards, chit fund organisers sit on four places in the open air to collect money from their clients. In the meantime, in a small room four batches of twenty members come together. They repay their credit to the treasurer. Moreover, loans are provided from the common fund of about Rs. 20,000; loans of Rs. 300 in three batches and Rs. 500 in one. To obtain this credit, the participants of each batch have to bid for a loan with a minimum amount of Rs. 15 for a loan of Rs. 300, and Rs. 25 for a loan of Rs. 500. The highest bidder receives the loan and has to pay the auction amount as interest. The next month, new loans can be provided when the outstanding credit and its interest has been repaid.
>
> This chit fund with its four batches has its roots in 1976, when twenty people joined and came to the house of the slum leader to pay their monthly contribution of Rs. 300 each. This creates a fund of Rs. 6,000 from which loans can be provided to the participants. When sufficient money was available in the fund, it was decided to stop paying the contributions. Later on new members were accepted one by one, but had to be vetted by one of the members.

The chit funds in this example are accumulating savings and credit associations, which are also known as non-rotating savings and credit associations or 'informal' credit associations. The accumulating savings and credit association (ASCRA) resembles the credit co-operatives or the credit union. In an ASCRA, just as in a SAVA, the pooled savings are not directly redistributed, but accumulate in a fund for a specific period. The difference is that the fund created in an ASCRA can be used partly or completely to provide loans either to members only, or also, but less common, to non-members. Part of these savings may be kept in a fund for emergency cases, or used for community development or joint investment (Bouman 1994: 376). In contrast to the SAVA, loans can be provided from the common fund.

An ASCRA, like other financial self-help organisations, can be organised on the basis of geographic location, age, gender, community, ethnic background or the place of work (see also Mehta and Mehta 1991: 1110). In Hyderabad, I found only a few properly functioning ASCRAs with a more or less endless cycle, as illustrated in the example at the beginning of this section. In these ASCRAs, the collection of savings ceased when the common fund was large enough to cover the loan demands. This may result in ASCRAs with hundreds of participants. In Sangli, there are even ASCRAs with more than 1,000 participants, but with a cycle of about one year to ensure a proper functioning (Smets 1992).

Loans are either made available each week, month or at another time interval. The provision of credit can be in a predetermined order, on a first-come-first-served basis, or decided by consensus, negotiation, seniority, bribery or decision of the organiser. Loans may even be granted to a member who offers the highest interest payment (Mehta and Mehta 1991: 1110). Normally, the loan size is such that it corresponds with the repaying capacity of the recipients. To ensure repayment of the credit a guarantor is often needed. During any given period, some members may take out more than one loan, while others do not need to borrow from the fund and use the ASCRA more as a savings club with the option of making profits or saving for future consumption or security. The credit taken out can be repaid in a lump sum or in instalments within a prescribed period. If the loan cannot be repaid in time, the savings are taken from the savings account of the borrower, and/or guarantors at the ASCRA. After closing down the cycle, the accumulated fund will be partly or completely redistributed among its members. The most common period is about one year, during which participants may use their fund for a specific purpose, for example, paying taxes and school fees or a religious ceremony such as Diwali, Eid-Ul-Fitr or Christmas (Bouman 1994: 376; Smets 1992: 67). To enlarge the common fund, entry fees, shares, and penalties on delayed payments of contributions and/or loan instalments, and (high) interest rates on loans may be charged. The interest rates charged are up to 13% per month. High interest rates on loans (5-10% per month) are not uncommon in Sangli (India), which helps the fund to accumulate rapidly (Smets 1992: 29-32). However, a share in the profit made will often compensate for these high rates of interest. ASCRA participants may decide to distribute only a part of the fund at the end of the cycle and start a new cycle with the remainder. Consequently, the accumulation process extends over a longer period and the financial mediation becomes of a more permanent nature, which creates opportunities for long-term credit. However, risks of safekeeping, embezzlement and loan defaults, besides administration and transaction costs, increase (Bouman 1994: 376; Smets 1992: 67).

If there are a large number of members paying high contributions, substantial amounts of money may circulate in an ASCRA. To manage such an ASCRA properly, strong self-discipline on the part of the organiser(s) and members is necessary (Smets 1992: 72). Participation in an ASCRA appears to be profitable even for employees at Indian banks. Participation can be attractive to people whose aim is to gain maximum profit. Such people may join an ASCRA where high interest rates are given on their savings and refrain from taking credit from the ASCRA fund. In this way, they can make the same or even more profit on their savings than they would at a local bank. In general, people do not only participate to make money out of their savings, but also to get relatively easy access to credit.

Compared with ROSCAs, ASCRAs are less socially and more financially orientated. The value orientations of the members of an ASCRA do not need to be homogeneous to ensure its smooth functioning. The social control mechanism is partly replaced by a system of rules and regulations and control by an organiser or board (Smets 1992: 66-68). Thus far, different types of financial self-help organisations have been described. In the next section, I shall discuss the concept of collective action for the operation of the different types of chit funds.

5.5 Collective action in chit funds

People join in a chit fund to meet their common needs, having a safe place to deposit savings and access to a lump sum. In general, working together in chit funds is instrumental for meeting individual needs, unless sources are pooled for a common purpose. In order to gain access to a chit fund people should belong to a network, because participation in a chit fund is dependent on introduction by a known person or the potential participants should be known to the organising body or person, who consider the new member trustworthy. There is not much flexibility in accepting new members in a new cycle of a financial self-help organisation. In other words, access to a financial self-help organisation is restricted to those who are part of a network and considered trustworthy.

Dependent on the behaviour of the chit fund participants, collectively preferred ends can be properly met. However, when people do not want to bear the costs of the collective good and only opt for the benefits a free-rider problem can occur. In other words, people have to make timely contributions to the financial self-help organisation, but when they only obtain a lump sum and refrain from the compulsory payment of contributions later on, free rider behaviour becomes manifest. All individuals who are not able or willing to contribute to the common purpose will enjoy the advantages of participating in a financial self-help organisation. In such a situation, selective incentives will be offered to those who contribute and withheld from those who do not. Furthermore, free riders can also be punished by, for example, excluding them from consumption. Non-payers of contributions can be excluded from, for example, access to a lump sum or credit.

Collective action depends also on the type of organisation. In this section, I will discuss the specific characteristics of collective action in the following chit funds; ROSCA, SAVA and ASCRA respectively.

In a ROSCA, selective incentives of a material nature are reflected in the lump sum, which can be gained when contributions are paid to the kitty. Social incentives are the encouragement of the savings behaviour of its members, and their social status within and outside the ROSCA. A group feeling can be strengthened when the participants act as expected. Outside the ROSCA group the social status of members can rise, because they demonstrate that they can save and buy certain goods, or spend money on important ceremonies or festivals. A psychological incentive is the increase in self-confidence. Moreover, in a ROSCA where social gatherings are of importance, members can be freed from the pressures of daily life by exchanging gossip, jokes, and stories (see e.g. Smets 1998; Smets and Broekman 1996).

The potential for default is small due to the link between savings and credit in a ROSCA. People are expected to pay their contribution in exchange for a lump sum, which may be obtained during the cycle.

A careful selection of participants for a specific ROSCA is, however, still necessary to maintain a generalised reciprocal relationship. The organiser can make such a selection, by all members or a group of (potential) participants together. It may, therefore, be decided, for example, that only members of the same sex are allowed to join. Other selection criteria may be, according to Hechter (1988: 110-111) admission for relatives only, admission only for people who are not expected to leave the community, admission only for 'credible' individuals. New members and (potential) defaulters have restricted access to the fund. They may only obtain the fund at the end of the cycle. This attitude can be established and maintained when there is a strong leader, or members of a more or less homogeneous socio-economic and socio-cultural background. Furthermore, the number of participants should not be too large nor the cycle too long, to ensure observability and social control (Smets 1992: 73-79). In extreme cases of social and psychological pressure to ensure the compulsory payments, this may even result in suicide (see Ardener 1964; Smets 1992: 65-66).

Free rider behaviour in a ROSCA directly damages the interest of other participants. If a person, who has already received the fund, stops paying his contributions, the collected pot will decline. The people, who still have to receive their share, are faced with a smaller kitty unless the organiser makes up the difference. Naturally, this can lead to fierce quarrels. To avoid default, peers in a ROSCA exercise social pressure on each other, which often leads to self-constraint on the part of its participants resulting in timely payment of contributions and continuous payment after receiving the fund. Such social pressure is reduced if the ROSCA is leader-centred. If such means of social pressure do not work properly, then the threat of violence may be used.

In a SAVA, material incentives refer to the purpose that the group saves for the prize that can be gained. Social incentives are the improvement of the participant's social status by contributing to a common goal or saving for an individual purpose. Psychologically this can lead to the enhancement of self-confidence among its members.

In a SAVA, there is no link between savings and credit, because no credit is provided at all. When people save, they do not have access to their savings until the target has been reached. If the period involved is too long, the motivation to deposit can decline. In such a situation, self-discipline is of crucial importance to the proper functioning of the SAVA. However, the separation of savings and credit does not necessarily support self-discipline. Social pressure is often needed to encourage people to keep paying their contributions on time. Moreover, if the participants save for a common purpose, the generalised reciprocal relationship among its participants may erode. Consequently, a free rider problem can easily arise. Some members may refrain from paying their contributions since they anticipate that the common target will still be reached without their contribution. For example, an improved road cannot be withheld from non-contributors. To encourage payment of the contribution a lottery system with prizes can be introduced. Such external inducements can encourage people's involvement.

In an ASCRA, the main material incentive is access to credit and/or the savings deposited. Social incentives are prestige within and outside the association from demonstrating your credibility. Furthermore, access to a lump sum to enable a member to meet expenses for rituals and festivals and certain material goods can improve somebody's position in society. Psychological incentives refer to the creation of a measure of self-confidence among the members.

The operation of an ASCRA is based on generalised reciprocal relations, even when the association is organised and managed by a leader or body. Such a relationship is maintained by denying free riders access to credit. Borrowers have to pay contributions, the size of which may be related to the loan that can be taken out. In order to obtain a higher amount, guarantees of other participants are often required. In other ASCRA, the contributions are limited to a share, which has to be paid by new members. By delinking savings and credit, the possibility of default may increase. For coping with default, rules and regulations are introduced to substitute for group control mechanisms, which are only applicable to small groups. Moreover, guarantors can be introduced to force borrowers to repay the loan. Guarantors are especially important when a bigger association is concerned where face-to-face relations between all participants are lacking. By creating links between a lender and a guarantor with social standing in society, social pressure can be exercised to encourage the lender to repay his debt to the ASCRA. In case of default, a guarantor may visit the defaulter when he/she is receiving relatives or friends at his home. In front of the guests, the guarantor can start complaining about the bad repayment behaviour of their host. The idea that this might happen has a preventive effect.

5.6 Chit funds and the poor

Chit funds in Hyderabad are mainly organised by relatively better-off people with a dynamic nature, who have learned to organise and manage a chit fund from those already organising a chit fund or through their own participation in one. Moreover, people choose specific types of chit funds, which fit their employment conditions, income flows, and savings and credit needs, as well as their psychological, socio-cultural and religious needs (see e.g. Hospes 1992a: 17; Smets 1992; 1996b; 1998). Therefore, we may conclude that people make their own financial self-help organisations, or as Hospes (1992a: 17) describes it:

> 'It is people that count: people make rules, adapt rules and compare rules and resources of different saving and credit arrangements.'

Objectives in participating in a chit fund can include obtaining access to a relatively safe haven for savings. A safe haven for savings means that relatives cannot easily make claims on the savings available and that the keeper safeguards them carefully. Chit funds do not only help to pool the savings of those who have the capacity to save, but also encourage the poor to put something aside for a rainy day (Nayar 1973: 143). However, access to savings can be problematic, especially in SAVAs. Members of a SAVA do not have access to their savings with the SAVA unless their request meets the regulations of the SAVA concerned. ROSCA and ASCRA participants get access to their deposited savings when they receive the kitty, part of the kitty or obtain a loan from the common fund. Below I will discuss the credit criteria that fit the poor's livelihood strategies for the different chit funds: (1) accessibility, (2) the use of non-conventional collateral, (3) self-determination of the purpose of the loan, (4) not too large a loan, (5) a short or medium-term, and (6) a flexible repayment schedule.

Firstly, access to finance is important for the poor. However, access to chit funds is restricted to members who belong to certain networks, the person has to be trusted to pay contributions, and for ASCRAs to also repay loans. Once a person has been accepted as a member, the question arises of access to finance if required. ROSCA members, however, cannot get the fund simultaneously, for example, for certain festivals, at the beginning of the agrarian production cycle or to overcome a drop in income for hawkers during the rainy season. SAVA participants do not have access to finance, since they are saving in a common pool. ASCRAs provide the opportunity of obtaining a loan. However, if too many members opt for credit from the kitty, it is possible that the amount asked for cannot be provided.

Secondly, loans, if provided, are awarded on the basis of savings deposited and/or the use of guarantors. In case of default, the savings deposited by the borrower and probably those of the guarantor will be taken. In other cases, group pressure forces participants to pay their instalments. Guarantees that one will not leave the neighbourhood can be demanded; only people living in their own house may be accepted as members to avoid the risk of people absconding while participating in a chit fund. Therefore, tenants will usually be refused as participants. In this respect, Hechter (1987: 110) says that only people 'who are unlikely to leave the community' will be accepted as participants. Once a participant has proved him/herself to be a good saver and repayer of credit in a chit fund, a loan can be obtained more easily from, for example, a moneylender.

Thirdly, the borrower should define the purpose for which the loan or lump sum obtained will be used. Finance, obtained from a chit fund, can generally be used according to the wishes of the person concerned. In other words, financial self-help organisations do not determine the purpose for which the finance required have to be used for. One exception is the SAVA, where members usually contribute for a predetermined purpose.

Fourthly, the size of the loan should not be too big. Since the loan size and the ROSCA fund are dependent on the contributions, the loan size is generally not too large. In other words, the loan size is small enough to be manageable for the borrower. However, the size is often considered too small to meet projected expenses. Consequently, more loans are often needed, but mainly from other sources.

Fifthly, the term of the loans provided is often short, with a period of less than a year. In exceptional cases, the term is longer.

Sixthly, some flexibility in loan repayment schedules is necessary for the poor. However, if contributions are delayed for any reason, this harms the other ROSCA participants directly, contrary to an ASCRA.

The urban poor are not always able to pay their contributions to the chit fund, even when they are willing to do so. Such practice harms the other participants. For Hyderabad, Radhakrishna and Galab report, on the basis of their case studies in slums, that the poorest of the poor are excluded from participation:

> 'Some of the families who are non-participants are so poor that they are not able to meet certain ritual obligations and they are not able to invite relatives and neighbours while performing crucial ritual obligations. This is the reason why they have cut off socially from the neighbours and relatives. In fact, inviting neighbours and relatives for the crucial rituals provides an opportunity for a family to expand helping networks and increase social wealth. Expansion of reciprocal networks increase the probability of meeting cultural and biological needs under extreme scarcity conditions.' (Radhakrishna and Galab 1997: 67-68)

This is reconfirmed for South Asia (Streefland 1996) and more specifically for Sangli, India (Smets 1992: 43-48). Moreover, licensed chit funds (auction ROSCAs) exclude the participation of the poor, since the monthly contributions are rather high (Rs 1000- 10,000) and the term of payment 50 months. However, housing finance derived from these chit funds is cheaper than housing finance from private 'formal' housing finance organisations (see Smets 2000).

I will try to construct a more differentiated model in which the potential of the different organisational types of financial self-help organisations in serving the poorest sections will be explored and compared. Due to their small and irregular incomes, the poor are not always able to pay their contributions on time. In a ROSCA, this often affects the other members directly. When an ASCRA participant, just as a SAVA participant, does not pay his contributions on time, the other members are not directly affected. In such cases, the fund can act as a kind of buffer. In an ASCRA, members who face problems with payment of their contributions may drop out and shut down their account. Normally, this is only permitted when the person concerned has no outstanding debt with the ASCRA. In some ASCRAs, the savings collected can be repaid directly (after deduction of a penalty), while in other cases members have to wait until the end of the cycle. In other words, for the poor it is easier to participate in an ASCRA than in a ROSCA or SAVA due to their irregular income. Participation in a ROSCA, compared with a SAVA, is less accessible to the poor since a delay in the payment of the contributions generally does hurt the other members directly, which can damage the poor's social network.

It may be contended that the irregular and low income of the urban poor is the main determinant of the potential of financial self-help organisations to serve the poorest of the poor. Figure 5 shows the participation bottom lines for ROSCAs, SAVAs, and ASCRAs respectively. All income groups above such a line are potentially able to participate in a ROSCA, SAVA or ASCRA respectively. In brief, an indication is given of the potential of going downmarket for the different financial self-help organisations. The down-marketing potential appears to be the greatest for ASCRAs and the least for SAVAs and ROSCAs respectively.

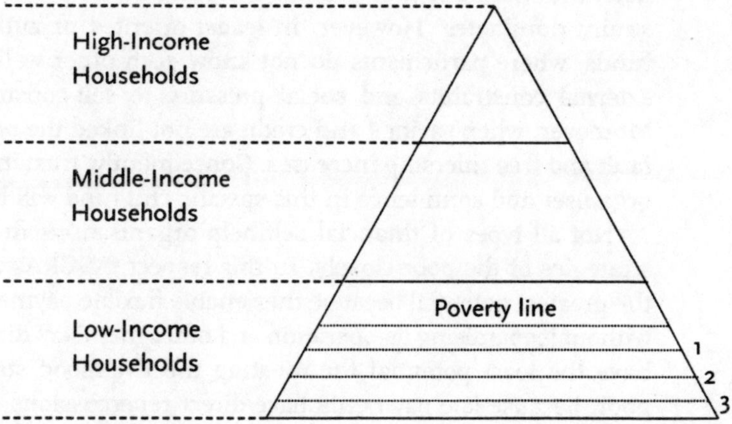

1 ROSCA participation bottom line
2 SAVA participation bottom line
3 ASCRA participation bottom line

Figure 5 Participation in financial self-help organisations

Conclusion

About a quarter of the surveyed households in Hyderabad used chit funds to financing their shelter exclusively or in combination with other sources. Participation in a ROSCA and ASCRA can be seen as social collateral when these participants demonstrate that they are good savers and repayers of loans. This can help them in obtaining loans from, for example, moneylenders.

Participation in chit funds is based on balanced reciprocity. Obligations stemming from participation in a particular chit fund are specified and cannot be withheld for a long period, but are instead specified within a relative short period. People join chit funds to meet their financial, but also socio-cultural needs. It may be suggested that the socio-cultural and psychological needs of participants can be met more effectively in smaller chit funds, which are often of a ROSCA nature. When a chit fund is larger, financial and economic functions tend to dominate. These differences also have repercussions on the operation of the groups concerned. In smaller groups face-to-face relations often enforce social control, if required. In larger organisations, these mechanisms are (partly) replaced by the introduction of guarantors and rules and regulations. In chit funds where face-to-face relations dominate, the mechanism of process trust and social pressure to self-constraint dominates. However, in leader-oriented or authoritarian chit funds, where participants do not know each other well, a mixture of external constraints and social pressure to self-constraint operates. Moreover, when savings and credit are not linked the potential for default and free ridership increases. Consequently, trust in especially the organiser and confidence in this specific chit fund will be jeopardised.

Not all types of financial self-help organisations fit the livelihood strategies of the poor closely. In this respect, ASCRAs appear to have the greatest potential because they enable flexible payments to the kitty without jeopardising its operation and other members directly. ROSCAs have the least potential for meeting the livelihood strategies of the poor, because late payments have direct repercussions on a ROSCA's operation and maintenance and on its members. Default or delay in payments in a SAVA does not hurt the other participants directly, but access to savings deposited is restricted. In brief, the potential for down-marketing is highest for ASCRAs and the most restricted for ROSCAs. The potential of SAVAs to serve the poorer sections of society is in between that of ASCRAs and ROSCAs.

6 Public housing finance in housing schemes for the urban poor

Amrut, his wife Shenama and their three daughters (4, 6 and 19 years) and son (12 years) live in a concrete house on the ground floor of an apartment complex designed for the economically weaker sections of the population. Amrut is the only income earner and works as a cleaner at a private office where he makes an income of Rs. 700 per month. In 1991, the title deed for the plot of about 40 square metres was provided free of costs in Shenama's name. A year later the government has constructed a concrete frame structure of pillars, roof and floor, for which it provided the beneficiaries with a loan of Rs. 13,000, to be repaid in monthly instalments of Rs. 98 over a period of 20 years. The beneficiaries had to construct their walls, doors, windows, etc. within this framework. For the completion of the dwelling Amrut and Shenama had to mobilise finance by themselves. Before the construction activities started in 1991, Amrut participated in a chit fund in his village of origin. He had to pay 16 monthly contribution of Rs. 500 in the auction ROSCA. In fact, the sum is much lower, since a share of the highest discount offered is divided among all participants. When he obtained the fund, he received Rs. 9,600. This he supplemented with Rs. 7,000 from his savings. Further to this, two Amrut's friends provided two interest-free loans of Rs. 3,000 and Rs. 2,000. In 1994, Rs. 3,000 was still outstanding and the Rs. 2,000 loan had been repaid in thirteen monthly instalments of Rs. 100-200. In addition, a sum of Rs. 5,000 was obtained from a moneylender, guaranteed by Amrut's brother-in-law, with an interest rate of 5% per month. In 1994, Rs. 3,000 was still outstanding. In the meantime, Amrut decided that the repayment of the government loan could wait. These debts would probably be waived in the future. Amrut commented on his habitat situation: 'My previous house was good. When the housing scheme came I got a concrete roof. Now, I have a lot of loans, I have to repay. I lived peacefully in my own house. There I did not have to worry about such huge loans.'

Amrut had a strategy of repaying the private housing loans one after another. However, the repayment of the government loan did not have any priority. It appears that Amrut and Shenama have obtained a 'beautiful' new house, but are not at all happy about it. In order to understand this situation, I will focus on these housing schemes in detail. Firstly, I will provide an overview of the agencies involved in the housing schemes for the economically weaker sections of the population. It appears that the housing schemes for the poor do not function as the government policy intended. In order to analyse the friction between theory and practice, I will focus on the following criteria; the selection of the beneficiaries, the implementation of the schemes, building activities and its affordability, and financial terms and conditions. I will show that these housing schemes do not help the economically weaker sections of the population. In reality, many other actors directly or indirectly involved in these schemes are the winners, while the poor lose out.

6.1 Housing schemes for the Economically Weaker Sections and their agencies

Different housing corporations are, or were, involved in these housing schemes in Hyderabad; the Andhra Pradesh State Housing Corporation (APSHC), and the Andhra Pradesh Urban Development and Housing Corporation (APUD & HC). APSHC was established in 1979 with the aim of formulating, promoting, executing and implementing housing schemes for the economically weaker sections of society, in short EWS housing schemes, in Andhra Pradesh. Until 1989 APSHC dealt with EWS housing schemes in urban as well as rural areas. During this period the Municipal Corporation of Hyderabad implemented the schemes in Hyderabad. In August 1989, the housing corporation APUD & HC was created with the main aim of providing EWS housing schemes in urban areas on a larger scale. The Municipal Corporation of Hyderabad only continued with the schemes already in progress. The State Government of Andhra Pradesh is proud of its 'successful' EWS housing schemes. This can be illustrated by, for example, the text of an advertisement published by the Government of Andhra Pradesh.

> 'Brick by brick, Andhra Pradesh built its reputation as leader in housing the weaker sections. Andhra Pradesh houses many records in the field. 2.64 *lakh* [264,000] permanent houses were constructed for the

> weaker sections at the rate of 1 permanent house per 1½ minutes. The highest ever in the country. 7.8 lakh SC [780,000 Scheduled Castes], ST [Scheduled Tribes] and BC [Backward Classes] families were provided assistance for construction of permanent houses. For 2 consecutive years, the HUDCO Award for maximum loan withdrawals added another feather. And what better way to ensure the success of its schemes than involving the beneficiaries themselves. Thus laying the foundation of a sound future. For Andhra Pradesh, the best years have just begun.' (Frontline 1994: 59; explanation in between brackets PS)

Every year the Government of Andhra Pradesh sanctions a specified number of houses for the economically weaker sections of society and makes a district-wise allotment of these houses. EWS housing schemes are based on self-help and contributions from the beneficiaries in the form of labour, materials and finance. In the next section, I will focus on the official rules and regulations of these housing schemes.

6.2 Housing schemes for the Economically Weaker Sections

In this section, I shall describe the EWS housing schemes, paying special attention to the schemes in Hyderabad, by focusing on the selection of beneficiaries, the implementation of the schemes, building activities, and financial terms and conditions.

6.2.1 Selection criteria

This housing scheme is intended for households that belong to the economically weaker sections of society, which encompass those households with an income of less than Rs. 1,250 per month. In addition, the beneficiaries should also be selected according to the following criteria, which are applicable at the district level: 50% scheduled castes, 10% scheduled tribes, 30% backward classes and 10% other economically weaker sections. Muslims belong to the latter group. Furthermore, a household in this target group is excluded if they already own a house in an EWS housing scheme (Sivasubrahmanyam and Prasado Rao 1992: 77).

Before they are able to participate in an EWS housing scheme, beneficiaries must possess land. To cope with this problem the Government of Andhra Pradesh may release *pattas* (title deeds) up to a size of about 170 square meters[1] to the beneficiaries. *Pattas* of less than of approximately 85 square meters are free from costs for households with a maximum of Rs. 10,000 p.a. Households with an income from Rs. 10,000 to 20,000 p.a. must pay half of the market value for a *patta* of less than 90 square meters. For both income groups, an area of 85-170 square meters has a price equal to the market rate and for plots of more than 170 square meters twice the market rate (GAP 1991: 2-3).

For several years the release of *pattas* and the participation in an EWS housing scheme have been linked in Hyderabad. From 1984 onwards, *pattas* had to be released in the name of a female member of the family. The theory was that the women tend to be more hesitant in selling houses in times of emergencies. Moreover, women are considered to have a better loan repayment record than men.

6.2.2 Implementation of the housing schemes

Plans for the EWS housing schemes, including the standard type designs of the housing units, are made and modified by the town-planning department of the Municipal Corporation of Hyderabad. The implementation has taken place under the supervision of different agencies. From 1976 onwards, the Urban Community Development Department of the Municipal Corporation of Hyderabad has implemented housing schemes for the Economically Weaker Sections. Until 1989, the Urban Community Development Department was the only executor of these housing schemes in Hyderabad. In that year APUD & HC was created since it was found that the Municipal Corporation of Hyderabad had not reached its targets owing to its being overburdened with all kinds of other activities. Moreover, members of the state legislative assembly could increase their influence on the housing schemes by limiting the schemes in which city councillors controlled the selection of beneficiaries and consequently the sanctioning of housing loans. This has led to the allocation of all new EWS housing schemes to APUD & HC. In the meantime, a Housing Cell was created, which is under direct supervision of the District Collector. This Housing Cell implements and monitors the housing schemes in Hyderabad. However, all schemes already in progress remained under the control of the Municipal Corporation of Hyderabad.

In general, EWS housing schemes are developed and implemented in neighbourhoods where the beneficiaries are already living. The ben-

1 The figures used for defining the size of the plots are 170, 85 and 90 square meters, which correspond to the size of 200, 100 and 110 square yards.

eficiaries are divided into construction groups, whose leader co-ordinates the construction works. The construction activities are guided and supervised by grassroots workers, such as slum development officers, community development officers, and members of the engineering staff. Meetings are held together with the beneficiaries to discuss the construction activities and related problems. The houses should be constructed according to a fixed time schedule. The implication is that the old houses should be demolished and/or replaced before the new ones can be built. If this is done carefully, building material can be recycled.

6.2.3 House construction

Standard designs are made for the construction of the houses. These designs are drawn up with the intention of creating 'cheap' housing for the economically weaker sections of society. Subsidised construction materials, namely cement and steel are employed. Moreover, self-help in the construction activities can reduce the costs, because it can minimise the involvement of middlemen and possibly the number of construction labourers that need to be employed. A problem regarding self-help can be a lack of construction skills. A solution is the provision of technical guidance. It is also anticipated that self-help will ensure the beneficiary's occupation of the house concerned.

Due to the scarcity of land under government ownership, houses with one and two floors were introduced in Hyderabad. The construction of these multi-storey buildings became more complicated. The foundation and pillars had to be strong enough to carry more floors. Initially the pillars were made of bricks, but in view of their bad quality and poor load-bearing capacity, a shift was made to the use of cement and steel. Within the contractor-built skeleton, the beneficiaries are expected to construct walls, door(s), and window(s).

6.2.4 Financial terms and conditions

First, I shall discuss the financial conditions of the loans taken out by the Municipal Corporation of Hyderabad and the housing corporation APUD & HC, and then move to the lending terms and conditions of the loans given to the beneficiaries.

Initially, the Municipal Corporation of Hyderabad borrowed directly from commercial banks for the housing schemes. Later on the national public agency, Housing and Urban Development Corporation (HUDCO), became the main financier. The Government of Andhra

Pradesh guarantees these housing loans. Until 1984, the Municipal Corporation of Hyderabad dealt directly with commercial banks and HUDCO, and was directly responsible for the repayment of the loans. In 1984, the loans were channelled through APSHC and from 1989 through APUD & HC. The repayment of the loans provided through the housing corporations is the responsibility of these corporations. For its own housing schemes, APUD & HC obtains credit from HUDCO and through the Government of Andhra Pradesh from the insurance companies LIC and GIC. The housing schemes are implemented on a no profit/no loss basis. In addition to subsidies for the beneficiaries, the housing corporation receives a managerial subsidy from the Government of Andhra Pradesh (GAP 1994a: 37).

The financial terms and conditions of the HUDCO loans for urban housing schemes are recorded in Table 31. The rate of interest for the housing schemes for the economically weaker sections of society (9% p.a.) is kept low by measures of cross subsidisation. Consequently, the urban housing schemes for low-income groups (LIG), middle-income groups (MIG), and high-income groups (HIG) bear a higher rate of interest. It was expected that a cheaper rate of interest for units would make housing more affordable to the poor.

Table 31 Financing pattern of HUDCO, for urban permanent housing schemes (effective from April 1994)

Category	Cost ceiling per unit	Max. loan ceiling	Rate of interest (% p.a.)	Term (years)
EWS	26,400	19,500	9	15
LIG	80,000	55,000	12-13	10-15
MIG	–	175,000	15-15.5	10-15
HIG	–	300,000	16.5	15

By delivering the title deeds, called *pattas,* for free and incorporating self-help in the scheme of unit costs could be brought down. The estimated cost of a housing unit is Rs. 13,000, which is lower than the maximum loan ceiling of Rs. 19,500 as defined by HUDCO. The unit costs are set by the Secretariat. The sum of Rs. 13,000 is made up as follows:

Loan	Rs. 11,700
Subsidy	Rs. 1,000
Beneficiary contribution	Rs. 300
Unit costs	Rs. 13,000

The beneficiary has to pay an additional amount of Rs. 61 as an admission fee. The housing loan is secured by mortgaging the title deed, which is usually a *patta*. Furthermore, beneficiaries are required by the housing corporation concerned to insure their dwelling against different kind of risks. The rate of interest, charged on the housing loan, is 10% p.a. This credit should be repaid in 240 monthly instalments of Rs. 98 each. The recovery of the loan starts one month after the completion of the house. A rebate of 3% can be given in the event of prompt repayment, which can be reimbursed from the state government (ibid.: 56-58). As soon as the loan is repaid, the *patta* will be returned to the beneficiary. However, the *patta* should be mortgaged for a minimum period of 5 years.

The housing loan is released in instalments. The first instalment is paid out only after the beneficiary has financed the costs of the groundfloor. The period of payment depends on how the construction proceeds. The size of the payments and the number of instalments differ. After completion of the building, the subsidy of Rs. 1,000 will be released. For an overview, see Table 32.

Table 32 Release of housing finance

Stages	Instalment
Foundations finished	Rs. 3,000
Plinth level reached	Rs. 3,500
Roof level reached	Rs. 3,300
Roof cast	Rs. 2,200
After completion	Rs. 1,000

For the construction of multi-storey buildings, the release of the instalments is adjusted. If the government provides the building materials, the costs thereof will be deducted from the loans.

6.3 Housing schemes and the urban poor

The implementation of the EWS housing schemes for the urban poor differ from the policy as described above. This can be illustrated by the selection of the beneficiaries, the implementation of the housing schemes, building activities, and its housing finance.

6.3.1 The selection of beneficiaries

The price of *pattas* is dependent on the income of the beneficiaries. The beneficiaries had to be selected on basis of their household income, which is a rather arbitrary criterion. In reality, the sizes of households differ. A small household is better off than a household of a larger size with an identical income. Furthermore, the respective incomes of different members of the household are not necessarily pooled. In practice, the checking of household income is often limited to the inspection of ration cards and the possession of luxury items, such as a television set.

When people have to pay (half of) the market value of the land, they are not eager to have the restrictions connected with a *patta*. Moreover, *pattas* of an equal size were given to beneficiaries whose respective households differed in size and composition. The size of the *pattas* given in the neighbourhoods investigated was 25-50 square meters. The rule requiring registration of a *patta* in the wife's name is often violated. There are known cases where males oppose this and succeed in getting the *patta* registered in their name. In the case of a polygamous household, the patta will be registered in the male's name.

Beneficiaries have to pay the middlemen bribes (often Rs. 1,000), which can be paid in instalments, to obtain the *patta* desired. The bureaucrats involved get their share. The profit gained can be increased by the construction of multi-storey buildings. Moreover, the allocation of EWS housing units is politicised along party lines. The allocation of housing units is under control of the Municipal Corporation of Hyderabad. However, in 1993 a pamphlet was circulated at the office of APUD & HC reminding the employees to consult the MLAs (Members of the state Legislative Assembly) concerned before allocating houses, In fact, the MLAs decide who the beneficiaries will be. At the root of this lies competition for political influence between the councillors and MLAs. Beneficiaries can also buy a patta or (partly) completed house. The local leaders demand their share of the transaction costs. One leader said that it is easy to sell the units, because the government only checks, if at all, 10 years after completion of the scheme. This encourages leaders to sell pattas to outsiders. Slum dwellers have filed several court cases against the local leader(s) and government officials.

6.3.2 Implementation in practice

Until 1993, APUD & HC was only able to construct 10,000 units per year in Andhra Pradesh, which is far fewer than its yearly target of 100,000 houses (GAP 1994a: 45). In Hyderabad, similar problems have occurred. In addition, if a housing scheme is taken up, this does not necessarily guarantee that the houses will be completed (for an overview see the Tables 33 and 34). The progress of housing schemes' implementation has slowed down because most slums with pattas have been covered. In the remaining neighbourhoods land has to be acquired by the government, which leads to delays in the implementation process (Reddy 1991: 216). The construction of multi-storey buildings has not solved the problem of constructing sufficient units.

When the Municipal Corporation of Hyderabad faced problems of completion of the housing units, the schemes were allocated to APUD & HC. However, APUD & HC faced similar problems of implementation. The formation of a separate housing corporation, APUD & HC, to boost the housing production in urban areas was not successful (GAP 1994a: 45). Nevertheless, the government of Andhra Pradesh wants to maintain high targets, mainly for election purposes. Bringing down the targets may benefit opposition parties.

The operation and maintenance of the EWS housing schemes is rather complex, which creates ample opportunity for manipulation. Many decisions are made according to subjective criteria. For example, procedures for reporting costs and achievements are not standardised. This makes it difficult to acquire adequate knowledge about the operation and maintenance of, for example, the engineering divisions of the Municipal Corporation of Hyderabad and the Housing Cell. Engineers work according to a short-term perspective, for example, to get houses constructed, while slum development officers or community development officers must consider long-term perspectives, for example, of community development. Moreover, there is a lack of control and supervision over the field staff, which has led to poor construction and even the collapse of houses (GAP 1994a: 64).

To reach targets or obtain the sanctioned houses completed, slum dwellers can be forced to participate. As a result, protests arise. Several beneficiaries have filed court cases. One of the cases is reported below:

Table 33 Progress EWS housing schemes of the Municipal Corporation of Hyderabad

Programme year	Targets fixed	Houses sanctioned	Houses finally taken up	Houses completed
pre 1983-84	n.a.	4468	4105	3950
1983-84	n.a.	1592	1171	1126
1984-85	n.a.	0	0	0
1985-86	n.a.	1555	734	650
1986-87	n.a.	0	0	0
1987-88	n.a.	749	336	247
1988-89	n.a.	846	740	554
1989-90	n.a.	0	0	0
1990-91	n.a.	1570	974	717
1991-92	n.a.	0	0	0
1992-93	n.a.	0	0	0
1993-94	n.a.	0	0	0

Source: Progress report EWS housing programme of the Municipal Corporation of Hyderabad, May 1994.

Table 34 Progress EWS housing schemes of APUD & HC in Hyderabad

Programme year	Targets fixed	Houses sanctioned	Houses finally taken up	Houses completed
1989-90	n.a	956	846	523
1990-91	1,000	2,944	1,570	693
1991-92	1,000	706	706	323
1992-93	7,540	1,202	858	152
1993-94	4,300	494	110	–

Source: Progress report of APUD & HC, May 1994.

An elderly lady lived on a plot of 60 square meters for a period of 40 years. In the beginning of the 1980s, she built a new house with two rooms, a latrine and a bathroom. The construction costs of this house with plastered walls and a corrugated iron roof were Rs. 50,000. She financed this construction with a gift of Rs. 15,000 from relatives and a loan of Rs. 35,000. However, in the beginning of the 1990s she discovered that she was participating in an EWS housing scheme and that her self-built house had to be demolished for this purpose. The curious

> fact is that nobody had asked her if she actually wanted to join the housing scheme. She was forced to participate, despite the fact that she had not paid an application fee. A local leader had paid this fee. When people of the housing cell and the local leaders asked her to remove her self-built house, her daughter and son in law with their children moved in to give her moral support. In 1992, they filed a court case against the Housing Cell, the Municipal Corporation of Hyderabad and the collector. The case was filed against all three, because it was not clear who was dealing with the scheme. They obtained a stay order and all building activities in the direct surroundings of the old lady's house had to be stopped.

The allocation of pattas is often leader-centred. *Pattas* for a specific neighbourhood are given to a middleman and not directly to the slum dwellers. The leader has the power to exclude specific slum dwellers, including (relatively) richer beneficiaries in the application list. In one scheme, an office of the World Bank-funded Andhra Pradesh Habitat Society had illegally occupied two housing units on the ground floor of an EWS housing scheme. Naturally, this contradicts the Andhra Pradesh Habitat Society's aim to improve the habitat conditions of the poor.

In several neighbourhoods people oppose initiatives of patta delivery because they do not want to participate in such a housing scheme. Others disagree with the lay out, house design and/or the allotment procedure (Reddy 1991: 197). The secretary to the Government of Andhra Pradesh, Department of Housing said:

> 'When people are forced, they will not co-operate fully. It is like you take one step forward and drive them ten steps back. If you force people to do things, they will hide in their shell.'

Despite this, the Government of Andhra Pradesh still emphasises the quantitative dimension of housing rather than concentrating on the qualitative side. Furthermore, it may be suggested that personal gain and housing the EWS is not the first priority.

6.3.3 Building activities

The standard designs for the houses may be modified slightly, in consultation with the beneficiaries. Reddy (1991: 213) reports a scheme, where each house is enlarged to such an extent that it is directly surrounded by three other houses. Therefore the scope for light and ventilation is limited. This is in contravention of standards laid down in the Town Planning Act. Furthermore, the construction of multi-storey units limits horizontal or vertical expansion, which may be required if the size of the household increases in the future. The units of a specific scheme are uniform in size. This often conflicts with individual household priorities, which change according to the family cycle or changes in the life of migrants in the city (see also Turner 1976).

Before construction work can begin, beneficiaries who are living in the neighbourhood concerned often have to vacate their plot. To bridge the period until the new house is built, the beneficiaries must temporarily rent a house or room, or construct a temporary dwelling. To rebuild their dwelling at another location, building materials cannot always be reused on account of their poor quality. Shifting to temporary housing leads to an additional (financial) burden. For the construction of temporary shelter, costs of Rs. 3,000 are not unexceptional.

In the schemes of the Municipal Corporation of Hyderabad and the Housing Cell beneficiaries obstructed the progress of the scheme by not co-operating in the construction and completion of the houses despite sustained official persuasion. The Municipal Corporation of Hyderabad tried to speed up the scheme in at least one slum by sending in bulldozers to destroy the old dwellings. The district manager of the Housing Cell has sent notices to another neighbourhood. A fragment of such document follows:

> 'The beneficiaries are further informed that who do not cooperate in completing the houses with brick work shall be removed from the scheme and their house site pattas will be cancelled by the Authority and the amount of Rs. 361/- contributed by him will be forfitted [sic, forfeited] and the house will be reallotted to other eligible beneficiary and further action will be taken as per G.O. [Government Order] Ms. no. 2, Housing Department, dated 17.01.1992.' (Explanation in between brackets PS)

The houses are supposed to be built with involvement of the beneficiaries. However, information concerning this self-help is not always shared with the beneficiaries.

> 'The leader told us to demolish our house, because the government is creating a house for you. We demolished our house 15 months ago and rebuilt it elsewhere. When I demolished it, I expected that a complete house would be made by the government. Then I discovered that I got only some pillars and a slab. I feel cheated.'

Another beneficiary said:

> 'They told us that the government provides houses. Then they only deliver a core house. Before the scheme started the minister said that they have to fill it up. We thought we got two rooms. But when the schemes started we got only one slab. The minister said you have to live here. Make a house of mats. You have to adjust. When you do not have money you use mats. When you have money, you make a real house.'

The self-help potential is limited in Hyderabad. Building your own house partly or completely means a drop of income, because people can only be in one place at a time. Through the establishment of construction committees, the opportunity of the beneficiaries to gain some income increases. Nowadays, a core house is often built through a contractor. Such a contractor, for example, a mason or middleman, obtains authorisation letters from the beneficiaries and collects the instalments for the work undertaken. The construction costs of the core house often exceeds Rs. 12,000 on account of increasing costs of building materials and the type of foundation required, which is dependent on the nature of the land (e.g. rocky or river bed). The contractor is, therefore, only eager to build if the beneficiaries are able to pay the additional amount of Rs. 2,000 to 3,000. In a neighbourhood where the contractor ceased his construction activities, a beneficiary constructed the foundation, pillars and slab himself, for which he needed an additional Rs. 4,400.

Building materials are needed for the construction of the houses. The reuse of building materials is difficult. Stored old bricks are stolen, despite their poor quality. They also fall apart easily. When building materials could be obtained through government channels at a subsidised rate, the delivery of materials, especially cement, was delayed for 2 to 185 days (GAP 1994a: 73). Building materials, cement and steel, must be obtained from government quotas.

In practice, centring (shuttering) materials are not supplied (GAP 1994a: 75). When building materials are obtained from the private sector, an advance sum may have to be paid.[2] A contractor who had used cement from the private market found himself in deep water with the government; the engineer of the Municipal Corporation of Hyderabad ordered that the pillar be demolished and rebuilt with government ce-

2 It is reported from Mabub Nagar district, in Andhra Pradesh, that a contractor was paid for the supply of building materials without recovering the costs from the beneficiaries (See GAP 1994a: 77).

ment. The beneficiaries told me that they had problems in removing the cement. They also thought that the quality of this cement was much better than the quality of government cement. In one case, the money allocated for government cement was embezzled by government employees.

If slum dwellers are involved in the construction of their houses, we can expect that time-bound targets will probably not be met (Marsden 1990: 59). Moreover, the construction activities are likely to be delayed by problems in the mobilisation of funds, the release of subsidies, lack of interest on the part of beneficiaries, disputes about location, non-affordable housing units for the target group, delays in the selection of beneficiaries, inadequate unit costs, and a lack of proper planning (GAP 1994a: 47). Furthermore, construction materials are not always available in time and beneficiaries are not always eager to invest their share.

Despite all delays the beneficiaries have methods for economising on the construction of their new house. They may, for example, use mud instead of cement in between the bricks, postpone plastering the walls, and use gravel instead of sand. Moreover, cheap labour and finance can reduce the construction costs.

6.3.4 Housing finance in practice

The Municipal Corporation of Hyderabad and APUD & HC obtain housing finance for the EWS housing schemes from HUDCO. In the event of default, HUDCO does not normally provide a new loan until the old ones have been repaid. However, retro-active financing is preferred whereby outstanding debts are deducted from the payments for new projects. The Urban Community Development Department of the Municipal Corporation of Hyderabad complained that HUDCO is very strict. They send telegrams and even charge a punitive interest of 2.5% p.a. on the principal amount and interest. The Municipal Corporation faces delays in repaying credit directly taken from HUDCO. According to HUDCO section Hyderabad, the total has reached about Rs. 5,000,000 since September 1989. The government of Andhra Pradesh has instructed APSHC to repay a part of the outstanding debts. In March 1994, APSHC paid Rs. 44,380,000 and the remaining debt of Rs. 910,000 is still outstanding, which has to be repaid by the Municipal Corporation of Hyderabad. In the meantime, the Municipal Corporation of Hyderabad has tried to repay these debts by transmitting the instalments collected from the beneficiaries.

The loans through the housing corporations are paid on schedule. However, APUD & HC faces problems with repayment and has asked the government of Andhra Pradesh for a non-planned budget provision to be able to repay the loan. The state government guarantees these loans and when the number of loans rises, the burden on the government increases.

The beneficiaries must pay an admission fee and beneficiary contribution in order to qualify for a house. It is reported that in some cases these payments are not refunded, even when units are not allocated. Furthermore, beneficiaries did not always insure their houses as required (GAP 1994a: 57-58).

From 1989-90 onwards, the unit costs for an EWS house were fixed at Rs. 13,000. In the mean time the prices of building inputs have increased to such an extent that the unit costs used are no longer accurate. However, the same unit costs are still used.[3] Today, Rs. 13,000 is not sufficient to build a house according to the standards prescribed (cf. Reddy 1991: 194). It is also assumed that people can mobilise additional finance. These sources of finance are personal savings, gifts from friends and relatives, credit from friends, relatives, moneylenders or through participation in a chit fund. These sources of finance are used exclusively or in combination. APUD & HC and the Municipal Corporation of Hyderabad suggests that an additional amount of Rs. 5,000 to 6,000 is needed. In the cases investigated the amounts used are much higher; Rs. 15,000 to 85,000 as reported by the beneficiaries. For many EWS dwellers the expenditure of such amounts within a relative time period delivers them high debts, which jeopardises their livelihood strategies. Especially in case of unexpected financial needs, they were forced to sell and leave the housing unit and start their housing process from the beginning onwards. In the meantime, the relatively better off obtain these housing units and the gentrification of such a neighbourhood gradually takes place. This is reflected in the low number (approximately 25%) of the surveyed EWS households in the housing schemes.

The Municipal Corporation of Hyderabad and APUD & HC use loan application forms in English. They can be filled in with the help of, for example, a slum development officer or local leader and signed by the beneficiary. The beneficiaries may be even asked to pay to have the release of the housing loan organised. Leaders often claim payments of

3 An exception will be probably made for some schemes that were temporarily stopped due to the communal riots of 1992. The Municipal Corporation of Hyderabad made attempts to raise additional sources of finance from banks.

up to Rs. 500 as service costs to cover expenses made. Beneficiary contributions are not always collected and loan ledgers are not maintained for the loans sanctioned; recoveries are also poor for occupied completed units (cf. GAP 1994a: 50-51). To enable the start of the housing scheme, leaders are even eager to pay the compulsory beneficiary contribution on their behalf. This is done without knowledge of the beneficiaries, which has led to protest of the beneficiaries who never wanted to participate in the housing scheme. In addition, beneficiaries are often not aware of the terms and conditions of the loan.

When the house is finished, the recovery of the loan can take place. It seems that there are limited guidelines for the release of a certificate of completion, which therefore becomes a rather subjective matter. The only specified item of construction, which should be checked, as mentioned on the completion certificate is the 'w.c. unit comprising of w.c. pan, connecting pipe including junction box, 2 leach pits properly covered/septic tank'. In reality, such measures encouraged people to refrain from constructing toilets to avoid having to repay the governmental housing loan.

The recovery rate of loans issued through the Municipal Corporation of Hyderabad and APUD & HC is poor. For urban and rural Andhra Pradesh the rate is 5.1% of the total amount due up to 1992-1993 (GAP 1994a: 55). For 1993-1994, the recovery rate of the Municipal Corporation of Hyderabad loans varied from 7.04% to 15.86%.

Not all beneficiaries attempt to avoid repayment. Some may rent out a part of their house for this purpose. The reasons for default varied. Firstly, people may not be satisfied with the quality of the building. In some cases even toilets were not installed. The persons living on the first floor squatted in a corner of their house to defecate or urinate. Consequently, faeces and urine dripped through a small pipe in the backyard of the ground floor. Secondly, the repayment of private loans has a higher priority than repayment of the government loans. Thirdly, the beneficiaries may also face other financial pressures, such as medical treatment and the education or marriage of offspring. Under such circumstances, the repayment of a government loan will be postponed. Fourthly, some expect that loans will be waived in the near future. (Party-political) leaders encourage beneficiaries to anticipate governments waiving loans, as happened in the case of the agricultural and rural debt relief scheme of 1990. Fifthly, the norms and values of the community define individual views on default behaviour. People do not repay, because others consider the non-repayment of government loans to be normal. Sixthly, no systematic programme for recovery has ever been worked out. Despite this, efforts are made to recover the loans from the beneficiaries. For example, Marsden (1990: 62) reports that uncollected instalments have been deducted from the salaries of the grassroots workers.

The grassroots workers in the housing schemes faced problems in collecting the instalments. Beneficiaries often opposed or even escaped them. A slum development officer told me that he takes locks from the municipality office and locks the houses of defaulters until they pay their instalments. This tactic is not always employed. One beneficiary said:

> 'I cannot direct money for repayment. The SDO [slum development officer] comes monthly for collecting our repayments. I always ask her whether I can pay next month, because I do not have the money. She says when you do not pay, the government will lock your house. This she has been telling already for one year and nothing happens.'

Some grassroots workers though have become very strict in recovering instalments by indeed locking the house of the beneficiaries until the outstanding debts have been repaid. However, one slum development officer, who was successful in collecting the instalments from the beneficiaries, embezzled the money.

The respective legal backing provided to grassroots workers of the Municipal Corporation of Hyderabad and APUD & HC varies. APUD & HC has been allocated powers under the Revenue Recovery Act. The Municipal Corporation of Hyderabad aims to obtain such powers. This is in fact just a matter of paperwork. In practice, the power to recover outstanding debts by attaching the property of the defaulter is limited. The recovery officer of APUD & HC explained it as follows:

> 'I have powers to attach the properties of defaulters. First, I will pay the defaulters a few visits to convince them to repay the loan. In case of continuing default goods can be attached. However, we go for soft tactics. The attachment of defaulter's property is problematic. The influence of politicians is too big.'

Politicians can break or support recovery officers. When recovery officers are too strict in their task, political leaders may harm the officer's position in the government bureaucracy or even transfer them to less popular areas. In addition to this fear among recovery agents, the allocation of housing units is done by people who are not responsible for the repayment of the loans. Both factors have a negative impact on the cost recovery of housing schemes.

In short, it may be said that the cost recovery of the EWS housing schemes is far from successful. In the next section, I shall attempt to illustrate who benefits from these schemes.

6.4 Who helps who?

By building as many EWS units as possible the Government of Andhra Pradesh can demonstrate that they are doing a lot to benefit the poor. However, almost all the actors involved try to manipulate the creation of policy, the selection of beneficiaries, and/or implementation of the housing schemes for personal gain. Almost none of the government officials are really bothered whether or not the target group is helped. Furthermore, control mechanisms appear to be absent. A government official said:

> 'Politics are the cancer of EWS housing schemes. It is like the expression operation succeeded, but the patient died. There are so many things, I pretend not to see and keep just to the official things.'

Let us shed some light on the process. The recovery rate of EWS housing loans is poor, which implies that the schemes can only be implemented at the expense of the tax payer. (Party-political) leaders allocate and sell *pattas* and (half) completed houses to people who do not necessarily belong to the target group. For this purpose, beneficiaries have to pay the slum leaders. These leaders in co-operation with political leaders create a vote bank by getting the housing scheme sanctioned. Later on, these politicians try to maintain their vote bank by telling the beneficiaries that they do not need to repay the housing loans provided by the government. These leaders have to bribe bureaucrats and other political leaders to get housing units allocated to people of their choice. Bureaucrats, who do not co-operate, face being transferred to unpopular districts. De Zwart (1992) analyses the dynamics of this mobile Indian bureaucracy. Apart from transfers to unpopular districts, transfers can also be to popular places. It is hard to distinguish where routine and bureaucratic procedures stops determining the transfers and where political-financial manipulation begins, where politicians aim at establishing a network of loyal contacts and damaging the network of competitors. In other words, market corruption, in which the supply and demand of transfers obtains a prominent place, is supported while parochial corruption will be challenged (ibid.).

Despite payments, which have to be made to (political) leaders and government officials, EWS housing schemes tend to be gift schemes. The allocation of these gifts is exchanged for political support. The network of the actors involved can be called a political-machine-like organisation (Bax 1978: 36-37; De Wit 1993: 37-39). The slum leaders are a crucial cog in this political machine. They have to please the political leaders and contractors and avoid protests from the beneficiaries. To maintain their position, slum leaders tend to monopolise information. In one area, where settlers wanted to ask their leader about the scheme, they were sent away. One settler gave a description of his meeting with the leader.

> The leader said: 'I do not have time now. Your formalities are over. Go away!' The leader always has 4-5 followers who are with him. They prevent us even from talking with him.

When these slum dwellers try to consult political leaders or bureaucrats, they are often directed to their slum leader. In short, slum leaders, politicians and government officials are involved in the manipulation of EWS housing schemes.

The target group is not helped by these housing schemes, because most units are sold to the (relatively) better off. The beneficiaries who belong to the target group are often pushed out of the area because the units are considered too expensive. One complaint is :

> 'The scheme was arranged by the leaders. I went with them to government offices. We do not know what they arranged. If we do not participate in the housing scheme, our land will be given to others.'

Another dweller described it as follows:

> 'Why did I have to leave my old house, which had mud walls and an asbestos roof. Where I was living, I was happy. Now I have a nice house but I am terribly indebted. How can I get my children married with all these outstanding loans.'

The EWS housing schemes encourage the beneficiaries to invest their 'own' money in their dwelling, but do not insist on their having savings, nor do they offer opportunities for savings to be deposited in a relatively safe place. Is the credit provided by the public agencies adjusted to the needs of the target group? Firstly, the housing loans provided by the Municipal Corporation of Hyderabad and the housing corporations are not very accessible to the economically weaker sections of society. When the beneficiaries succeed in applying for a housing loan a bureaucratic procedure is required, which is even made more difficult by middlemen demanding bribes. Secondly, the title deed provided is used as collateral for the housing loan. Non-conventional collateral is not requested. Thirdly, there is no flexibility in determining the use of the loan; it has to be used for construction purposes. Fourthly, the size of the loan (Rs. 11,700) is large and the beneficiaries are forced to obtain additional loans to be able to complete their housing unit. Fifthly, the loan has a long-term (20 years), while the poor prefer short or medium-term credit. Sixthly, the repayment of the loan has to take place in fixed monthly instalments and has an inflexible nature. However, in practice the instalments are not always paid in time or not at all, which affects the cost recovery of the housing schemes.

It appears that participation of EWS often leads to their early departure from the neighbourhood concerned. Furthermore, many of the poor have to borrow to pay the inevitable bribes. Huge debts to, for example, moneylenders force the poorest to sell their houses to people with higher incomes. Consequently, a process of the relative gentrification of the neighbourhood takes place.

The (relatively) better-off then profit from the subsidies involved in the schemes. Land and infrastructure costs are not included in the unit costs. Moreover, the housing loans from the government will often not be repaid. The main financial costs carried by the occupants are met from private loans and savings.

Although the recovery of the EWS loans is poor, the loans issued by the housing corporations are repaid to HUDCO since the government guarantees their repayment. In effect, the Government of Andhra Pradesh repays these loans at the expense of the taxpayer. The main financier of the EWS housing schemes is proud of the good recovery rate, and these lending operations are financially sound. However, the recovery rate of loans given directly to the Municipal Corporation of Hyderabad is still poor. Appointments are made with the Municipal Corporation; all the loans collected from the beneficiaries have to be channelled to HUDCO as soon as possible. It can be said that HUDCO shows good recovery records for the loans given through the housing corporations, but HUDCO, just as its financiers such as the National Housing Bank, can be blamed for closing their eyes to what happens at the grassroots level.

Conclusion

In spite the good intentions of some of those involved, it may be concluded that the EWS housing schemes are heavily politicised. Many people, except the majority of the target group, benefit from these schemes through the manipulation of the laws concerned, the selection of the beneficiaries and the operation and maintenance of the housing schemes. Many government employees tend to deliberately create and maintain their incompetence, or turn a blind eye to it. In this way, profits can be channelled to the actors involved. In the meantime, the public can be told that efforts have been undertaken to help the poor. It is a matter of selling the scheme politically and covering corrupt practices. These practices damage confidence in the EWS housing schemes. Instead, individuals in the game of manipulation, especially slum leaders, try to establish and maintain relationships with the beneficiaries based on process trust.

Self-help in the EWS housing schemes refers not only to the construction activities, but also to the partial self-financing. The beneficiaries must invest their self-help initiatives in the construction and financing of complete housing units, where possibilities of horizontal and vertical extension are non-existent.

The target group considers the units in an EWS housing scheme far too expensive and the conditions too difficult to fulfil. The idea of making the units affordable for the target group by providing cheap housing finance with a long term may be questioned. For the poor, affordable housing means that the financial burden of a housing loan should be short enough for them to cope with other expenditures needed within a relative short period of time. Consequently, relatively small amounts over the short and medium term are required; this also corresponds with an incremental building process. Moreover, cheap interest rates are not considered crucial; the key issue is access to finance on terms and conditions that suit the livelihood strategies of the poor.

7 Private housing finance: reaching downmarket?

> Yusuf, a motor rickshaw driver, has brought a client to a huge concrete building in the centre of Hyderabad. In the same building, a housing finance corporation is located. Yusuf takes the opportunity to visit the office of the housing finance corporation on the fifth floor. Yusuf does not want to make use of the elevator and climbs the stairs to the fifth floor. When he enters the office to ask for a small housing loan to improve his dwelling, the employees chase him out. He feels uneasy being dressed in a *lungi* and a t-shirt, while these employees wear wonderful trousers and beautiful shirts. When he tells them that he has come for a housing loan, the employees laugh and reply that he could never repay the loan. They tell him to leave.

Yusuf, the slum dweller, wants to get a small loan in order to improve his dwelling, but did not succeed in obtaining it from the housing finance corporation. They will not help him, because he was seen as too great a risk to lend to. Yusuf is only one example, many fellow slum dwellers generally lack access to 'formal' housing finance. However, housing finance corporations are encouraged to serve the poorer sections of society, or in other words to downmarket housing finance. This chapter will look into their failure to do so.

Private housing finance corporations are a relatively new phenomenon in the Indian housing finance market, which started with the establishment of the Housing Development and Finance Corporation in 1977. This private agency formed the basis for remarkable developments in the Indian housing finance system throughout the past few decades. In the meantime, the National Housing Bank, as a subsidiary of the Reserve Bank of India, was established in 1988. Simultaneously, a gradual process of liberalisation of the financial market has taken place, as a result of which private housing finance corporations were promoted. In 1999, 354 housing finance corporations were registered, while 95% of the housing finance sanctioned through housing finance corporations rests in the hand of the 29 major corporations. The remaining registered corporations are very small or not even active in the Indian housing finance market (Vora 1999: 5).

In order to discuss this policy of downmarketing housing finance through the private sector, this chapter is built up as follows. Firstly, the National Housing Bank's policies will be focused upon. This is necessary to understand the operation of the housing finance corporations, which will be described in the second section. Thirdly, the impact of the policy of serving the poorer sections of society will be critically analysed. Finally, this chapter will be brought to a close with a conclusion.

7.1 National Housing Bank

The National Housing Bank is expected to regulate and supervise the housing finance market in India. This apex body promotes housing finance corporations in India and provides (financial) support to these housing finance corporations. It aims to mobilise household savings, facilitate easy access to institutional credit for housing, increase the supply and improve the use of scarce land and building materials, and keep housing affordable for different income groups. For this purpose the National Housing Bank can raise funds by issuing bonds/debentures, and by borrowing from, for example, the Reserve Bank of India, government institutions, and foreign agencies (NHB 1990: 1-4).

7.1.1 Promotion of housing finance corporations

The National Housing Bank promotes housing finance corporations. These corporations have to pass through the various stages of registration, classification and recognition. Starting housing finance corporations should be registered with the Registrar of Companies. Such housing finance corporations are not screened, but are expected to allocate 50% of their business activities to housing finance. A registered housing finance corporation may be classified as a housing finance corporation, the decision based on written information provided by the housing finance corporation concerned. However, if a commercial bank, an insurance company or another government body has initiated the housing finance corporation, it will be classified more easily and quickly than an housing finance corporation established on private initiative. For final recognition, a housing finance corporation has to act in accordance with the guidelines and directions of the National Housing Bank and prove itself to be well managed and financially healthy (NHB 1991). Furthermore, a minimum equity share of Rs. 100,000 is needed. Out of this amount only 75% should be allocated to housing finance. To check these requirements, the head office and branches of the housing finance corporation concerned are visited by National Housing Bank employees (Struyk and Ravicz 1992: 16). It should, however, be noted that the National Housing Bank could even participate in an housing finance corporation by buying shares in it.

7.1.2 Lending regulations

The National Housing Bank expects that the main intention of housing finance corporations will be the provision of long-term credit for the construction or purchase of residential houses in India for individuals. The supply of finance for the enlargement or repair of residential houses is not permitted as the main activity. Lending should take place on adequate terms and conditions as defined by the housing finance corporations. An exception is interest rates (NHB 1990: 2-7). The interest rates that a housing finance corporation may charge individuals for a housing loan are related to the loan size. Project loans, except for slum redevelopment schemes, are exempted from this measure. The last column in Table 35 shows the effective interest rates charged by housing finance corporations. To make housing credit affordable to the poor, a lower interest rate is prescribed for small loans by taking into account the assumption that the poor will seek small loans. By charging higher interest rates for larger amounts the cheaper rates, will be cross-subsidised.

In addition to financial arrangements for the individual, the National Housing Bank also finances schemes on a project basis through public and private agencies, such as slum redevelopment schemes for the Low-Income Groups (LIG) and Economically Weaker Sections (EWS). The National Housing Bank finances such schemes undertaken by governmental or non-governmental organisations, if available, in all urban areas except Mumbai, Bangalore, Calcutta, Delhi and Chennai. In these schemes housing and infrastructural improvement can be combined. Moreover, incremental building on a low-cost basis is encouraged. The project loan should preferably be secured by mortgaging properties or by a government guarantee. For each unit, a loan can be given of a maximum of 80% of its costs or Rs. 45,000, which should be repaid within 15 years. Table 36 displays the effective interest rates concerned.

Table 35 Interest rates for loans with effect from 1-5-1994

Loan size	Interest rate p.a. charged by	
For new units & allottees of National Housing Bank's land development and shelter projects	National Housing Bank (refinance)	Housing finance corporations
up to Rs. 25,000	10.00 (fixed)	12.00 (maximum)
Rs. 25,001 - 100,000	14.25 (fixed)	15.50 (maximum)
Rs. 100,000 - 200,000	14.25 (fixed)	*
For upgradation upto Rs. 30,000	14.25 (fixed)	15.50 (maximum)
Project loans		
public agencies	15.50	16.50
housing co-operatives	15.50	16.50
rental housing	17.00	18.00
professional developers	17.00	18.50

* Housing finance corporations are free to decide the interest rates for these loans.

Table 36 Interest rates for shelter improvement in a slum redevelopment scheme with effect from 1-5-1994

Loan size	Interest rate
up to Rs. 25,000	9%
Rs. 25,001 - Rs. 45,000	12%

For each housing loan overhead costs are incurred. To meet the expenses of checking the title deeds and the administration costs involved, front-end fees are charged. However, registration charges for documents and stamp duties are not included in the front-end charges. These front-end charges, which can be deducted from the credit provided, may not exceed 2% of the housing loan. Over time, the amount involved should not exceed 1.5% of the credit outstanding, which forces housing finance corporations to keep the administration costs as low as possible (NHB 1990: 7).

7.1.3 Refinancing facilities

In 1991, the National Housing Bank introduced refinancing facilities. The National Housing Bank can raise cheap funds relatively easily on the financial market, which can be of help to housing finance corporations that face difficulties in sourcing. Housing finance corporations have to compete with commercial banks for deposits with a term of less than two years (Struyk and Ravicz 1992: 16). Refinancing is expected to make it easier for housing finance corporations to serve low and middle-income families.

The National Housing Bank completely refinances loans provided by recognised housing finance corporations and commercial banks, for the purchase or construction of new housing units with a built-up area of less than 40 square meters or costs of less than Rs. 150,000 (including the costs of land). 100% refinance is also provided for credit of up to Rs. 30,000 for the upgrading and major repairs of a house (NHB 1990: 8). Furthermore, all loans issued under the Home Loan Account scheme will be refinanced, but to a maximum of 60% of housing finance corporation's overall lending.

The National Housing Bank has also started to refinance loans for developing plots to encourage banks and housing finance corporations to allocate credit to this sector. The National Housing Bank joined the public agency Housing and Urban Development Corporation (HUDCO), which was originally the only financier in this sector. The loans refinanced will be lent at an interest rate below the rate that a housing finance corporation is allowed to charge. The margin between the rate charged by such a housing finance corporation and the refinance rate by the National Housing Bank is dependent on the loan size, of which Table 34 provides an overview.

7.1.4 Home Loan Account Scheme

The Housing Development and Finance Corporation was the first housing finance corporation to initiate a housing-linked contractual savings scheme, the Home Savings Plan. This scheme inspired the National Housing Bank to start the Home Loan Account scheme on a national level. In July 1989, the National Housing Bank launched the Home Loan Account scheme to encourage potential house owners to save for part of the costs of their desired house in advance. Any individual, major or minor, can open a Home Loan Account at any branch of a scheduled bank and at approved housing finance corporations. However, the condition is that an applicant for a Home Loan Account may not already possess a dwelling anywhere in India. Initially, the Home Loan

Account scheme was instituted for banks, because the National Housing Bank did not trust the housing finance corporations' financial strength. In this way the Home Loan Account scheme was able to spread quickly throughout most of India. From January 1991 onwards, housing finance corporations could join the scheme (Struyk and Ravicz 1992: 34-35).

A participant in an Home Loan Account scheme must save a minimum amount of Rs. 30 per month, which can also be paid in quarterly, half-yearly and annual instalments of Rs. 90, Rs. 180, and Rs. 360 respectively. This comes close to the idea of saving a minimum of Rs. 1 per day. If preferable, a saver can vary his contributions in multiples of Rs. 10. However, a participant cannot withdraw savings from the account until a minimum period of five years has lapsed. An interest rate of 10% p.a. will be paid for these savings. A Home Loan Account scheme offers an opportunity to save as much as possible, as regularly as possible, and for as long as possible.

The savers will be eligible for a housing loan after they have saved regularly for a minimum period of five years[1] from the time of opening the account. Here 'regularly' means that at least one instalment should be paid within a period of 12 calendar months. A loan can only be taken out for the purchase of a new house or flat from any public or private housing agency or co-operative society. A new house or flat means that the first registration of the dwelling should be in the name of the Home Loan Account participant. In general, there is no ceiling on the loan amount, which can be sanctioned under this scheme. However, the size of the housing loan will depend on the borrower's repaying capacity, the savings accumulated in her/his Home Loan Account (maximum 4 times this amount) and the costs of the new house or flat.

The repayment period for the loan is a maximum of 15 years against interest rates, which are dependent on the loan size (see Table 37). The participant who has taken a housing loan is eligible for tax concessions on instalments of an Home Loan Account loan up to a maximum of Rs. 10,000 p.a., according to the present provisions of the Income-Tax Act 1961, section 88. Furthermore, interest can be deducted in the calculation of income from house property as per section 24. The savings accumulated in a Home Loan Account, including its interest, to a maximum of Rs. 500,000 are exempted from wealth tax under section 5 of the Wealth Tax Act. These tax benefits are especially beneficial to the middle and high-income groups.

1 This period of 5 years becomes 3 years if the allocated house or flat is in a National Housing Bank financed project.

Table 37 Lending rates for Home Loan Account loans

Loan as multiple of savings	Loan size	Interest rate p.a. (excluding interest tax)
4 x	upto Rs. 50,000	10.5%
3 x	Rs. 50,001-100,000	12.0%
2 x	Rs. 100,001-200,000	13.5%
1.5 x	above Rs. 200,000	14.5%

It was anticipated that an increasing number of people would join the Home Loan Account scheme, which would lead to a considerable growth in the pool of savings. However, the scheme is not self-financing. If too many savers borrow, the pool of savings would soon dry up. Consequently, additional finance from attracting more savers or from external financial sources is required to meet the loan demands. A solution to this problem was to make all housing loans provided to Home Loan Account participants eligible for refinancing.

It was expected that the poor and the informally employed could prove their capacity for consistent saving through participation in the Home Loan Account scheme. In this way their creditworthiness could be proved and their access to housing finance improved. The scheme is made attractive to the poor by providing them with favourable conditions, such as four times the savings amount for loans and a cheaper interest rate. This is made possible through cross subsidising the interest rates.

7.2 Housing finance corporations

The Housing Development and Finance Corporation was the first private company in the housing finance market. Later on, other housing finance corporations joined and the National Housing Bank established rules and regulations for housing finance corporations concerning, for example, lending, refinancing and the Home Loan Account scheme. The impact of these measures on the operation of housing finance corporations will be discussed in this section.

7.2.1 Housing Development and Finance Corporation and the newcomers

From 1977 onwards, the Housing Development and Finance Corporation (HDFC) was able to establish a good position in the housing finance market, from which other housing finance corporations were initially absent. Its funds come mainly from financial institutions such as the LIC, the UTI, the ICICI, commercial banks and since 1984 from international development agencies. In addition, the HDFC has enlarged its working capital by issuing bonds. In this way, HDFC was able to escape the centralised rules and regulations affecting India's financial system. Moreover, the HDFC's mismatch between sourcing and lending is low. In short, the HDFC proved that an Indian institution can mobilise financial resources without subsidies or mandated credit allocations (Struyk and Ravicz 1992: 34-35).

The HDFC's commercial success inspired others to start housing finance corporations. Since 1984 an increasing number of housing finance corporations have been registered. However, the number of registered housing finance corporations does not give a clear indication of the private housing finance market, because some of them are either dormant or not engaged primarily in housing finance.

The Al-Ameen Islamic Financial and Investment Corporation (AIFIC) as a newcomer has a specific position in the housing finance market. It is a non-banking institution, whose activities include leasing, project financing and housing finance. AIFIC is recognised by the Reserve Bank of India and is allowed to deal with finance according to the Islamic principles as laid down in the Shariah.[2] It is agreed that AIFIC does not need to co-operate with financial institutions such as the National Housing Bank, which charge interest. Consequently, AIFIC arranges its working capital outside the regular financial system.

Many newcomers who operate within the regular financial system complain about the difficulty of obtaining enough working capital. Housing finance corporations often have to pay a higher price to raise funds, while the interest they are allowed to charge for these loans is declining. There is often a conflict for them between mobilising short-term deposits and providing long-term credit. The interest rate on de-

2 According to Shaghil (1989) the Shariah refers to 'the complex of Islamic injunctions related to variegated aspects of life and constitutes the backbone of the Islamic faith and is supposed to govern the individual and collective behaviour of the faithful' (ibid.: x). However, the interpretations of Islamic principles are not always identical, which can be illustrated with, for example, the discussion on interest principles (ibid.: 83-89).

posits must be increased to attract funds from the market. However, the interest rates and the front-end fees that may be charged remain the same. Thus the profit margin declines, which led to complaints against the National Housing Bank.

The National Housing Bank imposes a liquidity requirement of 10% of the deposits with a housing finance corporation, which is much lower than the 45% prescribed for a bank. A certain liquidity requirement is necessary to maintain public confidence in the stability of a housing finance corporation and protects both depositors and creditors against losses. Housing finance corporations are allowed to invest a maximum of 25% of their assets according to their own preferences. This money is often invested in the very profitable bridging loans extended to land developers and builders. Bridging loans have a short term (between six months and two years) and can carry interest rates of 19-21%. This potentially profitable business is not popular among all housing finance corporations due to a lack of skill in recovering the loans.

7.2.2 Lending in practice

Housing finance corporations lend not only to individuals, but also to public organisations, such as housing boards and private companies for (rental) housing and land development projects, for example. The latter loans can be a line of credit 'through' or 'to'. 'Through' indicates that the loan is given to an enterprise that lends it again to its employees. A line of credit 'to' means that the individual employee takes out the loan from the housing finance corporation and the employer guarantees the repayment.

To obtain capital, public institutions often require a government guarantee. Through such public institutions, special housing schemes for EWS can be financed. Since 1990, the HDFC has been able to mobilise foreign funds for EWS housing by means of cheap credit from the KFW (Kreditanstalt für Wiederaufbau).

Individual loans may be promoted by providing gifts such as accidental-death insurance,[3] free accident-risk cover and/or property insurance. The credit size is dependent on, amongst other things, the applicant's income. The size of the repayment instalments should not be more than 35% of the gross income of the applicants' household. This

3 Accidental death insurance covers the credit outstanding with an housing finance corporation if the borrower dies in an accident. In such a way the next of kin are exempted from repayment.

implies that expenditure for repayment of the housing loan, and the payment of income tax should not exceed 50% of the beneficiaries' income. The remaining 50% should be left over to meet other living expenses. However, it should be realised that often about 10% of the budget available has to be allocated for regular expenses and bribes[4] to get the documents and permissions required.

A housing finance corporation always takes some risk in lending. This is dependent on (1) the loan conditions, (2) the repayment capacity of the borrower, (3) the security involved, and (4) the loan approval procedure (Struyk and Ravicz 1992: 145).

Firstly, housing finance corporations try to minimise risks by adjusting their loan conditions. The average loan to value ratio is 51-75% (ibid.: 76), with the remaining amount paid by the beneficiary himself. The loan term varies from 5-20 years, and its interest rate is prescribed by National Housing Bank. However, some managers of housing finance corporations complained that the National Housing Bank does not follow the Reserve Bank of India's lending rate. In March 1994, the Reserve Bank of India decreased their lending rate by 1%, while the National Housing Bank stuck at a reduction of 0.5%.

Loans can be repaid in equal monthly instalments, whereby principal and interest are calculated on a monthly basis and the instalment remains equal for the period of repayment. The amount of the instalments (principal and interest) is dependent on the loan amount, interest rate and the loan term. However, if the repayment is delayed, a penalty may be charged. In one housing finance corporation, a penalty of 2% per month is charged if the payment of an instalment is delayed by only one day, or in the more generous cases 15-20 days.

The HDFC developed specific loan schemes, each with its own target group. Since 1986, the HDFC has experimented with the Step-Up Repayment Facility (SURF) whereby the instalments of repayment will increase at regular intervals, which anticipates an increase in the borrower's income. In this way, young borrowers can be helped to obtain

4 This can be illustrated with an example of a manager of an housing finance corporation. In Hubli he bought a flat of 700 square feet for Rs. 2,500,000. To get things done properly he had to bribe a lot of people. What follows is only an impression. To get the land involved (costs Rs. 40,000) registered he had to pay 12% of the value of the land as stamp duty and 2% as registration charges. To get the things done he had to pay an additional 9% of the amount already paid. After the registration of the land he went to the survey officer of the municipal record office to deposit his land tax. The government employee would not accept his tax payment, unless he bribed him with Rs.100. After a lot of haggling a receipt was given. To get an income certificate, Rs. 200 had to be paid extra to the normal costs of Rs. 250. The manager added that people who construct their own house have to bribe even more persons.

a larger loan. Two years later, the TLP (Telescopic Loan Programme) was introduced to make large loans more affordable. In this scheme the term can be shortened or lengthened depending on a rise in or decline of the borrower's income. In 1992, the TLP did not seem to be very successful in attracting (poor) clients and it was discontinued (Singh 1994: 37, 68). In addition to these schemes, there is a short-term finance facility for people who have to bridge the period between selling an old house and buying a new one.

Secondly, the borrower's repayment capacity is taken into serious consideration by housing finance corporations. There are no hard and fast rules for checking the credibility of a person and the decisions made are partly of an intuitive nature. The repayment capacity of the borrower may be measured by looking, for example, at his type of employment, income, the number of dependants, the applicant's age and his children's age.

Male as well as female employees in the formal private and public sector are given a housing loan relatively easily, since they can prove their income by showing their salary slips. To obtain a housing loan, one housing finance corporation even requires a minimum period of employment of five years. Credit will be provided more easily if an applicant can ensure that the loan taken out can be repaid by deduction from his salary at source. Self-employed applicants have to show their tax records, which are often underestimated if they exist at all. In general, housing finance corporations are very hesitant about dealing with self-employed applicants. For the applicant's income, his spouse's income, business income and rents may also be taken into consideration. It is very rare for children's income to also be taken into account, because they may separate too easily from their parents. If additional incomes of the household are included, the applicant will be eligible for a larger housing loan.

Applicants are screened by age to be sure that the borrower is assured of his income during the period of repayment. Loans are more easily provided to persons who can repay them before their retirement, which is usually at the age of 58.[5] The minimum loan term is five to seven years. Thus, people older than 51-53 are often excluded from housing loans through housing finance corporations. However, some housing finance corporations are more flexible and take into account the retirement benefits that an applicant will obtain in the future. More-

5 Retirement from public institutions is the age of 58, while it is 60 years in the private sector. However, some managers of housing finance corporations report problems of default when the borrower gets voluntary retirement.

over, the applicant's children's age and marital status may be taken into serious consideration to avoid the expected costs of dowry in the near future obstructing the repayment of the housing loan.

Thirdly, housing finance corporations require a legal marketable title deed as collateral for a housing loan. Such a title deed, in the applicant's or co-applicant's name, will be mortgaged. Housing finance corporations tend to use the 'equitable mortgage'. The mortgage provider keeps the title deed as long as the housing loan is outstanding. In this way, a formal registration process including its stamp tax (at least 10% of the price of the unit) can be avoided. Consequently, the affordability of a house and a housing loan increases. Disadvantages are the restriction on using an equitable mortgage as collateral for another loan, and that title claims by others can easily lead to conflict (Struyk and Ravicz 1992: 106-107).

Mortgaging a title deed can be a good means to ensure repayment of the loan issued. However, in the Indian context, such a mortgage is not as effective as may be expected. The foreclosure practice in India, which is governed by the Transfer of Property Act of 1882, is unworkable. All mortgages must be foreclosed through a judicial process, but there are possibilities for delaying the procedure, such as provided by order no. 34 of the Code of Civil Procedures, which requires inclusion in the judicial proceedings of anyone with an interest in the mortgaged property. This encourages borrowers to transfer their interests to third parties, aiming for delay. If a decree is obtained, the problems of enforcement arise, which may be even further complicated by, for example, corrupt practices. In general, a period of 8-15 years is needed to obtain a foreclosure decree and get it enforced (Madway 1989: 12).

To address the problems of foreclosure, one or more guarantor(s) may be added to the equitable mortgage. The number of guarantors may be dependent on the applicant's character, his income, the availability of insurance policies and the type of house (flat or a separate dwelling). A guarantor is seen as a person who can use peer pressure to discourage default. Such a person is supposed to convince a borrower to pay his instalments on time and to avoid default. This is effective if the guarantor has a good job and some status in society. One motivation can be that the guarantor does not want to be involved in a court case, which may stigmatise him.

In many housing finance corporations the number of guarantors, if any at all, will be decided by taking into account the borrower's character, a proved good repayment record, regularity and size of income, and available (life-)insurance policies. Some housing finance corporations, such as GIC Housing Finance Ltd., demand insurance against the risks of fire and other related risks. Furthermore, if the applicant dies, his life insurance policy and the pension benefits will be requisitioned to cover the outstanding debts. Furthermore, the guarantor is often expected to have at least more or less the same repayment capacity as the borrower. A proof of the guarantor's income and age may be required. In general, housing finance corporation employees report that the use of guarantors is very useful, providing that the guarantor is not a relative or close friend of the borrower. Such a relation is considered too close to enforce repayment. If clients are well known to the housing finance corporation concerned, a guarantor may not be needed at all. The selection and use of guarantors is not the same for all housing finance corporations, and selection criteria are often subjective. In addition to the use of guarantors, housing finance corporations tend also to request documents like salary slips, reference letter(s), and a copy of a ration card to prove the place of residence. Housing finance corporations make use of other security measures to cope with the shortcomings of India's foreclosure procedures. Box 3 provides an example of a list of documents required for obtaining a housing loan.

Fourthly, the loan-approval procedure is also designed to minimise risks, whereby applicants are screened before they are provided with a housing loan. Regarding this point, some managers of housing finance corporations said that they treat the application forms (costs Rs. 5 to 15) and the documents required at face value, while others employ a lawyer to check the official documents. Only when doubts arise, do the staff of the housing finance corporation concerned check all documents involved.

The loan approval can take 1-6 weeks after the complete set of documents needed is handed over, dependent on the housing finance corporation concerned. After approval, letters may be written to the employer, guarantors and references, while in the meantime the documents will be processed. When the loan is sanctioned, it will be paid in three-four instalments to the applicant by taking into account the progress of construction. However, the beneficiaries' share should be invested in the new dwelling first. If a housing loan is intended for an apartment, the builder/contractor can obtain the instalments directly from the housing finance corporation concerned.

7.2.3 Refinancing in practice

In 1994, 19 housing finance corporations, including HUDCO, were eligible for getting housing loans refinanced through the National Housing Bank. The loan size eligible for refinancing is often lower

BOX 3 Example of documents required for obtaining a housing loan

1 Proof of income
   a Original, latest slip with deduction
   b Pay slip should be authenticated
   c pertaining certificates for outstanding loans
   d Annual Income Certificate
2 Proof of age
3 Photocopy of ration card
4 Proof of qualifications
5 Photocopy of Life Insurance Policies
6 Sale deed
7 Link documents for last 13 years.
8 Encumbrance certificate for 13 years till date
9 Building permit letter along with sanctioned plan from competent authority
10 Approved lay out
11 Estimated costs of the approved house
12 Bank passbook
13 Other savings, certificate of shares or any savings
14 Collateral securities
15 Receipt of amount paid to the builder in the case of purchase of flat
16 Company's profile and brochures in case of private company
17 Patta pass book, land documents
18 Agreement of sale and agreement of construction (for flats)
19 Land tax papers
20 Urban land ceiling concessions (if applicable)
21 Property tax receipt
22 Occupation certificate

Source: Leaflet of Dewan Housing Finance Corporation Ltd.

than the actual housing costs, which increase due to inflation (Struyk and Ravicz 1992: 89). The amounts involved in refinancing are considered too small. The costs of an average house in a metropolitan city like Hyderabad are higher than the limits the National Housing Bank sets for refinancing. The refinancing scheme is increasingly used for the larger amounts and small loan sums are avoided. Another reported shortcoming of the refinancing scheme is that home improvement loans are not included.

A housing finance corporation's lending portfolio can be refinanced up to 60% by the National Housing Bank. In reality, not all housing finance corporations make use of this refinancing facility to its maximum extent, while others complain that 60% is not enough to expand their business. This is dependent on the other financial sources available to the housing finance corporation concerned. If use is made of the opportunity to get loans refinanced, the National Housing Bank's performance is not always praised. One manager said:

> 'The NHB [National Housing Bank] is hesitant about refunding loans issued by us. This has to do with the SCAM [crash], which caused a loss of funds owned by the NHB.'

Briefly, refinancing facilities are not popular for smaller amounts, which is also a result of the lending practice of housing finance corporations described earlier.

7.2.4 Home Loan Accounts and other deposit schemes

In 1989, housing finance corporations lost the ability to take deposits from individuals for a term of less than one year. This measure was imposed by the Reserve Bank of India to protect the commercial banking system from competition for short-term deposits and to help housing finance corporations to reduce incompatibilities between their assets and liabilities. The advantage of housing finance corporations in competing for long-term deposits is that deposits held by housing finance corporations are subject to much lower reserve requirements than those at commercial banks. Some housing finance corporations have still become increasingly dependent on the National Housing Bank's refinancing programme for acquiring funds, while other housing finance corporations have had easy access to cheap loans from parent organisations (e.g. AB Homes Ltd. from the Andhra Bank, Canfin Homes Ltd. from the Canara Bank, and LIC Housing Finance Ltd. from the Life Insurance Company), or by selling bonds. It may be suggested that housing finance corporations have had little incentive to mobilise savings because they have had easy access to funds through refinance and/or from their parent organisations (Struyk and Ravicz 1992: 68-69).

Housing finance corporations, compared with banks, have an interest advantage. Housing finance corporations offer 14% p.a. on deposits, while commercial banks offer only 10% for deposits of 2 years. However, housing finance corporations have to face restrictions on advertising for deposit schemes. Moreover, income tax on interest earnings is collected at source for depositors at housing finance corporations but not for those at commercial banks, where it is the account holder's responsibility to pay tax. A person with a savings account at a housing finance corporation has to request a tax refund, while savers at a commercial bank may deduct it from their income tax. Furthermore, several well-publicised crashes and bankruptcies have led the investing public to be rather cautious about the trusting their savings to private housing finance corporations (ibid.: 69, 103).

Housing finance corporations can attract savings from the public through deposit schemes and savings-linked credit schemes. Contributions can be paid at the office of the housing finance corporation concerned or are collected by agents. In deposit schemes, people deposit a fixed amount daily or monthly or save money over time. Participation in such schemes can lead to preferential treatment when applying for a housing loan, but this is not necessarily so. Savings-linked credit schemes are schemes in which participants can obtain a housing loan if they have deposited a fixed amount or saved regularly in the account for a prescribed period up to seven years. The loan amount is dependent on the amount deposited in the account concerned. The maximum loan size is 0.75-4 times the amount saved within the scheme. Savings often cannot be withdrawn before the period agreed between both parties has lapsed. These schemes are called, for example, the Home Plus Plan (HPP), Home Invest Plan (HIP), the Home Shelter Plan (HSP), and the Home Loan Account scheme. Initially only banks were allowed to have Home Loan Accounts. However, when housing finance corporations were expected to promote Home Loan Accounts, competition with their own savings-linked credit schemes occurred. An exception is the Ashiana housing scheme of the Al-Ameen Islamic Finance and Investment Corporation, which is exempted from Home Loan Account competition. Box 4 provides information about this Islamic scheme.

The launch of the Home Loan Account scheme by the National Housing Bank was not appreciated by all. Housing finance corporations had to compete with the new scheme and their own schemes, such as the HPP and the HSP, were affected and had to close down. One manager of an housing finance corporation said:

> 'NHB [national Housing Bank] can open and close an account. When they say sit, we sit, when they say run we run, and when they say stand we stand.'

The Home Loan Account scheme has been introduced and each person can open a Home Loan Account if he/she does not already have a

BOX 4 Ashiana Housing Scheme

The Ashiana housing scheme is a savings-linked credit scheme of the Al-Ameen Islamic Financing and Investment Corporation. A savings account can be opened individually or jointly with, for example, parents, spouse, or children. Participants must save regularly for a period of minimum 3 years and maximum 5 years. The amount and regularity of depositing these savings is decided by the client. After a period of 3 years' saving the client is eligible for a loan to buy or build a house or flat, and additions or extensions to an existing dwelling. Such a loan comes from a fund consisting of savings from its participants. The allocation of the loans is based on the principle 'first-come-first-served'. The term of a housing loan will be 7 years and should be repaid in equated monthly instalments. The size of the loan will be twice the saved amount with a maximum of Rs. 200,000. The participant can use his savings and the loan provided for his dwelling.

The scheme is completely interest free. There will be no interest given on savings, nor charged for the credit. However, for the repayment instalments an additional amount called 'proportionate rent' is added. This will be calculated according the following formula.

$$\text{Proportionate rent} = \frac{\text{loan amount}}{\text{value of the house}} \times \text{rental value}$$

For this formula the value of the house and its rental value should be known, for which it is necessary to have a survey concerning the location of the property in the city, the type of road (e.g. main road, small lane), the market value and the availability of amenities. Yearly the proportionate rent will be recalculated, to adjust to the loan outstanding which decreases by 1/7 p.a.

The instalments should be paid between the 10th and the 15th of every month. No penalty system is used to stimulate people to pay their instalments on time. If people have to face a delay in repaying within one year, the same proportionate rent will be brought into account.

house. This entails that the poor, who build their shelter in an incremental way, are excluded from participation in the scheme.

The interest rate given on savings in an Home Loan Account is fixed at 10% p.a., which makes it possible to provide housing loans at an interest rate below the market rate. Despite this, people still hesitate about depositing their savings in an Home Loan Account, because they can gain more elsewhere. The interest rate on the savings is even less than the inflation rate of 11% for 1994 (ADB 1995: 141), which leads to reduction in the actual purchasing power of the money saved.

By offering tax concessions to Home Loan Account participants, it was hoped that the scheme would increase in popularity. However, people with an income of less than Rs. 40,000 p.a. do not have to pay income tax. Thus the tax benefits only apply to the (relatively) well to do.

In some housing finance corporations people joined the Home Loan Account scheme, since they believed that a regular housing loan applied for would be released easier. Such customers stop paying their deposits after a housing loan is sanctioned. However, when a Home Loan Account client has saved regularly for a period of five years, he/she can apply for a loan. Despite the National Housing Bank's refinancing facility, participants are not certain whether they will get the desired loan even after they have saved for the period of five years and possess a plot. Moreover, participants have to prove their capacity to repay. The account holder's savings behaviour is not always sufficient to do so. A manager of a housing finance corporation added:

> 'You have to save now and get a loan after five years. This does not fit in with the perception of the clients. They do not want to wait for such a long period. When you give a loan after five years the prices have increased. The building costs will rise yearly by 10%. The land costs will boom even much more.'

A bank or housing finance corporation where the Home Loan Account has been opened cannot be forced to release the housing loan after the prescribed savings period of five years. The savings gathered through a Home Loan Account do not need to be allocated for housing per se; banks can also use this money for commercial lending. Then the bank has gathered cheap sources of finance for a period of five years. Furthermore, a banker is not so eager to issue the housing loan, because the profit margin is relatively small. The profit margin for a refinanced loan through the National Housing Bank is dependent on the size of the loan. There will be a tendency for housing finance corporations and banks to lend to middle-income groups due to higher profit potential. The idea that the profit made on the bigger amounts could be used for cross-subsidising the smaller ones conflicts with reality. This leads us to the next section in which the question will be addressed of whether the 'small man' is reached by housing finance corporations.

7.3 Small man first: successful or not?

To discuss the impact of the National Housing Bank's motto 'Small Man First', I will focus on (1) the conditions under which housing finance corporations operate, (2) the attitudes of these housing finance corporations, and (3) financial considerations made by these housing finance corporations.

Firstly, the National Housing Bank's motto 'Small Man First' has been put into practice by putting effort into the provision of small loans. Smaller loans have a lower interest rate and are more easily refinanced. If benefits provided were dependent on the income of the household concerned, there would be a tendency to underestimate incomes. To verify such an income is extremely difficult. By focusing on small loans it is assumed that a part of the funds available for housing finance corporations can be allocated to poor households. Small loans are not restricted to the small man, but affluent families can also make use of small housing loans, even for upgrading purposes. Housing finance corporations are free to define how to 'carry on the business of providing long term finance (...) on such terms and conditions as the company may deem fit' (NHB 1990: 2).

Secondly, the conditions under which housing finance corporations operate determine their attitude towards their clients. The provision of small loans is not very popular among housing finance corporations. The manager of a housing finance corporation said:

> 'This target group needs small amounts, which create high service costs. For this purpose a higher rate of interest should be charged, but the government does not allow us to do so.'

The interest rates for housing loans, such as the front-end fees, increase when the loan size is larger. The total profit that housing finance corporations can make on a loan increases with the size of the housing credit. This encourages housing finance corporations to focus on the provision of larger loans (Struyk and Ravicz 1992: 91-93).

Many savings-linked schemes require too long a period before credit can be obtained, or is refused. For such loans the normal criteria are applicable, which means that the poor are considered a high risk. There is a fear that a loan will not be repaid in time or not at all. Poor households often lack a proven record of creditworthiness due to the absence of any prior indebtedness and experience in dealing with formal financial institutions. This may be caused by psychological, spatial, and/or cultural barriers between the poor and the financial institutions concerned. The poor, often illiterate or with a low level of education, face problems with the large amount of paperwork required to obtain a housing loan. Furthermore, these households often face difficulties in proving the size and regularity of their income, especially when it is earned in the so-called 'informal' sector.

The poor often cannot offer a clear land title as collateral for a housing loan. These households may be extended families, which creates difficulties in defining who should hold the mortgage and is responsible for the repayment of the loan. In cases of an unclear land title and a difficult determination of the repayment responsibility, housing finance corporations often refuse to issue a housing loan. It is surprising to note that housing finance corporations use the lack of a clear title deed as one for the reasons for not serving the poor. In reality, due to burdensome foreclosure procedures, a clear title is as good as useless.

The legal framework also places limitations on serving the poor. A manager of an housing finance corporation referred to the Minimum Wages Act, which prescribes that labourers with a wage of Rs. 1,595 per month or less cannot be asked to repay outstanding debts.[6] This appears to be an important reason for being very careful or even reluctant to deal with the poor. The margin on which housing finance corporations operate is small, so they want to minimise risk as much as possible. Housing finance corporations want to be sure that the loan provided can and will be paid back.

The repayment methods of a housing loan often conflict with the poor's repaying capacity. Their incomes may be irregular; during the rainy period their work will be affected and consequently their income also (cf. Smets 1992: 56; Wegener 1982: 427). This conflicts with housing finance corporations' demand for equal monthly instalments throughout the year.

Thirdly, housing finance corporations are profit-minded institutions that make financial assessments about serving certain target groups. Limited information is available with regard to the achievements made in serving the poor with formal housing finance sector. The NIUA (1992) reports that access to formal housing finance is lim-

---

6 The poverty line for Hyderabad is Rs. 297 per person per month, which indicates that it may concern a household of, for example, two adults and six children. As shown earlier in this book, these households often require credit for survival and improving their living conditions. When the take out a loan from the 'informal' financial sector, they are keen to repay the loan to be sure to have access to loans in the future, when required.

ited for the Low-Income Groups and Economically Weaker Sections. In 1991, only 15.91% of the volume of institutional housing finance went to families below median income of Rs. 2,800, which is 24% of the loans sanctioned (JPS associates 1993). In general, housing finance corporations and banks are hesitant to deal with the Low-Income Groups. There is a tendency to only do business with the households with a monthly income of more than Rs. 2,000-2,500. However, I did trace some exceptional cases where households with a monthly income of Rs. 1,500 were dealt with. Those had a permanent job in the formal sector. Furthermore, the small man is often not aware of the (theoretical) possibility of depositing savings or obtaining a loan from a housing finance corporation. And when he/she is aware of the possibilities, access to the housing finance corporation is very difficult, if not impossible.

It appears that the market for housing finance is expanding, but not really downmarket. A major part of the volume of housing finance is lent in the major metropolitan centres. In these large cities, competition in the housing finance market is very intense and housing costs are high. Housing finance corporations generally expand to smaller cities, where there is considerable unmet effective demand. Consequently, much of the growth of the housing finance market can be found in smaller cities and towns, where middle-income households are considered an important target group. To promote the housing loans, housing finance corporations use temporary premises in towns near the branch offices in the larger cities (Struyk and Ravicz 1992: 50-53).

It seems that it is easier to serve a well-known market segment rather than serve the poor who are considered too great a risk. Managers of housing finance corporations have formed their own ideas concerning serving the poor. According to the credit instruments used the poor are very risky. Downmarketing will be extremely difficult as long as the perceptions of housing finance corporation managers conflict with the needs, perceptions and possibilities of the poor. The notion that the poor need a ready-made *pucca* house of a middle-class standard conflicts with the way the poor build their shelter. One manager said:

> 'When people have an income of less than Rs. 2,000 per month it is very difficult for them to build a house in Hyderabad. They need land and a house will cost at least Rs. 100,000. However, there is also a loan of Rs. 40,000 given for the construction of a pucca [concrete] house with two rooms. But cheaper than that is impossible. The government has to take care of the poor.'

In the meantime, the government has to face a rising demand for housing and a shortage of finance to pay for the construction and improvement of housing. Nevertheless, the poor are considered difficult to serve. The HDFC has made some efforts to serve the Indian poor. The Shelter Assistance Fund was created with the aim of helping the disabled and marginalised sections of the Indian population. Up to May 1994 a small sum of about Rs. 400,000 had been disbursed as grants and subsidised loans. The grants are spent on training and research projects that support the Indian shelter sector. Housing loans with a subsidised interest rate for EWS are channelled to NGOs.

An initiative for investigating the possibilities of downmarketing housing finance has been started by the National Housing Bank in collaboration with USAID. The National Housing Bank has had discussions with housing finance corporations and NGOs about what can be done to reach the poor. The NGOs' role here can be seen as one of an intermediary or community-based finance institution. The crucial question is whether they should be willing to co-operate. The National Housing Bank wants housing finance corporations to come forward with credit, but fears that they will not. There is talk of organising a risk-sharing fund, although such a fund may not stimulate the collection efforts, which should be made by housing finance corporations.

The initiatives to develop financial systems for the poor as described above will probably be appropriated by middle-class households if schemes are not simultaneously developed to serve the different segments of the middle class. However, housing finance systems for the poor should not be ignored until the middle-class segments have been served. Financial reform of housing finance for middle and low-income households must and has to take place simultaneously.

Conclusion

The Indian housing finance market cannot be looked at independently of the government's role in the overall financial sector, which is nowadays characterised by a process of liberalisation. However, the Indian government has tried and is still trying, albeit to a lesser extent, to stimulate economic development by controlling interest rates and directing credit to priority sectors. Furthermore, private sector housing finance has been developed since 1977 and the creation of the National Housing Bank has helped the sector to develop further. In addition to specific guidelines and directions for housing finance corporations, lending regulations, refinance facilities, and the Home Loan Account scheme were established with the particular intention of serving the small man. However, these intentions conflict with reality. The poor still face problems of the accessibility, affordability and suitability of formal housing finance through housing finance corporations. Housing finance corporations mainly tend to serve the households with incomes above medium level since the lending criteria (conventional credit, fixed purpose of loan, large loan size, long-term credit, and tight schedules of repayment) fit most closely with the living style of this income group. This clientele is known to the housing finance corporations and can be served relatively easily, after careful checking of their repayment capacity, without fear of high default rates. The same lending criteria, apart from a lower interest rate, are used for the poor. The poor are then treated as extremely risky and officers are distrustful, rather than questioning the lending criteria. That is why the poor do not have confidence in these housing finance corporations. One may question whether the poor are so risky. Earlier it has been shown that there are still enough lenders who do not consider the poor as too risky to deal with. The poor generally repay their private loans, although government loans, in their view, have a low priority.

Government control of the Indian housing finance market limits its further development. Financial subsidies, such as those given on interest rates and tax exemptions generally benefit the better off. It would be wise to stop giving subsidies, such as tax concessions and subsidies on interest rates, which are a burden on the financial system and taxpayers. Further liberalisation of the financial market may be suggested to enable the development of a kaleidoscope of credit instruments for the different segments of the various income groups. However, the poor require non-conventional collateral and self-determination of the purpose of the loan, small loans, short to medium term and a flexible schedule of repayment.

8 NGOs, CBOs and housing finance

Apart from the public and private interventions in the housing finance market that were discussed in the previous chapters, it is thought that non-governmental organisations (NGOs) and community-based organisations (CBOs) can play an important role in the housing finance market. However, during my period of fieldwork, I could not find any NGOs, which dealt with housing finance in Hyderabad. Possible explanations for why NGOs refrained from housing finance to slum dwellers will be presented here. In the late 1990s, however, some NGOs made plans to enter the housing finance market for the urban poor in Hyderabad. One of these NGOs is SPARC, which has experience in this area in especially Mumbai. The focus will thus shift to the activities of the alliance between the NGO SPARC, the National Slum Dwellers Federation and the Mahila Milan (a federation of women collectives) in Mumbai and Hyderabad. Following this, the potential roles of NGOs and CBOs alone or in an alliance with public and/or private institutions will be discussed. Finally, the potential for serving the urban poor on a large scale through alliances will be reconsidered.

8.1 Housing finance, NGOs and CBOs in Hyderabad

As already demonstrated in chapter six and seven, public and private housing finance institutions face problems in adequately serving the poor with housing finance. They face difficulties in adjusting to the needs of the poor, or what Seibel (1997: 9) calls an institutional adjustment strategy of downgrading. Such an action of downgrading formal housing finance institutions is rather problematic, due to the predominant idea that housing finance should be characterised by large amounts, generally a mix of savings and credit. Moreover, the loans involved are generally long term in nature. To improve access of the poor to formal housing, NGOs and federations of CBOs can be seen as an alternative channel to serve them. Here, solutions are found in alliances with NGOs and/or CBOs. However, NGOs and CBOs often lack the capabilities of dealing with public and private agencies. This is why some institutionalisation and legalisation of the NGO and/or CBO is required to enable alliance with legal financial entities such as banks and housing finance corporations.

Before discussing the potential role of NGOs and CBOs in providing housing finance, I will first focus on the concepts NGO and CBO. NGOs denote a kaleidoscope of non-public organisations and institutions, whose main priority is not profit making. NGOs, mainly organisations committed to public interests and concerns, are self-governed by an independent body and support groups and/or individuals in need (Arrossi et al. 1994: 38-39). The NGOs can be categorised in many ways by using criteria such as their focus of work, their area of operation, their organisational structure, their approach, and their period of existence (e.g. Arrossi et al. 1994: 39; Bowden 1990: 142; Korten 1986: 313-315; Wils 1990: 17). In the context of this book, the term NGO refers to a development NGO providing, or enabling the provision of financial services to its beneficiaries.

CBOs encompass groups of people who associate with each other to meet common interest (Quinones 1987: 2). Financial self-help organisations, as a kind of CBO, establish possibilities of creating access to credit and/or depositing savings. This implies that 'risks, costs and benefits are shared among its members on an equitable basis and that its leadership and/or manager are liable to be called to account by membership for their deeds.' (Verhagen 1987: 22). Consultants and policy makers expect that an NGO will be able to establish CBOs. In this respect, Mitlin and Satterthwaite (1992: 172) describe possible routes for working with communities:

> 'a long-term programme of integrated support for a single community, the establishment of potentially independent housing co-operatives, and the formation of small groups from individual households for a programme or activity with the NGO.' (see also Mehta 1994)

However, if successful CBOs increase the scale of their activities and their area of operation, they tend to become NGOs (Hulme 1994: 258).

Some NGOs and CBOs have proved that they are able to cope with problems of access to public and private institutions. These NGOs and CBOs can bring financial services into low-income neighbourhoods and are expected to adjust their services to the needs of the poor. NGOs and CBOs, involved in habitat and urban development related activities, can be found in the major Indian cities such as Mumbai, Calcutta, Delhi and Bangalore, but NGOs and CBOs dealing with housing finance may also be found in the smaller cities. However, the number of NGOs dealing with housing finance are not widespread. For example, only four out of the 18 NGOs in Mumbai, which deal with housing combined with community finance, provide housing finance (Mehta 1994; Mitlin 1997). The reason for this, among other factors, is caused by 'the continued problem of illegal land tenure in many cities and the traditional role of NGOs as service delivery providers.' (Patel 1999: 163)

Hyderabad has even fewer urban-focused NGOs compared with, for example, Mumbai and Delhi. NGOs working in Hyderabad deal mainly with issues such as health, educational programmes, women, sanitation, solid waste management, green lands and the traffic. One of the reasons for this smaller number of NGOs in Hyderabad may be the slum development endeavour of the Urban Community Development programme in Hyderabad. The scheme started in 1967 with an emphasis on housing, environmental and socio-economic improvement through community involvement. The aim was to create stronger communities in slum areas with their own neighbourhood committees and leaders who would plan, finance and carry out self-help projects. Furthermore, the Urban Community Development Department of the Municipal Corporation of Hyderabad acted as an intermediary between the communities and agencies, who could deliver technical and welfare services. These activities were initially successful and did not encourage NGOs to partake in slum development. However, when the emphasis shifted from community development to the improvement of the physical infrastructure in too many slums within too short a space of time, the involvement of the communities declined. Moreover, a shift from a demand-led to a supply-led approach has demonstrated that the maintenance of the physical infrastructure does not appear very sustainable (for a broader discussion of this Urban Community Development Scheme see: Marsden 1990; Shah 1990; Smets and Sivaramakrishnan 1997). The activities under the umbrella of the Urban Community Development Department suggested that there was not much work that could be done by NGOs in slum communities. Consequently, they focused more on rural areas and in Hyderabad on specific topics such as pollution. It was only during the 1990s that NGOs contemplated also focusing on slum areas in Hyderabad. In order to extend their activities the alliance SPARC/National Slum Dwellers Federation/ Mahila Milan contacted the rural-oriented NGO IRDS to encourage them to start savings schemes in 15 slums in Hyderabad. In 1994, IRDS was very hesitant to do this, arguing:

> 'How can we organise and motivate people? There are already very influential government schemes for the slum areas. What can we do?'

Later on, IRDS gave in and was trained to take over the role of the Indian NGO SPARC in Andhra Pradesh and initiated the first housing finance schemes in Hyderabad by the end of 1999.

SPARC is mainly known for the creation and strengthening of community-based organisations, such as financial self-help organisations among slum and pavement dwellers in Mumbai. For this purpose, SPARC works together with the National Slum Dwellers Federation (NSDF), in which slum leaders are organised, and the Mahila Milan (MM), which is a federation of women collectives. The alliance SPARC/NSDF/MM has not only established ties with other Indian cities such as Bangalore and Kanpur, but also with other communities in countries such as South Africa, Namibia and Cambodia. For Hyderabad, the local affiliate of the NSDF is the Twin City Slum Dwellers Federation.

Through a financial self-help organisation that was established by the alliance, savings are pooled and a fund for crisis loans has been established. For a period of approximately three months, new female participants are expected to undertake a training process to learn how such a financial self-help organisation works. Once operational, additional external finance enables the provision of loans for income generation activities and for construction. However, before housing loans can be provided, other activities have to take place such as a survey of the slum concerned, conscious building, and training in communication skills resulting in a pilot project. If such a pilot project deals with housing, attention has also to be paid to construction skills, the costs of materials, production of building materials and the provision of basic facilities (e.g. Bolnick and Mitlin 1999; Patel 1999; Patel, Bolnick and Mitlin 2000).

In order to bring the shelter dreams of the urban poor alive, dwellers can display life-size house models made of a wooden frame covered with cloth at a housing *mela* or exhibition. Such a housing *mela* enables dwellers to communicate with bureaucrats and officials of the local and state government about issues of security of tenure, lending rates of housing loans, the establishment of infrastructure and basic facilities in the settlement and the norms and values associated with the construction process. This offers the possibility of discovering out how state-provided subsidies and subsidised housing loans in combination with other financial sources, and construction materials and techniques promoted by the building centres can be used to improve the habitat of slum dweller communities. In Hyderabad, the housing mela of 29 to 31 May 1999 was the first Indian mela to be funded through funds raised by SPARC and managed by the federation of slum dwellers, in addition to the Housing Corporation of Andhra Pradesh and two building centres (SPARC 1999). Following this impression of the habitat activities of NGOs and CBOs in Hyderabad, I shall focus on some more theoretical and policy-oriented themes.

8.2 NGOs, CBOs and housing finance

NGOs and CBOs have been ascribed manifold advantages above public agencies. Firstly, NGOs and CBOs are often praised for their knowledge of customs, creativity, resources and enterprise of the poor. This enables them to serve the poor in a more adequate way than public organisations can do (e.g. Annis 1988: 214; Arrossi et al. 1994: 25; Garilao 1987: 113; Umashankar and Misra 1993: x). Secondly, governments are assumed to be interested in the active role of NGOs and CBOs in the habitat sector, which enables the government to avoid political obligations concerning the extension of the delivery of services in the future. Moreover, cost sharing and cost recovery can also reduce the burden on public resources (Annis 1988: 214-215). Thirdly, NGOs are also often praised for their effective use of resources and decision-making processes, which are thoroughly tested in practice (Brett 1993: 271). However, the advantages of the 'NGOs above governments have never really been seriously tested. (...) the advantage lies more in the belief that NGOs can do no worse than governments.' (Devine 1996: 5). In other words, wishful thinking is ascribed to the role of NGOs and CBOs in the process of development.

NGOs also appear to have advantages above the private sector, because they are more accustomed to the target group of slum dwellers. They are believed to know more about the norms and values, livelihood and financing strategies of these dwellers. Private sector agencies hesitate to serve the poor, because they are not known as clientele. Being an unknown quantity means that they are risky and that it is better to refrain from serving them due to potential default.

An additional role for NGOs and CBOs has been promoted, because the Indian poor are not well served by the mainly supply-led and credit-driven public and private financial institutions. Moreover, access of the poor to public and private housing finance institutions is limited due to the location of the branch offices, high transaction costs for the borrower (e.g. transportation costs to and from the finance institutions, bribes, and paperwork expenses), socio-economic and socio-cultural conflicts between employees of these financial institutions and the poor, and their lack of conventional collateral (e.g.; Arrossi et al. 1992: 16; Peterson, Kingsley and Telgarsky 1991; Seibel 1997; Smets 1995, 1997a; Wegener 1982: 427).

Even when membership fees and contributions are charged for the delivery of services, NGOs and CBOs, often with a weak financial status, may not have sufficient financial means to serve their target group completely (Davidson and Peltenburg 1993: 13-14). In this respect, Schmidt and Zeitlinger (1996b) found a poor performance of 15 credit granting NGOs in Latin American countries. The service-oriented NGOs, as well as the commercial ones faced problems concerning efficiency in providing loans and financial viability. Abugre (1994) goes one step further and questions whether NGOs have the expertise to administer loan finance at all.

Some expertise in the administration of loan finance is required to procure external finance. Lines of credit from donors or formal financial institutions can be useful to increase the financial means. Here, grants and subsidies may be provided with the motivation that this would improve especially the access of the poor to housing finance. Credit, if repaid, is considered preferable to grants, because revolving funds can provide loans to more people. Moreover, credit demands a more active and self-reliant response from the beneficiaries. To meet the targets in a freshly-started scheme, financial terms and conditions may be more relaxed, but when the number of applicants increases the available budget appears to become strained. This encourages the financiers to make the financial terms and conditions more strict (Copestake 1996: 24, 28).

Attention has been increasingly placed on the improvement of the management and monitoring of the financial performance, efficiency and accountability of NGOs and CBOs (e.g. Brett 1993; Copestake 1996; Mitlin and Satterthwaite 1992). In this respect, it is important to make a distinction between banking with the poor and banking by the poor, which refer to institutions, who deal with the poor, and institutions owned by the poor respectively. The institutions, owned by the poor, can be distinguished in member-owned and community-owned institutions. Membership-owned institutions are normally contingent upon equity capital contributions, and their membership criteria could be based on characteristics such as gender, religion and occupation. These institutions rely completely or largely on their own financial means; equity and savings. Non-members may also be served, but at different terms and conditions. They can be co-operatively-owned or individually such as in stakeholder banks. For a proper functioning of community-owned financial institutions it is crucial that the members should consider the institution, people or local government-based, their own. Community members are then directly or corporately owners of the institution and have a recognised say in the operation and management of the institution (Seibel 1997: 7-8).

The NGOs and the CBOs can deliver only financial services or these should be combined with strategies of awareness building; for example enabling group formation for financing construction activities in which a modernising and an empowering orientation are combined. Such a combination is called a double-headed strategy, while a choice made for one option only is a single-headed strategy (Hulme 1994: 260). Another crucial question is whether financial services should be restricted to housing finance or whether finance for more purposes, such as consumption and income-earning activities should be available from the same source. The former option refers to minimal credit and the latter to composite credit (for a discussion on composite credit see: Lall 1994).

8.3 Scaling up and linking

Scaling up of NGOs and CBOs can be geographical, horizontal by adding sectoral activities to existing programmes, such as the linkage of housing to income generation schemes, or vertical by combining up or downstream activities to existing programmes such as adding processing units to production schemes (Edwards and Hulme 1992: 19). Methods of scaling up may, for example, be project replication, an additive strategy by separating organisational or programme growth, a multiple approach aiming at catalysing other organisations through, for example, influence, training and networking (Edwards and Hulme 1992: 15). Scaling up can also be seen as pulling in (financial) resources (Mitlin and Satterthwaite 1992).

When external finance is mobilised, the NGO's role can be that of a social intermediary, a financial intermediary and/or a loan guarantor. Firstly, the NGO as a social intermediary mediates between the poor, possibly represented in the CBOs, and the lending institution by looking after the selection of the beneficiaries, group formation, savings mobilisation, loan supervision, skill training, loan appraisal and contacts with the bank. Secondly, the NGO as a financial intermediary obtains funds (loans and/or grants) for lending on to the beneficiaries and is responsible for their repayment. A well-known example of such an intermediary is the Grameen Bank. Thirdly, the NGO can act as a loan guarantor for the poor, which enables them to borrow from banks. This concept is used by, for example, Women's World Banking (Scoggins 1996: 11-12).

Scaling up demands decisions concerning the scale of operation of the NGOs and the CBOs. Economies of scale demand large organisations with relatively complex management and co-ordination systems. However, scaling up can conflict with CBO's strong attitude of 'small is beautiful'. Small savings and credit groups, generally demand-led and savings-driven, are the basis for the cultivation and maintenance of social control mechanisms. When these small groups are forced to become large units, problems of manageability and social conflict may rise (Brett 1996: 12). However, scaling up can reduce overheads and extend the outreach of the programme (Brett 1996; Ghate 1994: 136; Seibel 1997; Wils 1990: 6). In order to manoeuvre between staying small and scaling up, the NGOs should have

> 'a high degree of decentralisation, a 'flatness of organisation', together with a system of consistent bottom-up planning of the poor (...), but also a centrally controlled monitoring and evaluation system; centralised technical, commercial and administrative services; and an 'intervention cycle.' (Wils 1990: 26)

The minimalist approach has become the dominant one in circles of micro finance for donors as well as NGOs (e.g. Copestake 1996). However, NGOs dealing with housing finance do not regard the creation of more efficient markets as an opportunity to tackle poverty. Instead they opt for strengthening local CBOs to enable them to represent their interests by, for example, mobilising collective credit. Under such circumstances, one may generally speak of a multi-faceted approach to poverty alleviation for which Jones and Mitlin (1999: 33-34) have identified four advantages. Firstly, housing finance schemes can lead to a physical improvement of shelter, infrastructure and tenure. If this is combined with income-generation schemes it can contribute to local economic development. Secondly, housing finance schemes, which act in accordance with informal networks, can help to strengthen local community ties and ultimately lead to poverty reduction by means of sharing financial and non-financial resources, mutual solidarity and the exchange of information (see also Trialog 1995). Thirdly, the provision of housing finance can help to empower local communities in their negotiation with external agencies who want to contribute to their habitat improvement. Fourthly, housing finance can be used as an efficient tool to allocate development assistance to a specific target group (see also Arrossi et al. 1994).

For linkages with public or private organisations some form of institutionalisation is required, because NGOs and CBOs often lack financial, technical and organisational skills, networking capacities and access to sources of refinance. Institutionalisation is a process, which aims at the establishment of an improved value and stability of the organisation(s) concerned, initiated by a special status and legitimacy acquired by proving that needs and expectations of the target group are met successfully (Schmidt and Zeitinger 1996a; Scoggins 1996: 3). This institutional enhancement of NGOs and/or CBOs can also be called upgrading. Institutional linkages between formal financial institutions and NGOs/CBOs may lead to an evolutionary sequence from indirect to direct linkages and finally to direct access to banking services. The ultimate idea may be that CBOs can be transformed into local banks, which can be guided by NGOs (e.g. Seibel 1997: 14-16, 19; Srinivas 1996), or that NGOs may evolve into efficient and social-oriented banks (e.g. Matin et al. 1999: 9; Schmidt and Zeitinger 1996a). Institutionalisation does not necessarily need to be accompanied by legalisation, but for financial transactions with the formal sector some legal status is required, especially when procedures and financial administration must fit the practices of the public and/or private institutions (cf. Davidson and Peltenburg 1993: 13-14).

Institutional linkages can, according to Srinivas (1996: 9), take shape in three ways; the top-down approach, the bottom-up approach and the cocoon approach. In line with a top-down approach, the formal financial institutions have designed and developed schemes to link with CBOs and NGOs (e.g. NABARD, Vysya Bank). When CBOs take the initiative to link up with a bank or another financial institution to mobilise housing finance, one may speak of a bottom-up approach (e.g. MYRADA, SEWA). The cocoon approach encompasses those dwellers, who refrain from external support or influence and just deal with their own financial resources (e.g. chit funds, federations of CBOs such as FTCA).

An institutional linkage should only take place when it has a synergetic nature. In other words, the co-operation between the different parties should have a better output than separate working parties. However, Jones and Mitlin (1999: 36-37) have identified three frictions in such co-operation. Firstly, 'the government bureaucracy has proved more resistant than expected to working in new participatory ways with the residents of low-income settlements.' Secondly, 'the expansion of support services and, in particular, of technical advice and assistance has been insufficient to keep pace with the people's enthusiasm and the loan allocation process.' Thirdly, 'government priorities change and the pressure from social movements and people's organizations has not been sufficient to maintain these programmes in their original form.'

Apart from an institutional development, some legal status by means of registration is required to link a NGO or CBO with the public or private sector. Nagarajan (1996) has provided an overview (see Table 38) of the possibilities of registration in India; societies or trusts, partnership firms, private limited companies, public limited companies, and co-operative societies.

Table 38 Options for registration of NGOs

	Profit oriented	Charitable	Mutual benefit
Dealing with members	Permitted	Not permitted	Permitted
Dealing with non-members	Permitted	Only permitted	Not permitted
Collection of deposits	Permitted, but restricted	Not permitted and non-members	Permitted from members
Borrowing from outside institutions	Permitted	Permitted	Permitted
Forms suggested	1 partnership firm 2 co-operative 3 limited company	1 section 25 company 2 society trust	1 public limited company 2 society, dependent on local laws 3 co-operative

Source: Nagarajan (1996: 3).

This list offers many possibilities for registration of NGOs, but the involvement of the slum dwellers is of great importance to secure loan repayments. In particular when the dwellers consider a housing finance scheme as theirs, they will invest more in its operation and management and consequently in its financial sustainability. This will be enabled when beneficiaries have to regularly deposit savings and the possibility of dealing with non-members is restricted or even forbidden. This leads to several options for registration listed under the headings 'profit oriented' and 'mutual benefit'. All possibilities for registration encompass a kind of blueprint. However, a registration as co-operative appears to be the most advisable given that the rules and regulations for co-operatives in Andhra Pradesh had been relaxed by the end of the 1990s, reflected in a lift of restrictions of borrowing from formal financial institutions and the obligation of having government representatives in the board of the co-operative.

8.4 Alliances with the public sector

The public agency HUDCO offers housing loans for the construction and upgrading of shelter for the Economically Weaker Sections with a maximum household income of Rs. 1,250 per month and the low-income groups with a household income of Rs. 1,251-2,650 per month. The NGOs, who want to take part in the scheme, have to submit a detailed project proposal and a loan application, for which Box 5 provides an overview.

BOX 5 Required information for loan application

1. Name and address of the organisation
2. Year of establishment and the legal enactment under which agency is registered
3. Profile of the organisation and the existing activities and recovery performance
4. A proposal for seeking housing loan:
   - the target clientele, the socio-economic conditions etc.
   - whether the target clientele have the land title or there is assurance of land tenure from appropriate authority
   - types of schemes and the amount of loan required
   - methodology proposed by agency for implementing the scheme and for recovery of the loans from the beneficiaries
   - what kind of security is proposed to be provided
   - method of repayment
   - annexures
     settlement profile
     proposed design of the house or repairs
     rough cost estimates

Source: HUDCO (1995: 3).

Along with the documents required, the NGOs have to pay an application fee of Rs. 1,000 per scheme. A clear and marketable land title, a bank guarantee, or a government guarantee is required as security for a housing loan. The beneficiaries can also be squatters who have already lived in the same neighbourhood for a long time where they are not going to be shifted from, which should be proved by government documents. Here, collateral could be the proved land tenure from an appropriate authority, a guarantee of the NGO concerned that the loans will be recovered from the beneficiaries and/or deposits of 10-25% of the loan, whereby the exact percentage equals the total amount of credit minus the recovery performance of the NGO. For credit up to Rs. 2,500 for upgrading or repair no collateral is required, apart from the NGO's guarantee.

HUDCO's terms and conditions are similar to the NGOs and the state housing agencies, of which Table 39 provides an overview. The NGOs can obtain a 2% interest spread over the HUDCO's interest rate for loans. Moreover, a margin of 2.5% for administrative and service charges can be offered once to the NGOs. If the NGOs want to lend at a higher interest rate the HUDCO will increase its lending rate in accordance. The NGOs have to repay loans in monthly or quarterly instalments (personal communication with V. Swarup, HUDCO).

Table 39 Guidelines HUDCO loans for NGOs

Category Urban	Cost ceiling (Rs.)	Maximum loan ceiling (Rs.)	Extent of finance (%)	Net gross interest rate (%)	Repayment period (years)
EWS houses	26,400	19,500	90	9.5	15
Repairs, Additions	13,200	9,500	90	10.5	10
LIG houses	80,000	55,000	85	12.5 13.5	10 15
Repairs, Additions	n.a.	27,500	85	12.5 13.5	10 15

Source: HUDCO (1995: 4).

HUDCO has provided SPARC several credit lines for serving slum dweller households throughout India by means of their network. By the end of 1999, households were organised in four co-operatives linked with the Twin City Slum Dwellers Federation and the Mahila Milan in Hyderabad. The co-operatives were linked to four recognised slums with a homogeneous caste structure. Here, the focus is placed on the completion of public housing units for which the co-operatives obtained credit from this line. For such a loan, a household has to forward a 10% deposit of savings, which SPARC has to pass on to HUDCO against which a loan of maximum Rs. 35,000 can be obtained. SPARC is held responsible for the repayment of the loan (personal and e-mail communication with Sheela Patel and Isa Baud).

8.5 Alliances with the private sector

The housing finance corporations are private sector institutions, which are regulated by the National Housing Bank. The Housing Development and Finance Corporation (HDFC), as the pioneer on the private housing finance market in India, channels housing loans with subsidised interest rates through the NGOs to serve the poor.

In 1989-1990, the National Housing Bank started the Indo-US housing finance extension programme together with USAID/Abt consultancies. One of the aims was to involve the NGOs in the market of housing finance and setting up some pilot projects. During a meeting on 'community-based housing finance' held in Hyderabad in 1995, housing finance corporations were not particular eager to lend to the NGOs and the CBOs. They still preferred expanding their services to the middle class, which they consider less risky. On the other hand, not all the NGOs and federations of CBOs were willing to link up with a housing finance corporation. One of these organisations was the Federation of Thrift and Credit Associations (FTCA), whose office is in Hyderabad but which works mainly outside the city. The FTCA works only with money mobilised from its participants and considers external sources of finance too risky for its operation and management. The leaders of the local groups face already difficulties in handling their own money. Adding money would only increase the burden and can make the directors and managers of the local groups less accountable. The National Housing Bank sees a problem that the NGOs with the CBOs have not come to an appropriate institutional framework and a legal backing. The National Housing Bank is not very clear about the kind of alliance, which should be established with the NGOs.

In addition to the institutionalisation and legalisation of savings and credit associations in urban areas, there are additional problems concerning land tenure and the availability of land. In the Indo-US housing finance extension programme there has been a shift from pilot projects to training activities to strengthen the NGOs including their financial management and resource mobilisation. The themes of the workshops are, among other things, women and housing finance, institutionalisation of the NGOs, and networking. Nevertheless, no housing finance corporation or bank in Hyderabad is eager to enter an alliance with NGOs and CBOs and vice versa. Such alliances between banks, NGOs and CBOs do not work, due to the shortcomings and weaknesses of all actors involved, their mutual mistrust and scepticism. Such shortcomings may be overcome by reveal such alliances in a broader context as will be done in the next section.

8.6 Attempts to capture the dynamics of the actors involved

To close the gap between demand and supply of housing finance to low-income households, Igel and Srinivas (1996) have developed a credit delivery model for squatter housing in Bangalore, India. The idea is that formal credit is channelled to low-income households through a model involving four groups of agents; representatives of public sector agencies, private sector financial institutions, NGOs and CBOs. The community-based credit committee should bring the 'most' attractive characteristics of the operations of the 'informal' financial market together; 'timely credit, obligation to save, flexibility and reciprocity to tap household savings and provide the means to channel formal finance to low-income borrowers.' (Igel and Srinivas 1996: 294-295).

The credit committee at the core of the model has to be formed from within the slum by leaders and members of CBOs. Each member must save a predetermined and specified amount with the credit committee on a daily, weekly or monthly basis. Loans of a maximum of twice the savings of a specific member will be provided. Apart from individual savings, chit funds can be organised, from which a round of contribution collection has to be handed over to the committee to establish a reserve and emergency fund. The savings can be used partly as collateral for future loans from commercial banks or housing finance corporations. The credit committee is constituted from within the settlement, which enables a good representation of the low-income borrower's view and interests. This would minimise power manipulations driven by greed and profit maximisation (Igel and Srinivas 1996: 295-298).

The structure and activities of the credit committee may change overtime. When the economic conditions of the participating slum dwellers improve, four stages can be distinguished. Firstly, the credit committee only deals directly with the slum dwellers and collects savings from individual slum dwellers. Moreover, several ROSCAs can be organised. In the second stage, the credit committee also extends its operations to formal financial institutions. The collected savings can be deposited with a bank, where loans for individuals or groups can be arranged. To enable a direct link between the financial institution and the slum dwellers in the third stage, external commission agents are appointed by the banks to pay out loans and collect repayments. Such agents can help to establish mutual understanding between the dwellers and the financial institution, and to facilitate drawing up of contracts between the two parties involved. The operation of the agent enables the credit committee to focus more on the slum dwellers. The agents are a step towards stage four in which slum dwellers can have direct links and financial contracts with the financial institutions. In this period, the credit committee employs a role of support and co-ordination by securing the loan by, for example, providing collateral or guarantees (Igel and Srinivas 1996: 300-303).

To overcome a negative attitude of the actors involved, Srinivas (1996) uses the 'Housing Finance Triangle' in which advantages of the top-down, bottom-up and cocoon approach can be combined and shortcomings may be circumvented. The actors involved are the NGO, the CBO and the Bank, which form nodes of the housing finance triangle. Each actor has to mediate in the problems, shortcomings and mistrust between the other two actors that demands the active role of each actor (ibid.: 9): NGOs are expected to deal with items such as management skills, workshops and seminars in financial matters, training of group dynamics, monitoring and evaluation. Banks must focus on group loans, policy, programme and project implementation, support and co-ordination and CBOs on 'joint liabilities and guarantees, collective savings, leadership, sharing experiences and ideas, information dissemination through meetings, field visits, support and solidarity.

The Housing Finance Triangle is based on the Folding Star Model developed by David C. Lane, London School of Economics. This model is a tetrahedron shaped structure, built up through operational research and management system simulation, which enables actors to connect their roles and activities. The position, role and activities of the actors have to be determined for each case by its specific circumstances. In different stages of folding, the strengths and weaknesses of a programme can be demonstrated and possibilities for coping with problems and their solutions offered in either a small triangle or a larger one within which a small triad emerges. Different actors designate the points of the star, which folds over inwards in three stages. Ultimately the basic triangle remains in which the Bank, CBO and NGO represent each point (Srinivas 1996: 10).

Figure 6 is applicable for the operation of the alliance SPARC/NSDF/MM in Mumbai and shows which actors are expected to co-operate. Although such models have some potential, it is more or less assumed that they operate within a political vacuum. As long as the specific political context is not taken into account, such models tend to ignore unequal power relations and related development concepts. Those who possess more power decide which perceptions will be taken seriously. These power differences can go hand in hand with institutional conflicts between the actors.

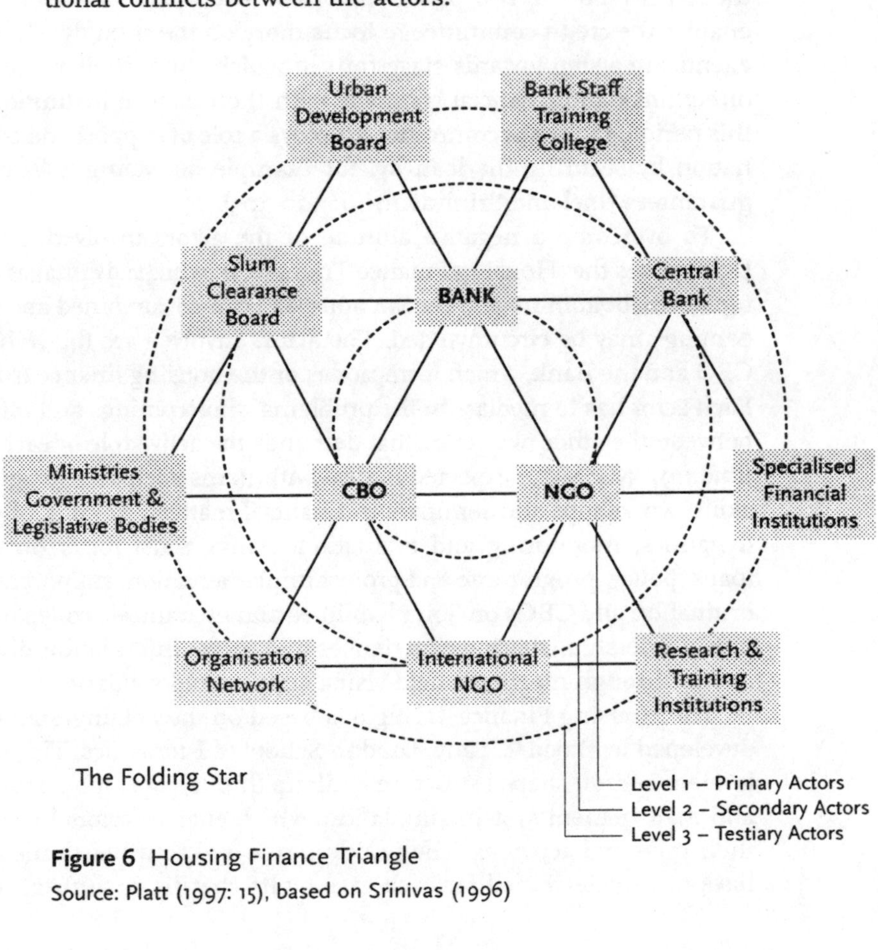

Figure 6 Housing Finance Triangle
Source: Platt (1997: 15), based on Srinivas (1996)

Sanyal and Mukhija (2000) illustrate such institutional conflicts in the Dharavi scheme, Mumbai, which aims at redeveloping the area by providing new infrastructure and housing, and establishing housing co-operatives for the local dwellers. In various stages of the preparation and implementation of the Dharavi scheme, conflicts arose between the stakeholders involved; housing finance agencies, public sector organisations (the Municipal Corporation of Greater Mumbai, the Maharashtra Housing and Area Development Authority, and the Prime Minister's Grant Project), private contractors, SPARC, NSDF, and the dwellers participated in a housing co-operative.

Conflicts arose at different stages of the scheme. At the planning stage, the original government project was challenged by SPARC, who surveyed the project area and discovered that more dwellers had to be involved in the scheme than the government had originally estimated. Moreover, a people's plan was created, which rejected the planned five-story buildings and proposed two-three stories that would lead to declining construction costs.

Table 40 Financial sources for housing in the Dharavi habitat improvement scheme

Source	Share of housing costs
Subsidy Prime Minister's Grant Project	10%
Interest free loan (also subsidised by Prime Minister's Grant Project)	20%
Housing finance agencies	35%
Beneficiaries own contributions	35%

Source: Sanyal and Mukhija (2000: 8)

To cover the housing costs, the Prime Minister's Grant Programme proposed a share of the costs as laid down in Table 40. In 1989, it appeared that the Prime Minister's Grant Project had insufficient finance to complete the Dharavi scheme. The Prime Minister's Grant Project was only willing to provide the direct costs subsidy and withdraw from the provision of interest-free loans and a guarantee for external loans.

In the meantime, the housing co-operative and SPARC started constructing houses, using a downpayment from the co-operative members to hire a private contractor. To obtain housing finance, SPARC approached HUDCO on behalf of the co-operative. HUDCO was willing to provide the credit, but demanded collateral. They suggested a guarantee of a state government housing authority, a land mortgage or a bank guarantee against a fixed deposit. However, the Prime Minister's Grant Project, as being the project's promoter, refused to advise that the state government housing authority should lease the land to the co-operative. Later on, SPARC managed to motivate the Municipal Corporation of Greater Mumbai to lease the land to the housing co-operation, so that it could be mortgaged for the HUDCO loan. Due to this lack of finance, the private contractor ceased construction activities. Nevertheless, SPARC attempted to find a way out and guaranteed the HUDCO loans from its own funds. HUDCO released 75% of the first loan instalment to the housing co-operative that was responsible for its repayment, withholding 25% for the interest payments. A new contractor was employed, who was a relative of a co-operative member. Finally, SPARC succeeded in arranging an interim bank guarantee for additional loans until the land lease was executed.

Later on, new financial problems arose and SPARC was not eager to double the downpayments and debt burden. Again, a new contractor stepped into the project and was willing to invest substantially in the scheme without further HUDCO loans. He/she was even eager to repay the HUDCO loans, reimburse SPARC for the bridge loans, and to return the subsidy granted. In return, he/she was allowed to sell 70% of the housing units on the free market. Only 30% had to be provided free to the residents. The co-operative members were pleased with the contractor's initiative and did not protest against the construction of additional floors. In practice, the dwellers had to pay an average cost of Rs. 35,000 for these 'free' houses. SPARC suggested that the co-operative members had been bribed to accept this offer.

As has been sketched above, different conflicts arose between the co-managing institutions during the preparation and implementation of the scheme. The conflicts between private entrepreneurs and SPARC led to SPARC developing a more market-oriented attitude. Moreover, the frictions between the public agencies and SPARC stimulated SPARC to gain control over a part of the public sector. These experiences led to the centralisation of SPARC's internal organisation. Furthermore, the way that SPARC dealt with the communities transformed 'from an open-ended, all inclusive and participatory way to a relatively selective style where it worked with a few trustworthy individuals.' Instead of advocacy only, the original mission of SPARC became one of social investment in profitable enterprises. Finally, it should be noted that the Mumbai case is unique; it took place against a background of rapidly increasing real estate prices and new private-sector-friendly governmental policies for low-income housing areas[1] in the 1990s (Sanyal and Mukhija 2000: 4-5, 28).

This case study not only reveals that institutional pluralism may be accompanied by conflict, but that such conflict does not necessarily have to have a negative impact on the institutions and the target group. Moreover, a possibility of institutional conflict require its acknowledgement, clear-cut devises and unambiguous rules about the division of labour when implementing habitat improvement schemes, and the creation of a centralised institution that may mediate disputes among the various parties involved in slum rehabilitation (Sanyal and Mukhija 2000: 27).

8.7 Downmarketing housing finance through scaling up reconsidered

In 1997, the Asian Development Bank released a loan of $ 300 million (Rs. 12.9 billion), which was intended for the provision of housing finance to the National Housing Bank, the HUDCO and the HDFC. The purpose of this loan was to strengthen linkages between housing finance corporations and CBOs not only with the aim of supporting low-income housing and slum improvement, but also enhancing the refinancing facilities of the National Housing Bank. For this purpose, greater insight is required into the operation and maintenance of the informal housing finance market and the willingness for alliances to channel 'affordable' credit to the urban and rural poor. In the same year, $ 600,000 was approved to ameliorate the institutional constraints of housing finance institutions. Another additional amount of $ 500,000 was approved to support the shift of the government's role as provider of houses towards a facilitator's role (ADB 1999: 3; Vora 1999: 10-11).

The financial injection from the Asian Development Bank could help in downmarketing housing finance, for which a minimalist approach has become increasingly popular. However, the NGOs generally face a shortage of funds for providing credit. As a consequence, external sources of finance should be mobilised in addition to the

1 'The public policy changes instituted to attract private developers included an increase in Floor Area Ratios (the ratio of the floor area of the built-project to the area of the site), larger allowance for free-sale of housing for cross-subsidizing the cost of housing construction and the introduction of Transfer of Development Rights (TDR – unbundles the development potential of a land parcel from a site specific context and allows property-owners to transfer the development potential from an "origin-site" to a "receiving site").' (Sanyal and Mukhija 2000: 5)

pooled savings from the associated CBOs. For this purpose, the NGOs have to be trusted by the financier, who tends to ask for conditions such as a complete building plan including targets before the credit will be released. The NGO SPARC (1996: 6) describes it as follows:

> 'Every agency which had lent us money behave with the alliance as though we need to be hundred percent definite about all aspects of the construction. Almost as though they are doing us a enormous favour to lend us money.'

Institutionalisation creates the possibility of co-operation between public and/or private institutions. The housing finance corporations in India spend a lot of money on hiring consultants to design systems. The same sums could be used to start pilot projects, which will create better knowledge on policy and procedures (SPARC 1996: 7). The alliance SPARC/NSDF/MM 'is working to secure land tenure, standardize house construction and design costs and negotiate with housing finance institutions to convince them of the need to lend directly to low-income households' (Patel 1999: 165).

The model of the alliance SPARC/NSDF/MM is vulnerable in four respects. Firstly, the complete process is dependent on trust; all individual members have to trust that all parties will behave and act in accordance with the collective's interests. Secondly, a growth of the decentralised development process may obstruct innovation and adaptation. Thirdly, it is of crucial importance to maintain a more or less balanced working relationship with the government. Especially when the alliance depends on public sector initiatives, there is a danger of encapsulation by the government or conflict between the actors. Only when some distance from the government can be established is the alliance able to develop new alternatives for housing and finance. Fourthly, the model is not financially sustainable and dependent on external finance (Patel 1999: 167-168).

Public or private sector agencies tend to demand the institutionalisation and legalisation of the NGOs and CBOs they are dealing with. However, institutionalisation and legalisation can lead to more bureaucratic procedures for the NGOs and CBOs, which are required to upgrade activities such as financial extension services, training personnel in book-keeping and financial management, promoting innovative savings schemes, internal resource mobilisation through debt instruments, in mediating contacts with banks or donors, collecting and safekeeping savings, checking the creditworthiness of clients, negotiating bank loans, as well as in practices of lending, collecting instalments, bearing the credit risk, and repaying bank loans (Seibel 1997: 15-16).

The financial terms and conditions for housing loans, including interest payments and the means of institutionalisation and legalisation, are often to a large extent determined by the lender. The housing loans provided by the housing finance corporations and the HUDCO are generally intended for complete housing units. Nevertheless, the loans are too small for the construction of a housing unit and a contribution from the beneficiary and/or the NGO is required. Still the housing loans are large and require a long term of repayment. Alliances between NGOs and formal housing institutions be backward due to the long term of housing loans and the short-term perspective of many NGOs, which are forced to work on a-project-to-project basis due to a shortage of internal resources (Garilao 1987: 117). Furthermore, many NGO projects tend to remain small scale and cover only small tracts of land in the target area (Bowden 1990: 146).

One alternative financial condition, which is more or less accepted by the HUDCO, the National Housing Bank and the housing finance corporations, is the social control mechanism as substitute for conventional collateral. Moreover, creditworthiness is accepted on the basis of proved savings behaviour. For such groups, community building may be required to enable the participation of the beneficiaries in a sustainable way. Bowden (1990), however, considers community building to not be very sustainable due to natural tension, which can affect each group, high turn-over of field workers, too much direct assistance given, lack of consensus about methods that enforce cohesion and sustainability, big role of charismatic leaders, problems in generating self-help decision-making capability (ibid.: 145-146). In addition, community-level action encourages external agents to refrain from lending their assistance, placing the burden of habitat improvement on the slum dwellers themselves (Douglas 1995: 25). The most encouraging community level action is characterised by

> 'households capable of pooling resources and dividing labor into complementary tasks; strong inter-household support networks; security of tenure; leadership arising from within that is also recognized by the state; the presence of NGOs that seek to empower rather than undermine community organizations; democratic regimes; and community-oriented support from international assistance agencies. While this exact profile is difficult to find in Asia, many of the elements exist or are appearing.' (Douglas 1995: 27)

In addition to the social control systems, relatively small loans require larger overhead costs, which may cause frictions with financiers. In this respect, an employee of the National Housing Bank complained that the overhead charges of the NGOs (8-10%) are very high compared with 3% of the housing finance corporations. The National Housing Bank aims at bringing down these overhead costs. In the meantime, the NGOs are held responsible for the repayment of loans. To make housing loans affordable for the poor, housing loans may be subsidised. The HUDCO subsidises housing loans for the poor, while the National Housing Bank and housing finance corporations subsidise relatively small loans for the poor and non-poor. Grants and subsidies for housing finance programmes can improve access to housing finance by the target group, but it reduces the potential of replicability of the scheme unless the grants or subsidies continue. Credit, provided it is repaid, is preferable to grants, because a revolving fund can cover more people in the long run. Furthermore, obtaining and repaying a loan requires a more active and self-reliant involvement of the beneficiaries (Copestake 1996: 24). Such involvement can be established through small savings and credit groups.

If a housing finance scheme becomes dependent on finance from donors in the West, the danger arises of what Garilao (1987: 118) calls 'the trap of dependency'. To avoid the trap of dependency, the NGOs have to mobilise local resources. The Federation of Thrift and Credit Associations even refused to accept external sources of finance. When it concerns finance from an Indian public institution, there is a danger that debts will be written off in a legal or illegal way. There is a tendency that borrowers will anticipate this and thus not repay the credit. In general, it can be said that it is 'the surest way to kill a movement is to smother it with money.' (Korten in Hulme 1994: 268)

In order to defend the interests of the poor and their own interests, NGOs can organise themselves in an NGO centre to strengthen their operation and maintenance by exchanging experiences (Steinberg 1994: 8). My case study on Hyderabad suggests that an incremental building process, instead of aiming at the construction of complete dwelling units, is beneficial to the poor. In practice, it appears that incremental building is increasingly seen as a good policy alternative. However, incremental financing is not commonly accepted. For example, the Indian Grameen Bank replica SHARE, working in rural areas of the state Andhra Pradesh, decided to provide housing loans with a term of four years after consultation with its beneficiaries. Such a term fits the livelihood strategies of the poor who have a short or medium term planning horizon. An additional result is that the friction between long-term financing and the relatively short to medium-term planning horizon of the NGO can be reconciled. A NGO's planning horizon is largely determined by funding agencies, which finance activities for a short to medium term only. NGOs engaged in the provision of long-term conventional housing loans require more surety for their own financial status.

> 'Operational external NGOs descending upon a community often assume that either financial systems do not exist where there are no banks, or that where they recognize the operation of informal systems, they are presumed inadequate. (...) It is assumed that formal financial systems will either more efficiently and cheaply reach all borrowers or are the conduit to modernization.'(Abugre 1994: 166)

However, informal financial systems are not always taken seriously, which can have serious consequences for the community where intervention takes place, as illustrated below.

> In one of the slum areas in Hyderabad a female representative of a Christian development organisation entered the neighbourhood and told the dwellers there to leave their chit fund (ROSCA) and join a savings and credit scheme introduced by the church. The dwellers gave up participation in their chit fund and started to participate in the new scheme after being motivated by the organiser to do so. However, when she stopped organising the scheme, everything collapsed. It was not clear where the pooled money had gone and how large the claims of the participants were, but the absent funds and outstanding claims catalysed the conflicts. Moreover, the co-operation between the dwellers was harmed and they did not trust each other any more. As a consequence, they did not dare to start their own chit fund again.

These cases, albeit two in number, hint at the importance of obtaining knowledge about the dynamics of the informal financial sector and its interaction with the formal and semi-formal financial sector. Thus far, I have focused on the theme of downmarketing housing finance through upscaling. Now, it is time to draw this chapter to a conclusion.

Conclusion

The role of NGOs and CBOs in the housing finance market in Hyderabad is very limited, but there are possibilities of expansion within certain limits. NGO's role in the delivery of housing finance is not only restricted in scope due to a lack of financial means available and the long-term bias of housing finance, but also due to an inadequate ability to cope with the provision of financial services. In addition, pre-existing financial services are difficult to expand due to institutional and environmental constraints. The financial terms and conditions are to a large extent determined by the formal housing finance institutions, which encompass mortgage lending, subsidised interest rates, mainly long-term and repayment in equated monthly instalments. In general, these loans are provided for buying a dwelling unit or for building one. In general, the beneficiaries have to take out a big loan amount. By subsidising the interest rate and enlarging the term the size of the monthly instalments can be reduced to an 'affordable' level. For community-based housing finance a double-edged strategy is preferred, in which modernisation and an empowerment orientation are combined. Here, savings and credit associations can play an important role by evoking trust and self-respect among the beneficiaries. Such a strategy must be proved successful in establishing CBOs. However, enlarging the scale of delivering housing finance is rather limited due to the finance available with the CBOs and the NGOs. In order to increase the funds, alliances can be sought not only among other CBOs and NGOs, but also with institutions in the private and public sector. If an NGO acts as a guarantor or borrows from a housing finance corporation, it obtains credit, but also has to deal with the housing finance corporations' norms and values. Their norms and values conflict with the short-term planning horizon of NGOs, and the norms and values of the poor, who build their dwellings in an incremental way. A better means of serving the poor with housing finance is to adjust the financial terms and conditions to the incremental building process of the poor. In other words, downmarketing housing finance through NGOs is limited unless the poor are given the opportunity to build in an incremental way. Therefore, the slum dwellers must be empowered, possibly with the help of an NGO, to be able to obtain such housing finance schemes to improve their living conditions over a long period. Furthermore, forming alliances among CBOs and NGOs can strengthen their negotiation capacity and position with other stakeholders in the housing finance market. Here is the challenge to overcoming periods of institutional conflict to obtain improvements of the urban habitat in a synergetic fashion.

9 Housing finance and the urban poor in conclusion: future perspectives

In this final chapter, I will relate the findings of this study to the existing debates on the match and mismatches between demand and supply of housing finance for the urban poor. There are two basic positions in the debate on demand. The economic school has been in favour of long-term integral financing of finished housing, whereas the self-help school argues for incremental financing based on short- and medium-term credit with a few restrictions. This study demonstrates that incremental financing for house construction helps the poor to improve their habitat conditions in a financial sustainable way. These results suggest that incremental-financing strategies, as viewed by the self-help school, are more in line with the livelihood strategies of the poor than the integral financing approach. As followers of this strand of thought say, short and medium-term housing loans coincide with the livelihood strategies of the poor.

The second part of this chapter briefly discusses the supply side debate, by paying attention to the relative importance of the segments of the financial sector to which low-income households have access. These include the 'informal' financial sector, 'semi-formal' financial sector, public financial sector, the 'formal' private sector, NGOs and CBOs. The focus will be placed on the requirements of low-income households and the financial terms and conditions used by the different suppliers of housing finance. This is followed by a discussion of the matches and mismatches between demand and supply. Finally, attention will be paid to innovative housing finance schemes with a view to the future.

9.1 Demand

The first question concerns the demand for housing finance. How do low-income households incorporate the need for housing finance in their livelihood strategies? In addition, different views on incremental financing as a livelihood strategy will here be discussed.

9.1.1 Households, livelihood strategies: integrating building and financing strategies

Investments in shelter do not rank among the most important priorities of the surveyed slum dwellers. However, privately-owned shelter, even a half-built hut, creates the possibility of improving their status, income and access to credit. Although there may be conflicting interests between household members, the self-help initiatives concerning construction and its financing provide a wealth of knowledge about the characteristics of housing finance as demanded by the urban poor.

The surveyed households require finance as well as land, building materials and skills for the construction of shelter. Land can be squatted upon, illegally bought, rented or obtained as a gift. In the Hyderabad sample, it appears that when a plot is bought, roughly half the households pay for it in instalments and the rest of the surveyed dweller households by a lump sum. No significant differences could be found among the strategies employed by the Muslim and Hindu households. Nonetheless some trends can be identified. Of those living above the poverty line, a majority appears to be able to pay a lump sum. Once land has been obtained one requires building materials that were bought new by 53%, second hand by 9%, and in a mix of both by 38% of the surveyed dweller households. Building materials generally had to be paid for by a lump sum. Apart from building materials, labour is required, for which the majority uses a combination of self-help and wage labour.

Investments in housing are in line with coping strategies, which Montgomery (1996: 293) distinguishes as low-stress, medium-stress and high-stress coping strategies. My research reveals that low-income households invest in housing in such a way that the stress of the coping strategies is minimised as much as possible. However, investments in housing generally cannot be met only with low-stress coping strategies (e.g. by economising on consumption, enlarging income by periodic migration of household members, and taking small debts from reiatives, friends and neighbours). They have to be supplemented by medium-stress coping strategies (e.g. using cash savings, pledging future wages, taking loans from family, friends, neighbours, moneylenders and shopkeepers, participation in financial self-help organisations) and high-stress coping strategies (e.g. mortgaging or pawning assets, sale of productive assets, sale of working capital or productive assets)

In Hyderabad, self-help initiatives for improving the urban poor's habitat are generally characterised by an incremental-building process through which shelter is constructed step by step and improved in quality and/or size over a long period of time. Although not all surveyed households have entered a second stage of such a building process, the case material reveals that these activities are accompanied by severe stress and render the poor vulnerable to further stress. The extent to which high-stress coping strategies are employed depends on the individual household member's priorities and the means available. Major factors influencing this are the family cycle or changes in the settling patterns of migrants in the city. As a consequence, one might speak of a continually changing pattern of individual and/or household needs, priorities and possibilities. By implication, shelter has to be judged according to its meaning for its users, rather than its physical appearance.

The surveyed urban poor prefer shelter that brings financial obligations for short or medium term to reduce their vulnerability. Consequently, renting shelter is not preferred since this requires a regular payment of rent over a long period, which reduces the available household budget continuously. Such a long-term reduction of the available budget limits the flexibility required in the urban poor's expenditure pattern. The same argument applies to shelter for which long-term credit may be employed. Again, flexibility in the expenditure pattern would be affected, which often has the greatest impact on the female household members. Income turns out to be a very poor indicator of what dwellers can and are willing to invest in their shelter. The use of conventional affordability criteria (see e.g. Lee 1990, Malpezzi 1991, Rodell 1990: 81-82) in the planning and implementation phase of a habitat scheme generally underestimates the amount of money available for investment among the poor.

9.1.2 Using sourcing and credit as livelihood strategy: terms and conditions

Even if income does not provide the easy indicator that formal sector financiers would prefer, attention must also be paid to the income of the surveyed dweller households. Although many women are contributors to the household income, the men earned the largest share of the household income, which is also necessary for survival. The majority of the surveyed slum dweller households are indebted. Paradoxically, those living above the poverty line turned out to be more indebted than those below it. For investments in housing, 45% of the surveyed households are indebted, with a majority of those living above the poverty line.

It may be suggested that one requires a certain income level to be trusted enough to repay credit. The surveyed dwellers try to build shelter and obtain housing finance of a kind that does not harm their livelihood strategies. This shapes the terms and conditions of the finance slum dweller households in Hyderabad attempt to obtain. The conditions appear to be similar for Hindus as well as Muslims, suggesting that cultural difference is not a decisive factor here. Instead, a survival culture is prevalent among both religious groups living in poverty. Both groups can, want and do save. They opt for a flexible savings method and a relatively safe place for depositing these savings. These poor households tend to avoid 'locked up' savings systems as much as possible.

The kind of loan the poor in Hyderabad prefer displays the following characteristics. Firstly, the loan should be accessible. In order to get access to credit it is important that the poor invest in their social network. Without contacts, financial help cannot be obtained, directly nor indirectly. Consequently, the poorest of the poor often have no, or limited, access to credit.

Secondly, the creditworthiness of the borrower should be based on non-conventional collateral since many dwellers lack a regular income and a job. They are often employed in the 'informal' sector and have irregular incomes. Furthermore, slum dwellers often lack a title deed, which may be mortgaged. In such a situation, only social control is an effective alternative to ensure repayment. However, when the poor have some items that can be pledged with, for example, a pawnbroker, a combination of social as well as conventional collateral will generally be used.

Thirdly, the borrower should define the purpose of the loan, not the lender. Only the borrower can decide whether he/she is willing and able to invest in a specific item at a specific moment. The borrower has to fix priorities of expenditure. However, once defined the purpose of the loan has to be monitored as to its purpose if it is not secured by, for example, articles pledged.

Fourthly, a loan should be small. Too big a loan amount can conflict with the budgeting capacity of the poor and can jeopardise their livelihood strategies.

Fifthly, credit should have a short or medium term with a maximum of five years. The poor tend to avoid long-term credit, because they try to maintain a flexible expenditure pattern so as to secure their survival in the future.

Sixthly, the schedule of repayment should be flexible to overcome periods in which the income of the borrower drops too much. Such problems may be seasonally dependent due to the monsoon or emergencies. Furthermore, payments in a lump sum or in bigger amounts should be accepted, especially when people contribute to a financial self-help organisation known as a chit fund and use the fund they receive for the repayment of a loan.

The criteria mentioned above do not include the interest rate, because accessibility and finance on terms and conditions the urban poor can manage is of greater importance. They appear to be willing to pay 'high' interest rates when they can obtain the kind of finance that is appropriate for them. Naturally, the poor like to pay low interest rates. When they have the option to choose cheap credit with similar conditions, there is no doubt what they will do so.

9.1.3 Incremental financing discussed

The relation between incremental building and its financing methods can be interpreted differently. Economists, such as Malpezzi and Pugh, state that housing finance should enable the poor to build and consume housing now and pay for it later incrementally. They contend that incremental building and incremental financing should be separated from each other. If incremental building and financing are not linked, people can build a complete housing unit and enjoy the benefits now. However, in constructing complete dwelling units, large loans are necessarily involved leading to financial obligations over a long period of time. The poor prefer to combine incremental building and incremental financing. Here, incremental financing refers to the terms, and not to the size of the instalments as Pugh and Malpezzi suggest. Even when, for instance, more flexible repayments could be developed by allowing periods of non-payment, a long-term loan tends to jeopardise the livelihood strategies of the poor.

A long-term loan blocks the poor from taking out credit for other purposes. A house under debt restricts its socio-economic security function, which would enable the owner to obtain financial or non-financial help at some future date. This is different from the ideas ventilated by the followers of the self-help school (e.g. Abrams, Mangin, Turner, Van der Linden), who emphasise that incremental building is not dependent on the terms and conditions of the housing finance to which the poor have access. The poor appear to build and finance their shelter incrementally, because it fits their livelihood strategies as highlighted below.

The repayment of a housing loan is dependent on the borrower's capacity and willingness to pay. The ultimate result of an incremental construction of a house may be that it is more expensive than the construction of the same unit in one go. Here, the concept of affordability comes into the picture. Although presumably it helps, affordability does not necessarily mean that credit should be cheap. It is more important that credit can be handled over time. Incremental building and servicing of the urban poor requires incremental financing. The characteristics of the loan used by the poor households suggest that loans with a maximum term of five years fit more easily their livelihood strategies in contrast to the view of Malpezzi (1994: 459) and Pugh (1994: 388), who, as stated above, both suggest that incremental building and incremental financing should be separate. They also assume that the poor will be helped by consuming quality housing now and pay for it later in instalments over a long period of time. However, housing finance, being user-friendly, requires that sufficient attention be paid to the livelihood dynamics within the household. Such finance is characterised by its accessibility, small or medium term, the use of social collateral, and a flexible repayment schedule. In conclusion, affordability is important, but it should be seen over a period of time. Affordable housing finance for the low-income households has a short to medium term character.

9.2 Supply

In this research, I have tackled the question of 'What financing methods can be distinguished in Hyderabad for the housing of the urban poor?' It is remarkable that the literature mainly deals with (semi) 'formal' financial institutions, while the urban poor are mainly dependent on the 'informal' financial sector. Below, I will provide a broad overview of the supply side and the related financial terms and conditions.

The suppliers of housing finance deal mainly with individual arrangements, except for the schemes in which savings and credit are combined. The supply side of the housing finance market encompasses many financial agents and institutions from different sectors, which will be discussed in the following order: 'informal' sector, semi-'formal' financial institutions, public sector, private 'formal' sector, NGOs and CBOs. To a great extent the literature focuses on public and 'formal' private sector financing intermediaries (both general and technical). Some attention has been given to financing through NGOs and CBOs, although their importance and capacity to set up and manage housing finance have been overestimated.

In the Hyderabad study, as elsewhere, the 'informal' private sector financial intermediaries is in practice many times more important to the poor than the public and 'formal' private sector institutions. Table 41 provides an overview of the terms and conditions of the housing loans in the different market segments as discussed above. Here, the characteristics are generalised to enable insightful comparison.

Table 41 Financial terms and conditions of housing loans in different Hyderabad sub-markets

	Accessible	Collateral	Purpose loan	Term	Repayment
'Informal' sector	More or less	Often social	Often defined by the borrower	Short-medium	Flexible
'Semi-formal' financial institutions	More or less	Often mix of conventional and social	Defined by the borrower or fixed	Short-medium	Flexible
Public sector	More or less	Conventional	Fixed by lender	Long	Fixed
'Formal' private sector	No	Conventional and social	Fixed by lender	Medium-long	Fixed
NGOs	More or less	Conventional and/or social	Fixed	Medium-long	Flexible
CBOs	More or less	Social	Defined by the borrower or fixed by lender	Short-medium	Flexible

Source: Own research.

Note: Term of the loans: short (<1.5 year), medium (1.5 - 5 year), long (> 5 year).

9.2.1 'Informal' sector

In general, credit providers in the 'informal' housing finance sector in Hyderabad are rather heterogeneous in nature. 'Informal' credit providers can be divided in personal lenders, commercial lenders and financial self-help organisations. Personal lenders encompass friends, neighbours, relatives, colleagues and employers. The relations between lender and borrower are characterised by personal, flexible lending arrangements. The relation is of a tit for tat nature, which requires a trust relationship between the borrower and lender. For employers who lend to their employees, the risk of default is minimised because the instalments for the repayment of the loan can be deducted from the employee's salary.

Moneylenders and pawnbrokers can be classified as commercial lenders, who offer credit in a business-like way. These lenders are often considered rather efficient with regard to the speed of the transactions, the distribution of credit to many borrowers rather than a few, the rate of return offered on borrowed funds, the rate of recovery, and their services. Other advantages of these lenders are the safeguarding of proper scrutiny of loan application and collateral, personal assessment, and follow up actions.

Financial self-help organisations encompass chit funds (ROSCA, ASCRA, SAVA), in which people are organised in groups with a possibility of combining savings and credit, sometimes including an insurance function. The rules and regulations of each association can be modified in such a way that they fit the needs of all their participants, whilst also functioning properly as a financial self-help organisation. The chit funds provide the opportunity of using financial means in a rather effective way.

In spite of differences in the 'informal' sector in Hyderabad, some general characteristics can be given. The 'informal' housing finance sector is relatively accessible to the urban poor. Accessibility is here to a large extent dependent on participation in a network. 'Informal' housing finance is generally characterised by non-mortgage lending. However, in an urban setting, such as Hyderabad, the ownership of a dwelling, even a hut or a shack without legal title deed, is mostly required to ensure that people, who still have financial obligations in a specific neighbourhood, do not disappear. However, a borrower is free to determine the purpose for which he/she wants to use the credit obtained. They may decide to use it for the improvement of their dwelling or for another purpose. The size of loans is small and relatively high interest rates are charged (3 to 10% per month is not unusual). Moreover, the term is short to medium, but with a flexible repayment schedule. Savings and credit associations offer the possibility of 'savings through' with a more or less continuous stream of savings combined with access to credit, while most other sources restrict themselves to the provision of credit. However, a proved savings and loan repayment record creates a trustworthy client.

9.2.2 Semi-formal financial institutions

Semi-formal financial institutions are institutions, which are recognised by the Central Bank of India, such as licensed chit funds, moneylenders, pawnbrokers, and finance corporations. This recognition offers the possibility of filing a court case in case of default, but these institutions are not permitted to undertake all banking activities. The surveyed dweller households borrowed from all these so-called non-banking financial institutions for housing purposes.

In Hyderabad, the licensed chit funds are auction ROSCAs with an authoritarian management structure. It is the leader who selects the participants, for this he/she will take the possession of social collateral into account. Once the participant has obtained the fund, the chit fund organiser does not bother about its expenditure, but insists that the payments will be paid on time until the cycle is finished. These chit funds offer cheaper housing loans than housing finance corporations, but exclude the poorest due the large sums involved for the contributions (see Smets 2000).

Moneylenders screen clients by looking at their trustworthiness with regard to social collateral. In addition, pawnbrokers use conventional collateral, namely pledging material goods. The borrower decides the purpose for which the loan will be used. The size of these loans varies enormously. The repayment schedule is short to medium term, but some flexibility in repaying the instalments is allowed. However, once repayments have been delayed extra interest will be charged for that specific period.

Finance corporations deal mainly with clients who are able to pledge conventional collateral. The loan (Rs. 6,000-30.000) is provided for a specific purpose. In practice, borrowers may manipulate the use of the loan and allocate it for housing purposes. The loan often has a fixed repayment schedule with a short term. Housing finance corporations are discussed separately in the section on private 'formal' sector.

Apart from non-banking financial institutions, salary-owners' co-operatives and housing finance co-operatives are classified as non-banking financial co-operatives, which are recognised by the Central Bank of India. These co-operatives deal only with co-operative members and combine social and conventional collateral to reduce the risk of default. Once a borrower has obtained a loan, he/she can decide the purpose for which he/she will use the loan. The repayment of the loan has to take place according to a fixed repayment schedule with terms of approximately 2-4 years. Until recently the co-operatives were heavily politicised. The new co-operative law of 1995 in Andhra Pradesh minimises such power manipulations, which had before that time been customary.

9.2.3 Public sector

Public housing finance for the urban poor of Hyderabad is accessible to a limited extent. The Economically Weaker Sections housing schemes encourage the beneficiaries to invest their 'own' money in their dwellings, but do not really insist on savings, nor do they offer opportunities to deposit savings in a relatively safe place. The finance is officially designated for the urban poor, but in practice the relatively better off make use of these loans and tend to push the poor out of the projects. The poor need to maintain a good relationship with other slum dwellers, who are part of a political-machine-like organisation to be able to participate in a housing scheme and obtain the related housing loan. In public sector housing schemes, an incremental method of building is incorporated, but the ultimate aim is the construction of a complete housing unit, as designed by the Municipal Corporation of Hyderabad. The beneficiaries are expected to take out a large housing loan. To make a housing unit affordable to the urban poor, direct subsidies on construction costs and/or indirect subsidies on the interest rate are provided. The formal housing loans are made affordable to the poor by lengthening the period of repayment by reducing the equal monthly instalments. However, the implicit assumption is that the income and intention to pay for housing will remain the same over a long period of indebtedness. The housing loans are thus characterised by conventional mortgage lending, subsidised interest rates, mainly long-term finance, and repayment in equal monthly instalments.

9.2.4 Private 'formal' sector

Access to housing finance from housing finance corporations in Hyderabad is rather difficult for the urban poor to obtain, if at all. Moreover, the lending criteria are more appropriate to the life style of above the medium level income group. For the provision of a housing loan, a combination of conventional (mortgageable assets) and non-conventional 'collateral', such as peer pressure, is required. Moreover, housing-linked contractual savings schemes are used, but compulsory 'saving up' beyond these schemes is not required. The size of a housing loan is large, because it is generally meant for the construction of an entire housing unit. So, the use of the loan is specific to housing and may not be used for other purposes. The term of the loan is medium to long and the repayment schedule is very strict, but can take different forms. To cover this risk, conventional collateral is generally required. One exception is made for the urban poor by charging a lower interest rate.

9.2.5 NGOs and CBOs

Many policymakers believe that NGOs and CBOs can cover a part of the housing finance market. They are thought to be more efficient and effective, because they are assumed to better understand the needs of the urban poor. In Hyderabad, this is a very badly developed market segment, although initiatives are slowly emerging. Potentially, it can be said that NGOs are more or less accessible to the poor. Moreover, the poor can demonstrate their trustworthiness by means of their savings behaviour. The use of the loan is generally fixed. To obtain a housing loan, which is often a large sum, conventional and/or non-conventional collateral is required. Non-conventional collateral is characterised by mechanisms of social control by peers. The loan term is medium to long and the repayment schedule can be flexible. However, irregular payments result in penalties and/or increased interest.

CBOs are relatively accessible, because access is restricted to a specifically determined group, whose members are screened by taking into account their earlier savings and loan repayment record. The purpose for which the loan should be used may be fixed or completely free. The credit size may vary from small, medium to large, but with an emphasis on small to medium. The repayment of the loan is flexible, but with a term of short to medium. The flexibility of the repayment schedule is often accompanied by charging penalties or additional interest.

9.3 Demand versus supply

This section will reveal the incompatibility between demand and supply of housing finance for the urban poor in Hyderabad and its underlying reasons. Moreover, attention will be paid to initiatives devised to overcome this incompatibility.

The ideas of the self-help school and the economist school to a large extent still determine housing finance policies. They use inductive versus deductive interpretations of the requirement of the urban poor. The ideas of the self-help school (e.g. Abrams, Mangin Turner, Van der Linden) are based more on experiences at the grassroots level, focused on the household level. The economist school (Malpezzi, Pugh) is more determined by theoretical economic models, which assume some hard and fast elements, which offer more security at first sight. Policy makers are more accustomed to middle and other upper-class experiences than those of the urban poor. In other words, there appears to be a conflict between perceptions.

Housing finance corporations are averse to risk and tend to invest in areas where they feel secure, which means they are familiar with the target group. It appears that the poor as a market segment are unfamiliar or are considered difficult to serve by private and public housing finance institutions. The affordability criteria used by the Indian 'formal' private housing finance sector are based on legal minimum incomes. The effect is that lower-income groups are excluded. On the other hand, the affordability criteria of the Indian public housing finance sector are based on maximum income criteria to preclude higher-income groups from specific housing and housing finance intended for the lower income brackets. For individual private sector housing loans, it is assumed that small loans with a subsidised interest rate will be taken out by the poorer sections of society. This would potentially enable a process of incremental building, but the housing finance corporations are not very eager to provide these small loans, because of their larger overhead costs and lower interest rates. Furthermore, the poor are considered risky, because they generally lack marketable title deeds and a high enough regular income. This encourages the housing finance corporations to focus on larger housing loans. Savings, if included, are generally seen as 'saving up' for specific purposes, neglecting the need for different savings systems such as 'saving down' for repaying loans and 'saving through', which are practised by many financial self-help organisations.

Serving the poor with housing loans is difficult as long as the perceptions of policy makers, economists and managers of housing finance institutions conflict with the needs, perceptions and possibilities of the poor. There are several prejudices concerning the poor. It is believed that the poor cannot decide which type of loan fits them and that they will overestimate their repaying capacity. Furthermore, the urban poor are often illiterate and lack experience with the 'formal' financial sector. However, they do have experience with finance (savings and credit), but this is restricted to the 'informal' financial sector where they demonstrate perfectly rational behaviour. Breaking away from conventional wisdom and introducing incremental financing can be an attempt to break the barriers formed by the (mis-)conceptions of middle and other upper classes. These perceptions determine the terms and conditions of housing loans and the actual release of these loans from the formal housing finance institutions. Contrary to the HUDCO, the policy of the National Housing Bank now attempts to break down the barriers by encouraging incremental financing for an incremental building process. However, in practice, housing finance corporations are still hesitant to accept this, because they use conventional criteria to determine creditworthiness, which exclude the poor.

If the financial terms and conditions of the housing loans fit the livelihood strategies of the urban poor, these loans are user-friendly. Under such circumstances, the loans are affordable and allow the poor to repay the credit. In addition to user-friendliness, cost recovery must be taken into account for sustainable housing finance schemes. Table 42 summarises how demand and supply coincide in the different sub-markets. The urban poor are helped in a sustainable way with finance, if the sub-market scores positive on user acceptability. In addition, the housing finance schemes are sustainable if financial agents in the sub markets have a good cost recovery.

Table 42 Sub-markets and their adequacy of housing finance for the urban

	User friendly (demand)	Cost recovery (supply)
'Informal' sector	+	+
Non-banking financial institutions	+–	+
Public sector	–	–
'Formal' private sector	–	+
NGOs*	+–	+–
CBOs*	+	+

Source: Own research.

* Although empirical data is lacking for Hyderabad, some expectations are provided. These are based on experiences of other NGOs and CBOs active in other urban areas.

By comparing the different market segments it appears that 'informal' sector loans are of a rather sustainable nature. The public sector scores negatively on these two items, which illustrates, despite possible good intentions, the incompatibility between the livelihood strategies of the urban poor and the public housing finance policy and its implementation. This would point to the non-sustainability of public financing schemes.

We could expect that private sector agencies would serve their clients better than the public institutions, which faced problems of inefficiency, bureaucratisation and a low rate of return on capital. However, the profit-oriented private sector agencies are only interested in investing in housing when they are certain that loans will be repaid. The private housing finance corporations consider the poor too risky and refrain from serving them. Here, notions of risk reflect a lack of understanding about the poor's livelihood strategies. Instead of opening up this niche of the market, the housing finance corporations prefer to serve known segments of the market as long as there continues to be enough demand for their financial products.

NGO's role in the delivery of housing finance is not only limited in scope due to a lack of financial means available and the long-term bias of housing finance, but also to an inability to cope with the provision of financial services as well. In addition, pre-existing financial services are expanded with difficulty due to institutional and environmental constraints.

The financial terms and conditions of housing finance are to a large extent characterised by mainly long-term mortgage lending, subsidised interest rates, and repayment in equal monthly instalments. In general, these loans are provided for buying a dwelling unit or for building one. If an incremental way of building is accepted at all, the ultimate aim is the construction of a complete house. Such a unit requires a large sum of cash, savings and credit. In general, the beneficiaries have to take out a big loan amount. By subsidising the interest rate and enlarging the term the size of the monthly instalments can be reduced to an 'affordable' level. NGOs are believed to roughly fit the two criteria, while CBOs meet both criteria well. CBOs thus appear to be in closer touch with the poor because they are grassroots based. It can therefore be assumed that they operate in line with the livelihood strategies of the urban poor. This would lead to the need for promotion of CBOs in the delivery of housing finance to the poor. However, one should take into account that these CBOs should be initiated from the grassroots level to understand how things are done there.

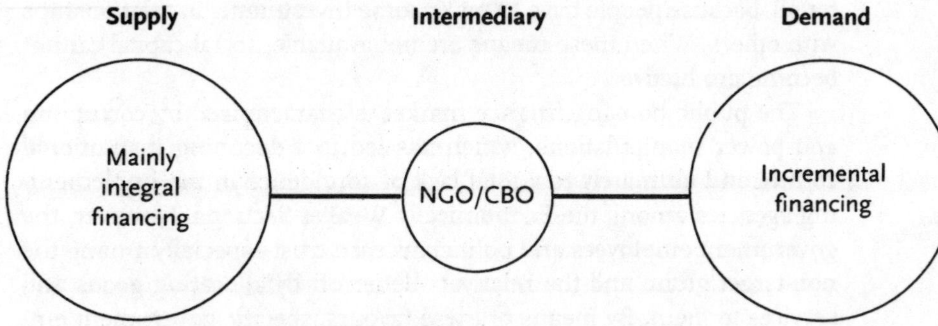

Figure 7 Demand and supply of housing finance for the urban poor in Hyderabad

For a schematic overview of the incompatibility between demand and supply of housing finance for the urban poor in Hyderabad see Figure 7. This illustrates how the largest supply of housing finance comes from the 'formal' financial sector and that its term and conditions fit integral financing as promoted by the economist school. The suppliers who meet the demand of incremental financing in line with informal sector agencies. Both clusters do not meet each other. In innovative schemes NGOs and CBOs are encouraged to link both clusters, which will be the focus of the next section.

What does this mean for trust, confidence and control mechanism in the different sub-markets in Hyderabad? Housing finance derived from 'informal' sector sources is generally characterised by non-mortgage lending, which is secured by trust earned by the lenders and borrowers (friends, neighbours, colleagues, moneylenders, employers, chit funds) where the lender's as well as the borrower's positively valued behaviour defines expectations of their future conduct. Other lender-borrower relations, such as those among relatives, are often based on ascribed trust due to blood ties. Once one earns trust from a friend or neighbour, it also acquires a frozen nature, while in all other 'informal' financial arrangements one may speak about process trust. In practice, trust goes together with social control mechanisms to enforce the expected savings and/or credit repayment behaviour. Once such social control works effectively, people are more easily trusted to pay instalments on time. For example, the threat of confronting defaulters with their default behaviour in front of guests generally forces them to pay their instalments on time.

Mortgage possibilities for the urban poor are limited, if available at all. These results support the view that social capital plays a major role in determining access to finance. However, social capital is not inclusive for all, because people have to make some investments in relationships with others. When these means are not available, social capital cannot become productive.

The public housing finance market is characterised by corruption and power manipulations, which has led to a declining institutional control and ultimately to a total lack of confidence in the implementing agencies among the Economically Weaker Sections. However, the government employees and politicians earn trust especially among the non-target group and the relatively better off by allocating goods and services to them. By means of these favours, specific government employees obtain earned trust, which has to be proved again and again over time reflected in the existence of process trust from their clientele. The political-machine-like relationships involved here are accompanied by social control mechanisms to maintain the dependency of the clients and brokers. It is no question that these personal trust relationships damage the poor's confidence in public housing finance institutions.

In the private 'formal' financial sector in Hyderabad, the clients are expected to have confidence in banking and non-banking financial institutions. The recognition of these institutions by the Central Bank of India provides them a label of being trustworthy, which is reflected in the ascribed and frozen confidence customers have in the institution and its institutional control mechanism. However, the poor lack this confidence due to access problems. Here, it is unlikely that employees of the financial institution will establish trust relations with this clientele. This affects the confidence in the institution.

The staff of an NGO has to earn trust from their target group. This trust will be tested over and over again and is typically a form of process trust. For the maintenance of this trust, social control mechanisms, such as group and individual pressure, appear to be powerful tools. Similar processes apply for the establishment, operation and maintenance of (financial) CBOs.

As a solution, stronger relations between institutions within the different market segments are proposed. If these are to be successful, it is of crucial importance that trust is established. Moreover, when a process of institutionalisation takes place earned and process confidence consequently develops. When trust and confidence are ascribed, such as within the caste system, this can also form a basis for co-operation. However, ascribed trust has still to be proved in practice. When people try to escape their obligations ascribed trust can change in earned distrust. On the other hand, ascribed distrust does not create opportunities for trust, thus restricting possibilities for co-operation. It may be suggested that earned and process trust and confidence go together in the development of innovative housing finance schemes, because the urban poor seriously mistrust the formal financial institutions. In this respect, participation in a savings and credit association can provide the participants with self-confidence, self-respect, and trust/reliance upon each other, which can be a vital instrument in negotiating within the CBO and with other CBOs, NGOs and financial institutions. However, to avoid the erosion of trust and confidence, it is of crucial importance to maintain the flexibility and dynamics of the group processes and institutions where ascribed and process trust play a crucial role.

The characteristics and dynamics of trust as part of social capital is context dependent. Social capital as used in the 'informal' financial sector differs from social capital promoted as substitute for conventional collateral. Social capital in the 'informal' sector is a powerful tool because there is always a threat of coercion, confiscation of material goods, destruction of one's livelihood and physical violence. The fear of this happening minimises default enormously. In the 'formal' financial sector these threats cannot be tolerated due to its legal status, which restricts or even forbids the threats and execution of above mentioned threats (see also Smets and Bähre 2001).

Apart from the legal status of the financial agencies, India's economic context is also of importance. As a consequence of macro economic reforms in India, the government budgets and grants for parastatal organisations declined dramatically in the 1980s and 1990s. In the mean time, government bodies still rely mainly on funds from public agencies such as the HUDCO for their housing schemes, because funds in the private market are more expensive. Furthermore, direct and indirect subsidies provided through public agencies to the urban dwellers are declining. The private sector, NGOs and CBOs have been increasingly encouraged to enter into the provision of housing finance, but many of them implement financially unsound habitat improvement schemes in slums and other low-income neighbourhoods.

In order to make better use of scarce resources and make more effective use of institutional strengths of specific agencies, alliances between public agencies, private agencies, NGOs and CBOs are promoted in policy circles. However, such partnerships and alliances are only useful when they become more effective than what the agencies have been able to provide on their own. Partnerships and alliances, including modes of institutional conflict resolution, are only useful when they lead to synergy with respect to the strategic planning, the allocation of budgets, co-ordination and regulation. It is of financial importance that attention paid to correct estimates of demand, project design and negotiation for risk sharing with appropriate contracts, and how foreign and domestic funds can be tapped. Moreover, if an NGO acts as a guarantor or borrows from a private sector agency it does not just obtain credit, but also has to deal with the norms and values of this agency. Those financiers generally still aim for the construction of complete housing units, for which large loans are required with long-term repayment. Furthermore, they decide how housing finance can be made affordable for the poor. Here, 'cold' money, coming from external sources, dominates the financial terms and conditions. This may conflict with the self-help strengthening 'hot' money, which is mobilised among the beneficiaries themselves. Their norms and values may conflict with the short-term planning horizon of NGOs, and the norms and values of the urban poor themselves, who build their dwellings in an incremental fashion.

9.4 Innovative housing finance options

Over time, innovations have been developed to serve the poor with housing finance. The options are the development of bank-like or community-based housing finance systems, but pre-existing financial institutions can also be encouraged to go downmarket by serving the poor. Other options are the development of public policies to improve access, institutional linkages, and the development of new housing finance institutions. Here, the minimalist approach dominates.

Apart from such top-down initiatives, bottom-up approaches may be employed to develop innovative housing finance schemes, where empowerment of the slum dwellers plays an important role. NGO activities in Hyderabad are, however, limited probably due to the former Urban Community Development schemes. One of the few NGOs active in Hyderabad is SPARC, which works together with the National Slum Dwellers Federation and a federation of women community-based organisations (Mahila Milan). This alliance is mainly known for its organisation of slum and pavement dwellers and their financial self-help organisations in Mumbai. To start housing finance schemes in Hyderabad, SPARC initiated alliances with stakeholders such as slum dwellers and housing finance institutions. This contrasts with the cocoon approach employed by the Federation of Thrift and Credit Associations, who deals only with their own financial resources and refrains from external lines of credit. This federation is fearful that 'cold' money will damage the operation of the carefully built-up social capital among its participants.

Once alliances between different stakeholders in housing finance schemes have been established, it appears that, within such co-management, the government bureaucracy is more resistant to working with other stakeholders than may be expected. The period for which such support lasts is also dependent on the priorities set by the government, which may easily change when a new government enters power. Even when the supply of support services expands, it is difficult to keep track with demand due to an enormous increase of the urban population.

Co-management is a relatively new concept promoted by the World Bank. In the policies for the improvement of the urban habitat, the World Bank generally has developed a kind of middle of the road approach. It combines elements from different theoretical viewpoints including the self-help school and various economists. However, in practice this has caused problems in the adjustment of habitat schemes to the poor, resulting in inadequate cost recovery. It appears that slum improvement and pilot projects mainly benefited the relatively better off instead of the targeted urban poor. The related subsidies on credit have benefited non-poor beneficiaries and the broader financial market became distorted. Moreover, the friction between short to medium-term planning of the poor and the long-term bias of housing loans created problems at the level of policy formulation of the World Bank. The Bank discovered that one universal policy cannot be made, and shifted from paradigm to paradigm when a specific model did not produce quick results.

In addition, they started to collect 'better' practices. In other words, the World Bank became a bank of information alongside its role as a bank of lending. The rapid change of development paradigms and the aim to achieve good results quickly can place the popularity of NGOs and CBOs alone or in alliance with public and/or private organisations and the gathering of 'better' practices in another perspective. How long will these options continue to be popular? On the basis of this research, my plea is to move away from fancy paradigms and take the practices of the urban poor as the point of departure. These practices can provide an important source of information, which has to be systematically researched. Once such research activities bear fruit, one can start thinking about replicating schemes elsewhere, but always in such a way that they are adjusted to the local circumstances.

Apart from the friction of information and perceptions, power relations can be of crucial importance in developing and implementing alternative policies. This is especially in the public sector where power manipulations are manifest. Despite the good intentions of some of those involved, it may be suggested that the housing schemes for the Economically Weaker Sections are heavily politicised. Here, a slum leader operates as a broker between the dwellers on one hand and bureaucrats and politicians on the other. The dwellers are dependent on the slum leader(s) for having access to goods and services to improve their living conditions and the slum leader is dependent in turn on politicians and bureaucrats to obtain the items he/she has to channel to the dwellers. Patrons and brokers aim to create and maintain artificial incompetence in their operation within the government bureaucracy. In this way, profits can be channelled to the actors involved. In the meantime, the public can be told that efforts are undertaken to help the poor. It is thus often a matter of selling a housing scheme politically and covering up corrupt practices.

Power manipulations of politicians, bureaucrats and slum leaders are determined to the implementation of the housing policy. Power holders are eager to defend their interests by adjusting housing finance schemes to their individual interests such as maintaining patronage relationships, which bring them goods, money, prestige and votes (see e.g. Baken 2000; De Wit 1993; Smets and Hanssen 1996). These political machine-like manipulations should be taken into account when dealing with the poor. In this context, the policy of privatisation fits rather strangely, because power holders in the public sector are probably not very eager to privatise parts of the public sector due to their benefits. This can also lead to practices where those previously employed in the public sector start a private agency, which only deals with profitable sectors of the market, excluding the urban poor. In my view, the government should return to guaranteeing the provision of services to the poor. For the Indian government decentralisation measures, as laid down in the Nagar Palika Act, form the potential for gaining closer contact with the target group. In the context of this law, new innovative housing finance schemes may be facilitated, enabled or even developed together with the urban poor. In such co-operation between co-managing institutions during the preparation and implementation of the Dharavi scheme in Mumbai demonstrates that institutional pluralism can go hand in hand with conflict. However, conflicts do not necessarily have a negative impact on the institutions and the target group.

9.5 Future perspectives

Since 80% of housing investments is expected to come from CBOs, NGOs and the 'informal' sector, it is of crucial importance that these sectors be enabled and facilitated. In this respect, I have formulated the following points, which should be taken into account:

- The urban poor require housing finance, savings as well as credit, which coincide with their livelihood strategies and ultimately help them to improve their living conditions. For savings, the accumulation of which requires some flexibility, access to a safe deposit site is required. Credit should be accessible and characterised by a relatively small size, a short to medium term, the use of social collateral (e.g. peer pressure) and a somewhat flexible repayment schedule. Moreover, it is important that the borrower should define the purpose of the loan, although once fixed, this has to be monitored by the lender and through peer pressure. If the loan is used for other purposes, peer pressure must enforce its repayment.
- A combination of housing finance and income-generating activities may help to establish a broader basis for the financial management of the household in such a way that flexibility in expenditures is ensured.
- The promotion and collection of savings among the target group can be a good starting point for establishing housing finance schemes.
- The practices of the urban poor and experiences of agents in the 'informal', semi-formal and formal financial sector can be an important source of information for agencies to design innovative housing finance schemes. The collection of better practices should be extended towards the 'informal' financial sector.
- The design and replication of (innovative) housing finance schemes must be context dependent. Attention should be paid to the different elements that influence their operation and management; structure and culture of the organisation, rules and regulations, the economic, political, socio-cultural and physical environment must all be studied and taken into account.
- Apart from designing innovative housing finance schemes for the urban poor, one may consider the possibilities of enabling and facilitating existing operations in the 'informal' financial market, such as moneylenders, pawnbrokers and financial self-help organisations.
- When institutions with different loyalties are expected to work together, attention has to be paid to the dynamics of institutional conflicts to enable a synergetic outcome. Such conflicts demand clear-cut devices and unambiguous rules about the division of tasks and the creation of

a centralised institution that may intervene and negotiate between the agencies involved.

- It should be taken into account that power manipulations are a part of human nature and that schemes should be developed in such a way that the issue of power manipulations and how to deal with them are included. As a consequence, blue print approaches should be replaced by process approaches.

What do these points indicate for the different actors at the supply side? Within the Indian context of an estimated housing shortage of 23 million units, including repairs and upgrading, the Ninth Plan (1997-2002) estimates that more than Rs. 1,500 billion is required. The expectation is that only one quarter of the amount can be mobilised through the public and private sector. Moreover, of the total housing investments in India the 'formal' financial sector only accounts for approximately 20% and the remaining part will have to come from the 'informal' financial sector, and CBO and NGO involvement. That is why in 1999 the Country Programming Mission of the Government of India requested the support of the Asian Development Bank for support in the preparation of a feasibility study for a loan 'to address the financial, institutional, and regulatory constraints to increasing the availability of housing finance, particularly to low-income households.' (ADB 1999: 1).

The Asian Development Bank believes that the public institution HUDCO is best suited to downmarket housing finance through CBOs also providing the technical support and training for improvement of their operations. Moreover, this is expected to contribute to the upscaling of CBO's lending modalities and geographic reach. For the housing finance corporations, the challenge is to establish financial alliances with commercial enterprises and co-operatives, which wish to provide housing for their employees and members respectively (ADB 1999: 2).

The Asian Development Bank ascribes the problems of the housing finance market in India mainly to the absence of a long-term debt market, which has lead to constraints in the availability and sustainability of commercial housing finance among the housing finance corporations. The refinancing provisions of the NHB provide some liquidity, but this option is not sustainable over time (ADB 1999: 3). In order to enable the preparation of a new Housing Finance Project, the Asian Development Bank agreed to provide technical assistance to the Government of India to a maximum of $ 405,000 (ADB 1999: 5).

Housing finance of HUDCO and NHB is linked to long-term credit, unlike the short and medium terms in the informal sector. Long-term housing loans are suited to the housing construction practices and perceptions of the middle and upper classes. Dominant middle and upper classes, as beneficiaries, can more easily afford to build a complete housing unit and finance it to a large extent with long-term credit. Here, supply and demand for housing finance do coincide. The urban poor, however, build their dwellings according to an incremental building process, which requires short- to medium-term credit. The provision of ready-made buildings with long-term credit obstructs their livelihood strategies, which encompass an avoidance of long-term financial obligations. The need for incremental building and financing is defined by the insecure living conditions of the poor. Here, income poverty does not necessarily lead to housing poverty if housing is built and financed incrementally.

The incompatibility between supply and demand implies that the poor will not be helped at all by a continuation of the dominant practices, but rather that they will be pushed below the poverty line or even further below it. Furthermore, the poor are not helped by credit alone. They are helped by access to finance on terms they can manage. For the housing finance institutions, making use of social control mechanisms instead of conventional collateral can solve the problem of screening the repayment of the loans provided to the poor. In other words, housing finance is trapped in a dilemma of perceptions among the middle and upper classes, who as policy-makers, economists, and managers of the housing finance institutions mainly fix the terms and conditions of housing loans for the urban poor, which must be challenged. The NHB's attempts to alter middle and upper-classes views on the financial terms and conditions and promoting incremental building and financing on a limited scale have not been successful. More efforts should be undertaken to demolish these ideas completely, to enable the delivery of micro housing finance to the poor. This is especially important for co-management practices, one of the recent developments in the housing finance sector, where the public and private sector housing finance corporations must negotiate with other stakeholders, including 'informal' financial agents. Such negotiation processes offer, particularly the urban poor organised in CBOs, the opportunity to stress their demands, which will hopefully encourage managers of housing finance institutions to set aside their middle-class perspective and start listening to the poor. Such a process of co-management has the potential to minimise incompatibilities between demand and supply.

In short, as long as a long-term bias of housing loans dominates the housing finance market in India, the urban poor have to cope with such an incompatible loan, if obtained at all. Instead housing loans should fit the urban poor's livelihood strategies, where it is a matter of obtaining housing finance that is compatible with their livelihood strategies. For this purpose, a process approach should replace the blue print ones. The outcome of a process approach is to a large extent open-ended. Consequently, the more powerful have to give up their desire to completely control the formulation and implementation of policies. Then more emphasis has to be placed on developing trust between the different stakeholders. Here, new opportunities for research arose, which will hopefully contribute to the improvement of the habitat conditions of the urban poor. Finally, I hope that this book has helped scientists, policymakers and practitioners to gain more insight into the needs of the poor as well as their own role in research, and policy formulation and implementation.

Abbreviations

AIFIC	Al-Ameen Islamic Financial and Investment Corporation
APPHC	Andhra Pradesh Police Housing Corporation
APSHC	Andhra Pradesh State Housing Corporation
APUD & HC	Andhra Pradesh Urban Development and Housing Corporation
ASCRA	Accumulating Savings and Credit Association
BC	Backward Classes
BHEL	Bharat Heavy Electricals
CBO	Community-Based Organisation
CDO	Community Development Officer
ECIL	Electronics Corporation of India
EWS	Economically Weaker Sections
FIRE	Financial Institution's Reform and Expansion Project
GIC	General Insurance Corporation
GPA	General Power of Attorney
HDFC	Housing Development and Finance Corporation
HFC	Housing Finance Corporation
HIG	High-Income Group
HIP	Home Invest Plan
HMT	Hindustan Machine Tools
HUDA	Hyderabad Urban Development Authority
HUDCO	Housing and Urban Development Corporation
IDPL	Indian Drugs and Pharmaceuticals Ltd.
KFW	Kreditanstalt Für Wiederaufbau
LIC	Life Insurance Corporation
LIG	Low-Income Groups
MIM	Majlis-e-Ittehad-ul Muslimin
MM	Mahila Milan
NFC	Nuclear Fuel Complex
NGO	Non-Governmental Organisation
NSDF	National Slum Dwellers Federation
QQSUDA	Quli Qutub Shah Urban Development Authority

RBI	Reserve Bank of India
ROSCA	Rotating Savings and Credit Association
SAVA	Savings Association
SC	Scheduled Castes
SDO	Slum Development Officer
SHO	Self-Help Organisation
SPARC	Society for Promotion of Area Resource Centres
ST	Scheduled Tribes
SURF	Step-Up Repayment Facility
UTI	Unit Trust of India

Literature

Abbott, J. (1996) *Sharing the city: community participation in urban management*. London: Earthscan.

Abrams, C. (1964) *Man's struggle for shelter in an urbanizing world*. Cambridge: The MIT Press.

Abrams, C. (1966) *Housing in the modern world*. London: Faber and Faber.

Abugre, C. (1994) When credit is not due: a critical evaluation of donor NGO experience with credit. In: F.J.A. Bouman and O. Hospes (eds), *Financial landscapes reconstructed: the fine art of mapping development*. Boulder, etc.: Westview.

Adams D.W. (1992) Taking a fresh look at informal finance, In: D.W. Adams and D.A. Fitchett (eds), *Informal finance in low-income countries*. Westview Press. Boulder.

Adams, D.W. and J.D. Von Pischke (1994) Micro-enterprise credit programs: déjà Vu. In: F.J.A. Bouman and O. Hospes (eds), *Financial landscapes reconstructed: the fine art of mapping development*. Boulder, etc.: Westview.

ADB (Asian Development Bank) (1990) *Asian development outlook 1990*. Manila: ADB.

ADB (1992) *Asian development outlook 1992*. Manila: ADB.

ADB (1993) *Asian development outlook 1993*. Manila: ADB.

ADB (1995) *Asian development outlook 1995 and 1996*. Manila: ADB.

ADB (1999) *Technical assistance to India for preparing the housing finance*. II project. TAR: IND 30204. Manila: ADB.

Afzal Mohammad (1995) *Socio-economic and spatial dimensions of Hyderabad Metropolitan area: 2011 a.d.* Hyderabad: Centre for Economic and Social Studies.

Alam, S. Manzoor, F. Alikhan and M. Bhattacharji (1987) Slums in metropolitan Hyderabad: a profile. In: S. Manzoor Alam and F. Alikhan (eds), *Poverty in metropolitan cities*. New Delhi: Concept.

Alcock, E.A., K.N. Misra, J.L. McGairl and C.B. Patel (1963) Self-help housing methods and practices in South-East Asia, *Ekistics*, vol. 16, no. 93, pp. 81-87.

Amin, A.T.M.N. (1996) The informal sector paradigm: analytical contributions and development role (editorial introduction), *Regional Development Dialogue*, vol. 17, no. 1, pp. vi-xxviii.

Anderson R.T. (1966) Rotating credit associations in India, *Economic Development and Cultural Change*, pp. 334-339.

Annis, S. (1988) Can small-scale development be large-scale policy? In: S. Annis and P. Hakim (eds), *Direct to the poor: grassroots development in Latin America*. Boulder/London: Lynne Tienner.

Ardener S. (1964) The comparative study of rotating credit associations, *The Journal of the Royal Anthropological Institute of Great Britain and Ireland*, vol. 94, pp. 201-229.

Arrossi, S., F. Bombarolo, J. Hardoy, D. Mitlin, L.P. Coscio and D. Satterthwaite (1994) *Funding community initiatives: the role of NGOs and other intermediary institutions in supporting low income groups and their community organizations in improving housing and living conditions in the third world*. London: Earthscan.

Aziz, A. (1997) *Miniature political economies: the survival strategies of the poor*. New Delhi: M D publications.

Bähre, E. and P. Smets (1999) Counting on people: trust and control in ROSCAs. In: P. Smets, H. Wels and J. van Loon (eds), *Trust & co-operation: symbolic exchange and moral economies in an age of cultural differentiation*. Amsterdam: Het Spinhuis.

Baken, R.-J. (1990) *The high price of cheap plots: the rising threshold to consolidation of low income households in Karachi (1974-1988)*. Urban research working papers, no.25. Amsterdam: Vrije Universiteit.

Baken, R.-J. (2000) *Plotting, squatting, public purpose and politics: land market development, low-income housing and public intervention in Vijayawada and Visakhapatnam, India (1990-1993)*. PhD Thesis. Amsterdam: Vrije Universiteit.

Baken, R.-J. and P. Smets (1999) Better a 'hut' on the ground than a castle in the air: public and informal housing finance for the urban poor in Andhra Pradesh, India. In: K. Datta and G.A. Jones (eds), *Housing and Finance in Developing Countries*. London: Routledge.

Baken, R.-J. and J. van der Linden (1992) *Land delivery for low-income groups in Third World Cities*. Aldershot, etc.: Avebury.

Baken, R.-J. and J. van der Linden (1993) 'Getting the incentives right': banking on the formal private sector. A critique of current World Bank thinking on low-income housing delivery in Third World Cities, *Third World Planning Review*, vol. 15, no. 1, pp.1-22.

Banck, G.A. (1980) Survival strategies of low-income urban households in Brazil, *Urban Anthropology*, vol. 9, pp. 227-242.

Batley, R. (1996) Public-private relationships and performance in service provision, *Urban Studies*, vol. 33, no. 4-5, pp. 723-751.

Baud, I.S.A. (2000) *Collective action, enablement and partnerships: issues in urban development*. Inaugurele rede 27 oktober. Amsterdam: VU uitgeverij.

Bax, M. (1978) *Jaap-Joop-Mies: leesplank van de netwerkanalyse*. Assen/Amsterdam: Van Gorcum.

Becker, G.S. (1973) A theory of marriage: part I, *Journal of Political Economy*, vol. 81, pp. 813-846.

Becker, G.S. (1974a) A theory of marriage: part II, *Journal of Political Economy*, vol. 82, pp. S11-S26.

Becker, G.S. (1974b) A theory of social interactions, *Journal of Political Economy*, vol. 82, pp. 1063-1093.

Benjamin, S. et al. (1985) The housing costs of low-income kampung dwellers, *Habitat International*, vol. 9, no. 1: pp. 91-110.

Bhatt, N. and S.-Y. Tang (1998) The problem of transaction costs in group-based micro lending: an institutional perspective, *World Development*, vol. 26, no. 4, pp. 623-637.

Bhattacharya, N., P. Chakraborty, M. Chattopadhyay and A. Rudra (1991) How do the poor survive? *Economic and Political Weekly*, February 16, pp. 373-379.

Bhole, V. (1988) *Housing and urban development in India*. New Delhi: Classical Publishing Company.

Biggs, S. and G. Smit (1998) Beyond methodologies: coalition-building for participatory technology development, *World Development*, vol. 26, no. 2, pp. 239-248.

Boleat, M. (1987) Housing finance institutions. In: L. Rodwin (ed.), *Shelter, settlement and development*. Boston: Allen & Unwin.

Bolnick, J. and D. Mitlin (1999) Housing finance and empowerment in South Africa. In: K. Datta and G.A. Jones (eds), *Housing and finance in developing countries*. London: Routledge.

Bottomley, A. (1983) Interest rate determination in underdeveloped rural areas. In: J.D. Von Pischke, D.W. Adams and G. Donald (eds), *Rural financial markets in developing countries: their use and abuse*. Baltimore/ London: John Hopkins University Press.

Bouman, F.J.A. (1978) Indigenous savings and credit societies in the Third World, *Development Digest*, XVI, 3, pp. 36-47.

Bouman, F.J.A. (1989) *Small, short and unsecured: informal rural finance in India*. Oxford University Press, Delhi.

Bouman, F.J.A. (1990) Informal rural finance: an Alladin's lamp of information, *Sociologia Ruralis*, vol. XXX, no.2, pp. 155-173.

Bouman, F.J.A. (1994) ROSCA and ASCRA: beyond the financial landscape. In: F.J.A. Bouman and O. Hospes (eds), *Financial landscapes reconstructed: the fine art of mapping development*. Boulder, etc.: Westview.

Bouman, F.J.A. and O. Hospes (1994) *Financial landscapes reconstructed: the fine art of mapping development*. Boulder, etc.: Westview.

Bourdieu, P. (1989) *Opstellen over smaak, habitus en het veldbegrip*. Gekozen door Dick Pels. Amsterdam: Van Gennep.

Bowden, P. (1990) NGOs in Asia: issues in development, *Public Administration and Development*, vol. 10, pp. 141-152.

Breman, J. (1980) *'The informal sector' in research: Theory and practice*. Rotterdam: CASP III.

Brett, E.A. (1993) Voluntary agencies as development organizations: theorizing the problem of efficiency and accountability. *Development and Change*, vol. 24, pp. 269-303.

Brett, E.A. (1996) The participatory principle in development projects: the costs and benefits of cooperation, *Public Administration and Development*, vol. 16, pp. 5-19.

Buckley, R.M. (1999) Housing finance in developing countries: a review of the World Bank's experience. In: K. Datta and G.A. Jones (eds), *Housing and finance in developing countries*. London, New York: Routledge.

Buckley, R.M., C.R. Dunham, J.C. Walker and T. Persand (1989) *Private housing finance for low-income households in India*. Washington, D.C.: The Urban Institute.

Burgess, R. (1978) Petty commodity housing or dweller control? A critique of John Turner's views on housing policy, *World Development*, vol. 6, no. 9/10, pp. 1105-1133.

Burgess, R., M. Carmona and T. Kolstee (1997) Contemporary spatial strategies and urban policies in developing countries: a critical review. In: R. Burgess, M. Carmona and T. Kolstee (eds), *The challenge of sustainable cities: neoliberalism and urban strategies in developing countries*. London, New Jersey: Zed Books.

Burgwal, G. (1993) *Caciquismo, paralelismo and clientelismo: the history of a Quito squatter settlement*. Urban research working papers, no. 32. Amsterdam: Vrije Universiteit.

Cabannes, Y. (1995) Community-based housing finance: a step ahead .. Who knows the direction?, *Trialog*, 47, pp. 54-58.

Caminos, H., J.F.C. Turner and J.A. Steffian (1968) *Urban dwelling environments: an elementary survey of settlements for the study of design determinants*. Cambridge, Massachusetts.

CEC (Centre for Environmental Concerns) (1985) *Hyderabad: the state of art of physical environment*. Hyderabad: CEC.

Chambers, R. (1989) Editorial introduction: vulnerability, coping and policy, *IDS Bulletin*, vol. 20, no. 2, pp. 1-7.

Chambers, R. (1995) Poverty and livelihoods: whose reality counts?, *Environment and Urbanization*, vol. 7, no. 1, pp. 173-204.

Chambers, R. (1998) Foreword. In: J. Blackburn and J. Holland (eds), *Who changes? Institutionalizing participation in development*. London: Intermediate Technology Publications.

Chant, S. (1991) Women's work and household change in Mexico. In: *The revolution: the challenge of reform in Mexico*, London: Tauris.

Cohen, M.A. (1983) The challenge of replicability: towards a new paradigm for urban shelter in developing countries, *Regional Development Dialogue*, vol. IV, no. 1, pp. 90-99.

Coleman, J.S. (1990) *Foundation of social theory*. Cambridge, Massachusetts: Harvard university Press.

Copestake, J. (1996) NGO-state collaboration and the new policy agenda - the case of subsidized credit, *Public administration and development*, vol. 16, pp. 21-30.

Crow, B. (1994) Finance in context: exploring diverse exchange conditions. In: F.J.A. Bouman and O. Hospes (eds), *Financial landscapes reconstructed: the fine art of mapping development*. Boulder: Westview.

Dandekar, V.M., P.V. Sukhate and C. Rangarajan et al. (1993) *Report of the expert group on estimation of proportion and number of poor*. New Delhi: Government of India, perspective planning division.

Datta K. and G.A. Jones (eds) (1999) *Housing and finance in developing countries*. London: Routledge.

Davidson, F. (1988) Capacity building for urban management. International Development Institutions: Strategies to Maximise Impact. Paper presented at the seminar 'Capacity Building for Urban Management. New Challenges, New Approaches'. 17-18 December. Rotterdam: IHS.

Davidson, F. and M. Peltenburg (1993) *Government and NGOs/CBOs working together for better cities*. Working Papers Series no. 6. Rotterdam: IHS.

Deb, K. (1997) Role of the state in city growth: the case of Hyderabad city. In: R.S. Melkote and S. Prasad (eds), *The Third World City: emerging contours*. Hyderabad: Delta.

Desai, V. (1996) Access to power and participation, *Third World Planning Review*, vol. 18, no. 2, pp. 217-242.

Desai, A.R. and S.D. Pillai (1972) *A profile of an Indian slum*. Bombay: Popular Prakashan.

De Soto, H. (1989) *The other path: the invisible revolution in the Third World*. New York: Harper & Row.

De Swaan, A. (1996) Onderlinge fondsen: toen en hier, nu en daar. Informele spaar- en verzekeringskassen in het negentiende-eeuwse Westen en in de tegenwoordige buiten-westerse wereld. In: M. Van der Linden and J. Sluijs (eds), *Onderlinge hulpfondsen: historische en etnografische essays*. Amsterdam: Stichting beheer IISG.

Devas. N. (1999) *Who runs cities? The relationship between urban governance, service delivery and poverty*. Urban governance, partnership and poverty theme paper 4. Birmingham: University of Birmingham.

Devine, J. (1996) *NGOs: changing fashion or fashioning change?* Occasional paper 02/96, Centre for development studies. Bath: University of Bath.

De Wit, J. (1989) *Slum dwellers, slum leaders and the government apparatus: relations between actors in slum upgrading in Madras*. Urban Research Working Papers, no. 8. Amsterdam: Vrije Universiteit.

De Wit, J. (1991) *Stedelijke armoede in India*. Utrecht: Landelijke India Werkgroep.

De Wit, J. (1993) *Poverty, policy and politics in Madras slums: dynamics of survival, gender and leadership*. PhD thesis. Amsterdam: Vrije Universiteit.

De Zwart, F. (1992) Mobiele bureaucratie: manipulaties met overplaatsingen van ambtenaren in India. PhD thesis. Amsterdam: University of Amsterdam.

Douglas, M. (1995) *Urban environmental management at the grass roots: towards a theory of community action*. East-West Center Working Papers, Environment Series, no. 42. Honolulu: East-West Center.

Edwards, M. and D. Hulme (1992) Scaling-up the development impact of NGOs: concepts and experiences. Scaling-up in urban areas. In: M. Edwards and D. Hulme (eds), *Making a difference: NGOs and development in a changing world*. London: Earthscan.

Elias, N. (1990) *Het civilisatieproces: sociogenetische en psychogenetische onderzoekingen*. Aula paperback 148. Utrecht: Het Spectrum.

Ellemers, J.E. (1969) Patronage in sociologisch perspectief, *Sociologische Gids*, vol. vi, pp. 432-440.

Environment & Urbanization (2000) UNCHS (Habitat) – the global campaign for good governance, *Environment & Urbanization*, vol. 12, no. 1, pp. 197-202.

ESCAP (Economic and Social Commission for Asia and the Pacific) (1991) *Guidelines on community-based housing finance and innovative credit systems for low-income households*. Bangkok: ESCAP

Fapohunda, E.R. (1988) The nonpooling household: a challenge to theory. In: D. Dwyer and J. Bruce (eds), *A home divided: women and income in the Third World*. Stanford/California: Stanford University Press.

Ferguson, B. (1999) Micro-finance of housing: a key to housing the low or moderate income majority?, *Environment and Urbanization*, vol. 11, no. 1, pp. 185-199.

Fiori, J. and R. Raminez (1992) Notes on the self-help housing critique: towards a conceptual framework for the analysis of self-help housing policies in developing countries. In: K. Mathéy (ed.) *Beyond self-help housing.* München: Profil Verlag & London: Mansell.

Fine, B. (1999) The development state is dead – long live social capital?, *Development and Change*, vol. 30, pp. 1-19.

Folbre, N. (1994) *Who pays for the kids? Gender and the structures of constraint.* London, NewYork: Routledge.

Frontline (1994) Andhra Pradesh, Special Feature. August, 26.

Fukuyama, F. (1995) *Trust: the social virtues and the creation of prosperity.* New York: Free Press

Gambetta, D. (1988) *Trust, making and breaking co-operative relations.* Oxford: Basil Blackwell.

GAP (Government of Andhra Pradesh) (1991) Government Order Ms. No. 331.

GAP (n.a.) *Shelter for all.* Hyderabad: Andhra Pradesh State Housing Department.

GAP (1994a) *Report of the Comptroller and General Auditor general of India for the year ended 31 March 1993*, no 1., commercial, Hyderabad: GAP.

GAP (1994b) *Recommendations of the collectors' conference, 2-4 May 1994.* Hyderabad: Revenue Department.

Garilao, E.D. (1987) Indigenous NGOs as strategic institutions: managing the relationship with government and resource agencies, *World Development*, vol. 15, supplement, pp. 113-120.

Ghate, P.B. (1994) Lending to micro enterprises through NGOs in the Philippines. In: F.J.A. Bouman and O. Hospes (eds), *Financial landscapes reconstructed: the fine art of mapping development.* Boulder: Westview.

Ghate, P., A. Das-Gupta, M. Lamberte, N. Poapongsakorn, D. Prabowo and A. Rahman (1992) *Informal finance: some findings from Asia.* Manila: Oxford University Press.

Giddens, A. (1995) *The consequences of modernity.* Blackwool: Polity Press.

GOI (Government of India) (1992) *National housing policy.* Delhi: Ministry of Urban Development.

Gonzáles de la Rocha, M. (1994) *The resources of poverty: women and survival in a Mexican city.* Oxford, etc: Blackwell.

Gopi, K.N. and Kalpana Markandey (1994) *Energy environment and well-being.* New Delhi: Concept.

Gupta, D.B., S. Kaul and R. Pandey (1993) *Housing and India's urban poor.* New Delhi: Har-Anand.

Haddad, L., J. Hoddinott and H. Alderman (1994) *Intrahousehold resource allocation: an overview.* Policy Research Working Paper 1255. Washington: World Bank, Policy Research Department.

Hancock, K.E. (1993) 'Can pay? Won't pay?' or economic principles of 'affordability', *Urban Studies*, vol. 30, no. 1, pp. 127-145.

Harriss, B. (1981) *Transitional trade and rural development: the nature and role of agricultural trade in a South Indian district*. New Delhi: Vikas.

Hasan, A. (1997) *Urban housing policies and approaches in a changing Asian context*. Karachi: City Press.

Hechter, M. (1988) *Principles of group solidarity*. Berkeley, etc.: University of California Press.

Hilhorst, T. and H. Oppenoorth (1992) *Financing women's enterprise: beyond barriers and bias*. Amsterdam: Royal Tropical Institute.

Hill, P. (1989) *Development economics on trial: the anthropological case for a proscecution*. Cambridge: Cambridge University Press.

Holmström, M. (1984) *Industry and inequality: the social anthropology of Indian labour*. Cambridge, etc.: Cambridge University Press/Bombay, etc: Orient Longman.

Holton, R.J. (1992) *Economy and society*. London/New York: Routledge.

Hospes, O. (1992a) People that count, Paper presented at the Workshop on Women's Use of Rotating Credit Associations, Oxford, 7th-9th January.

Hospes, O. (1992b) Evolving forms of informal finance in an Indonesian town, In: D.W. Adams and D.A. Fitchett (eds), *Informal finance in low-income countries*. Westview Press, Boulder.

Hospes, O. (1996) *People that count: changing savings and credit practices in Ambon, Indonesia*. Amsterdam: Thesis publishers.

HUDCO (1995) *Guidelines for loans for housing of rural and urban poor*. New Delhi: HUDCO.

Hulchanski, J.D. (1995) The concept of housing affordability: six contemporary uses of the housing expenditure-to-income ratio, *Housing Studies*, vol. 10, no. 4, pp. 471-491.

Hulme, D. (1994) Social development research and the third sector: NGOs as users and subjects of social inquiry. In: D. Booth (ed.), *Rethinking social development: theory, research and practice*. Essex: Longman scientific & technical.

Hulme, D. (2000) Impact assessment methodologies for microfinance: theory, experience and better practice, *World Development*, vol. 28, no. 1, pp. 79-98.

Igel, B. and H. Srinivas (1996) The co-optation of low-income borrowers by informal credit suppliers: a credit delivery model for squatter housing, *Third World Planning Review*, vol. 18, no. 3, pp. 287-305.

Izumida Y. (1992) The Kou in Japan: a precursor of modern finance, In: D.W. Adams and D.A. Fitchett (eds), *Informal finance in low-income countries*, Westview Press, Boulder.

Jatkar, S.D. (1993) The Marwari community of Hyderabad. In: M. Radha Krishna Sarma, K.D. Abhyankar and V.G. Bilolikar (eds), *History of Hyderabad District 1879-1950 (Yugabda 4981-5052)*, volume II. Hyderabad: Itihas Sankalana Samiti (Bharatiya).

Johnson, S (1998) Programme impact assessment in micro-finance: the need for analysis of real markets, *IDS Bulletin*, vol. 29, no. 4, pp. 21-30.

Johnson, S. and B. Rogaly (1997) *Microfinance and poverty reduction*. Oxford: Oxfam.

Jones, G.A. and K. Datta (1999) From self-help to self-finance: the changing focus of urban research and policy. In: K. Datta and G.A. Jones (eds), *Housing and finance in developing countries*. London: Routledge.

Jones, G.A. and D. Mitlin (1999) Housing finance and non-governmental organizations in developing countries. In: K. Datta and G.A. Jones (eds), *Housing and finance in developing countries*. London: Routledge.

Jones, G.A. and P.M. War (1995) The blind men and the elephant: a critic's reply, *Habitat International*, vol. 19, no. 1, pp. 61-72.

Jørgensen, N.O. (1977) *Housing finance for low-income groups with special reference to developing countries*. Rotterdam: Bouwcentrum.

JPS Associates (1993) *Baseline financial profiles of housing finance companies in India*. New Delhi: JPS.

Karmali, N (1998) Microsoft's passage to India, Forbes Global, 27 July. Available: www.forbes.com/global/1998/0727/0108030a.html

Kaufman, D. and D.L. Lindauer (1984) *Income transfers within extended families to meet basic needs; the evidence from El Salvador*. World Bank staff working papers no. 644. Washington, D.C.: The World Bank.

Keare, D.H and S. Parri (1982) *Evaluation of shelter programs for the urban poor: principal findings*. World Bank staff working papers, no. 547. Washington, D.C.: World Bank.

Khalidi, O. (1988) *Hyderabad: after the fall*. Kansas: Hyderabad Historical Society Wichita.

Khusro, A.M. (1958) *Economic and social effects of jagirdari abolition and land reforms in Hyderabad*. Hyderabad: Osmania University.

Kim, Kyung-Hwan (1997) Housing finance and urban infrastructure finance, *Urban Studies*, vol. 34, no. 10, pp. 1597-1620.

Klak, T. and M. Smith (1999) The political economy of formal sector housing finance in Jamaica. In: K. Datta and G.A. Jones (eds), *Housing and finance in developing countries*. London: Routledge.

Knorringa, P. (1995) *Economics of collaboration in producer-trader relations: Transaction regimes between market and hierarchy in the Agra footwear cluster, India*. PhD thesis. Amsterdam: Vrije Universiteit.

Knorringa, P. (1999) Trust and distrust in artisan-trader relations in the Agra footwear industry, India. In: P. Smets, H. Wels and J. van Loon (eds), *Trust and co-operation: symbolic exchange and moral economies in an age of cultural differentiation*. Amsterdam: Het Spinhuis.

Kooiman, D. (1998) The Nizam's last victory: Hyderabad on eve of Second World War, *Economic and Political Weekly*, vol. XXXIII, no. 12, pp. 645-660.

Korten, D.C. (1986) Micro-policy reform – the role of private voluntary development agencies. In: D.C. Korten (ed.), *Community management: Asian experience and perspectives*. West Hartford: Kumarian.

Kundu, A. (1993) *In the name of the urban poor: access to basic amenities*. New Delhi/London/ Newbury Park: Sage.

Kundu, A. (1996) Access of urban poor to basic services - the changing policy perspective. In: K. Singh and F. Steinberg (eds), *Urban India in crisis*. New Delhi: New Age.

Kuper H. and S. Kaplan (1975) Voluntary associations in an urban township, *African Studies*, Kraus Reprint [1944] vol. 3, pp. 178-186.

Lall, V.D. (1988) Savings in the midst of urban poverty: need for a new approach to assess poverty, *Nagarlok*, vol. xx, no. 4, pp. 11-21.

Lall, V.D. (1994) Institutional mechanism to reach out development inputs for Delhi urban poor. Theme paper for policy seminar 'Finance & Development Inputs for the Urban Poor in Delhi'. New Delhi: Delhi Slum Improvement Board/ Society for Development Studies.

Lee, M. (1990) The affordability criterion: inefficient, inequitable and immoral? .... In: Mulk Raj and P. Nientied (eds), *Housing and income in Third World urban development*. New Delhi, Bombay & Calcutta: Oxford University Press & IBH.

Lenten, R. (1991) *Cooking under the vulcanoes: communal kitchens in the southern Peruvian City of Arequipa*. Latin America Studies no. 68. Amsterdam: CEDLA.

Leonard, K. (1971) The Hyderabad political system and its participants, *The Journal of Asian Studies*, vol. xxx, no. 3, pp. 569-582.

Lewis, O. (1975) The culture of poverty. In: J. Friedl and N.J. Chrisman (eds), *City ways: A selective reader in anthropology*. New York: Crowell.

Lloyd, P. (1979) *Slums of hope? Shanty towns of the third world*. Middlesex, etc.: Penguin.

Lont, H. (1999) When we are broke ... Managing unbalanced cycles of money in urban households, Yogyakarta, Indonesia. In: P. Smets (ed.), *Money and culture: examples from Indonesia, South Africa and India*. Urban research working papers no. 44. Amsterdam: Vrije Universiteit.

Luhmann (1979) *Trust and power*. Chichester, etc: John Wiley & sons.

Madway, D.M. (1989) *Revision of India's mortgage foreclosure laws: report to the government of India*, Ministry of Urban Development. Washington, D.C.: The Urban Institute.

Majumdar, T.K. (1983) *Urbanising poor: a sociological study of low-income migrant communities in the metropolitan city of Delhi.* New Delhi: Lancers.

Malliswari, M.N. (1988) *Informal sector of Hyderabad: an analysis of credit policy effects.* M.Phil. thesis. Hyderabad: Centre for Economic and Social Studies.

Malpezzi, S. (1990) Urban housing and financial markets: some international comparisons, *Urban Studies*, vol. 27, no. 6, pp 971-1022.

Malpezzi, S. (1991) Discounted cash flow analysis: present value models of housing programmes and policies. In: A.G. Tipple and K.G. Willis (eds), *Housing the poor in the developing world: methods of analysis, case studies and policy.* London: Routledge.

Malpezzi, S. (1994) 'Getting the incentives right': a reply to Robert-Jan Baken and Jan van der Linden, *Third World Planning Review*, vol. 16, no. 4, pp. 451-466.

Mangin, W. (1967) Latin American squatter settlement; a problem and a solution, *Latin American Research Review*, no. 2, pp. 65-98.

Mangin, W. (1970) *Peasants in cities: readings in the anthropology of urbanization.* Boston: Houghton Mifflin Company.

Marsden, D. (1990) *A study of officials: an organizational analysis of the Urban Community Development Department, Municipal Corporation of Hyderabad.* University of Wales, Swansea Papers in International Development No. 4.

Marshall, G. (ed.) (1994) *The concise Oxford dictionary of sociology.* Oxford: Oxford University Press.

Martinussen, J. (1997) *Society, state & market: a guide to competing theories of development.* London/ New Jersey: Zed Books.

Mathéy, K. (1992a) *Beyond self-help housing.* München/London: Profil Verlag/ Mansell.

Mathéy, K. (1992b) Positions on self-help housing: bibliographical notes. In: K. Mathéy (ed.), *Beyond Self-Help Housing.* München/London: Profil Verlag/Mansell.

Matin, I., D. Hulme and S. Rutherford (1999) *Financial services for the poor and poorest: deepening understanding to improve provision.* Financial and Development Research Programme. Working Paper Series, paper no. 9. Manchester: University of Manchester.

McLeod, R. (1994) A changing financial landscape: the evolution of finance policy in Indonesia. In: F.J.A. Bouman and O. Hospes (eds), *Financial landscapes reconstructed: the fine art of mapping development.* Boulder, etc.: Westview.

Mehta, M. (1994) *Down marketing housing finance through community based financial systems: strategy for down marketing.* New Delhi: Abt Associates/ Indo USAID Housing Finance Expansion Programme.

Mehta M. and D. Mehta (1991) Housing finance system and urban poor, *Economic and Political Weekly*, april 27, pp. 1107-1114.

Mencher, J.P. (1988) Women's work and poverty: women's contribution to household maintenance in South India. In: D. Dwyer and J. Bruce (eds), *A home divided: women and income in the Third World*. Stanford/California: Stanford University Press.

Merrett, S. and K. Russell (1994) Non-conventional finance for self-help housing, *Habitat International*, vol. 18, no. 2, pp. 57-69.

Microcredit Summit (1997) *Declaration and plan of action*. Washington, D.C.: Micro Credit Summit.

Minhas, B.S., L.R. Jain and S.D. Tendulkar (1991) Declining Incidence of Poverty in the 1980s: evidence versus Artefacts. *Economic and Political Weekly*, vol. xxvi, no. 27/28, pp. 1673-1682.

Ministry of Urban Affairs & Employment (1999) *Urban Land Ceiling Act Repealed*. Available: urbanindia.nic.in/new.htm Date: 4 June 2001.

Misztal, B.A. (1996) *Trust in modern societies*, Cambridge: Polity Press

Mitlin, D. (1997) Building with credit: housing finance for low-income households, *Third World Planning Review*, vol. 19, no. 1, pp. 21-50.

Mitlin, D. (2000) Addressing urban poverty: increasing incomes, reducing cost, and securing representation, *Development in Practice*, vol. 10. no. 2, pp. 204-215.

Mitlin, D. and D. Satterthwaite (1992) Scaling-up in urban areas. In: M. Edwards and D. Hulme (eds), *Making a difference: NGOs and development in a changing world*. London: Earthscan.

Mitra, B.C. and P. Nientied (1989) *Land supply and housing expenses for low income families: a rational for government intervention*. Urban research working papers no.19. Amsterdam: Vrije Universiteit.

Montgomery, R. (1996) Disciplining or protecting the poor? Avoiding the social costs of peer pressure in micro-credit schemes, *Journal of international development*, vol. 8, no. 2, pp. 289-305.

Moore, H.L. (1991) *Feminism and anthropology*. Cambridge: Polity.

Moser, C.O.N. (1983) The problem of evaluating community participation in urban development. In: C.O.N. Moser (ed.), *Evaluating community participation in urban development projects*. Working paper no. 14. London: DPU, University College London.

Moser, C.O.N. (1989) Gender planning in the Third World: meeting practical and strategic gender needs, *World Development*, vol. 17, no. 11, pp. 1799-1825.

Moser, C.O.N. (1992) Women and self-help housing projects: a conceptual framework for analysis and policy making. In: K. Mathéy (ed.), *Beyond self-help housing*. München: Profil Verlag and London: Mansell.

Moser, C.O.N. (1998) The asset vulnerability framework: reassessing urban poverty reduction strategies, *World Development*, vol. 26, no.1, pp. 1-19.

Mosley, P. and D. Hulme (1998) Microenterprise finance: is there a conflict between growth and poverty alleviation?, *World Development*, vol. 26, no. 5, pp. 783-790.

Nagarajan, V. (1996) Institutionalising savings and credit groups: Strategic issues for NGOs. Paper for the workshop on organizational options for savings and credit groups wishing to formalize and expand their operations. 26-27 March, India, Cochin.

Nagarajan , G., R.L. Meyer and K. Ouatara (1994) Financial intermediation by NGOs: implications for indigenous village groups in the Gambia, *Savings and Development*, vol. XVIII, no. 2, pp. 211-223.

Naidu, R. (1990) *Old cities, new predicaments: a study of Hyderabad*. New Delhi, etc.: Sage.

Narsing Rao, B. (1997) Changing political profile of Hyderabad. In: R.S. Melkote and S. Prasad (eds), *The Third World city: emerging contours*. Hyderabad: Delta.

Navajas, S., M. Schreiner, R.L. Meyer, C. Gonzales-Vega and J. Rodriguez-Meza (2000) Microcredit and the poorest of the poor: theory and evidence from Bolivia, *World Development*, vol. 28, no. 2, pp. 333-346.

Nayani, P. (1987) Illegal Subdivision of land and housing consolidation in Hyderabad, *Urban India*, vol. 7, no.2, pp. 54-70.

Nayar C.P.S. (1973) *Chit Finance: an exploratory study on the working of chit funds*, Vora and Co, Bombay.

Nayar C.P.S. (1986) Can a traditional financial technology co-exist with modern financial technologies?: The Indian experience, *Savings and Development*, no. 1, pp. 31-56.

Nayar C.P.S. (1992) Strengths of informal financial institutions: examples from India. In: D.W. Adams and D.A. Fitchett (eds), *Informal finance in low-income countries*. Boulder, etc.: Westview.

NHB (1990) *National Housing Bank*. New Delhi: NHB.

NHB (1991) *Housing finance companies: guidelines and directions*. New Delhi/ Bombay: NHB.

Nientied, P., E. Meijer and J. van der Linden (1982) *Karachi squatter settlement upgrading: improvement or displacement?* Bijdragen tot de sociale geografie en planologie, nr. 5. Amsterdam: Vrije Universiteit.

Nientied, P. and J. van der Linden (1988) Approaches to low-income housing in the Third World. In: J. Gugler (ed.), *The Urbanization of the Third World*. Oxford: Oxford University Press.

NIUA (National Institute of Urban Affairs) (1992) *The informal finance for urban housing status and prospects*. Research Study Series, no. 47. New Delhi: NIUA.

NIUA (1995) *Handbook urban statistics*. New Delhi: NIUA.

Noponen, H. (1991) The dynamics of work and survival for the urban poor: a gender analysis of panel data from Madras, *Development and Change*, vol. 22, no. 2, pp. 233-260.

North, D.C. (1991) *Institutions, institutional change and economic performance*. Cambridge, etc.: Cambridge University Press.

Okpala, Don C.I. (1994) Financing housing in developing countries: a review in developing countries: a review of the pitfalls and potentials in the development of formal housing finance systems, *Urban Studies*, vol. 31, no. 9, pp. 1571-1586.

Olson, M. (1980) *The logic of collective action: public goods and the theory of groups*. Cambridge: Harvard University Press.

Olson, M. (1982) *The rise and decline of nations: economic growth, stagflation and social rigidities*. New Haven, London: Yale University Press.

Ostrom, E. (1996) Crossing the great divide: coproduction, synergy, and development, *World Development*, vol. 24, no. 6, pp. 1073-1087.

Papanek, H. and L. Schwede (1988) Women are good with money: earning and managing in an Indonesian city, *Economic and Political Weekly*, October 29, pp. WS 73-84.

Parthasarathy, R. (ed.) (1983) *Andhra Pradesh District Gazetteers*, Hyderabad. Hyderbad: Government of Andhra Pradesh.

Patel, S. (1999) Interpreting gender and housing finance in community perspective: the SPARC, Mahila Milan and NSDF experience. In: K. Datta and G.A. Jones (eds), *Housing and finance in developing countries*. London: Routledge.

Patel, S., J. Bolnick and D. Mitlin (2000) Sharing experiences and changing lives. Paper presented at the 'Urban Community Exchanges' meeting at DFID, London on 26 January.

Patel, S. and S. Burra (1994) Access to housing finance for the urban poor: institutional innovations in India, *Cities*, vol. 11, no. 6, pp. 393-397.

Peterson, G.E., G.T. Kingsley and J.P. Telgarsky (1991) *Urban economics and national development*. Washington D.C.: The Urban Institute.

Platt, R. (1997) *Ensuring effective provision of low cost housing finance in India: an in-depth case analysis*. Working Paper no. 9725. Asia Pacific Business and Development Research Unit. Bradford: University of Bradford.

Platteau, J.-P. (1988) *Traditional systems of social security and hunger insurance: some lessons from the evidence pertaining to third world village societies*. DEP, no. 15, London: London School of Economics.

Post, J. (1999) The problems and potentials of privatising solid waste management in Kumasi, Ghana, *Habitat International*, vol. 23, no. 2, pp. 201-215.

Pugh, C. (1990) *Housing and urbanisation: a study of India*. New Delhi/Newbury Park/London: Sage.

Pugh, C. (1994) Development of housing finance and the global strategy for shelter, *Cities*, vol. 11, no. 6, pp. 384-392.

Pugh, C. (1997a) The changing roles of self-help in housing and urban policies, 1950-1996, *Third World Planning Review*, vol. 19, no. 1, pp. 91-109.

Pugh, C. (1997b) Viewpoint. The World Bank's millennial theory of the state: further attempts to reconcile the political and the economic, *Third World Planning Review*, vol. 19, no. 3, pp. iii-xiv.

Putnam, R.D. (1993) *Making democracy work: civic traditions in modern Italy. Princeton*, New Jersey: Princeton University Press.

Quinines, B.R. (1987) Linkages between formal and informal sectors in rural financial markets: the role of self help groups. Paper presented for the workshop on issues in rural savings mobilisation. Dhaka, 27-29 April.

Radakrishna, R. and S. Galab (1997) Informal mutual credit associations in India: a case of slums in Hyderabad (draft report). Hyderabad: Centre for Economic and Social Studies.

Radhakrishnan S. et al. (1975) *Chit funds*, Madras: Institute for Financial Management and Research.

Rakodi, C. (1993) Planning for whom? In: N. Devas and C. Rakodi (eds), *Managing fast growing cities: new approaches to urban planning and management in the developing world*. Essex: Longman/ New York: John Wiley & Sons.

Reddy, A. Malla (1991) *Administration of slum improvement in Andhra Pradesh: a case study of Hyderabad*. Ph.D. thesis. Hyderabad: Osmania University.

Reddy, G.V. Krishna (1992) *The law of pawnbrokers and moneylenders in A.P.* Hyderabad: Asia Law House.

Reddy, Narayan K. (1996) *Urban redevelopment: a study of high-rise buildings*. New Delhi: Concept.

Reddy, V. Ramakrishna (1987) *Economic history of Hyderabad State (Warangal Suba: 1911-1950)*. Delhi: Gian.

Renaud, B. (1984) *Housing and financial institutions in developing countries: an overview*. World Bank Staff Working Papers, no. 658. Washington, D.C.: The World Bank.

Renaud, B. (1985) *Financing shelter*. Water supply and urban development department, operations policy staff. Discussion paper report no. UDD-78. Washington, D.C.: World Bank.

Renaud, B. (1987a) Another look at housing finance in developing countries, *Cities*, February, pp. 28-34.

Renaud, B. (1987b) Financing shelter. In : L. Rodwin (ed.), *Shelter, settlement and development*. Boston: Allen & Unwin.

Roberts, P. (1991) Anthropological perspectives on the household, *IDS Bulletin*, vol. 22, no. 1, pp. 60-64.

Rodell, M.J. (1990) Reviving affordability theory. In: M. Raj and P. Nientied (eds), *Housing and income in Third World urban development*. New Delhi, etc.: Oxford & IBH.

Rosenberg, R. (2000) Apexes: just the facts, ma'am. Available: Devfinance@lists.acs.ohio-state.edu, Date: 9 March 22:50:43.

Roy, K. (1987) Urban shelter programme and cost recovery issues, *Nagarlok*, vol. XIX, no. 4, pp. 85-97.

Rutherford, S. (2000) *The poor and their money*. New Delhi: Oxford University Press.

Sahlins, M. (1974) *Stone age economics*. Chicago: Aldine.

Sandhu, R.V. (1988) Savings and indebtedness among the poor, *Nagarlok*, vol. xx, no. 4, pp. 66-73.

Santos, M. (1979) *The shared space: the two circuits of the urban economy in underdeveloped countries*. London/New York: Methuen.

Sanyal, B. and V. Mukhija (2000) Institutional pluralism and housing delivery: a case of unforeseen conflicts in Mumbai, India. Report prepared for the Management Development and Governance Division of UNDP.

Sarupria, S. (1997) Political economy of city growth Hyderabad: a tale of three cities. In: R.S. Melkote and S. Prasad (eds), *The Third World City: emerging contours*. Hyderabad: Delta.

Satthertwaite, D. (1997) Urban poverty: reconsidering its scale and nature, *IDS Bullletin*, vol. 28, no. 2, pp. 9-21.

Saunders, P. (1981) *Social theory and the urban question*. London, etc.: Hutchinson.

Schenk-Sandbergen, L. (1988) *Poverty and survival: Kudumbi female domestic servants and their households in Alleppey (Kerala)*. New Delhi: Manohar.

Schmidt, R.H. and E. Kropp (1987) *Rural Finance: guiding principles*. Eschborn.

Schmidt, R.H. and C.P. Zeitlinger (1996a) Prospects, problems and potential of credit granting NGOs, *Journal of International Development*, vol. 2, no. 2, pp. 241-258.

Schmidt, R.H. and C.P. Zeitlinger (1996b) The efficiency of credit granting NGOs in Latin America, *Savings and Development*, vol. xx, no. 3, pp. 351-381.

Schmink, M. (1984) Household economic strategies: review and research agenda, *Latin American Research Review*, vol. XIX, no. 3, pp. 87-101.

Schrader, H. (1991a) *The socio-economic function of moneylenders in expanding economies*. Working Paper no. 153. Bielefeld: Sociology of Development Research Centre.

Schrader, H. (1991b) *Rotating saving and credit associations – institutions in the "middle rung" of development*, Southeast Asia Programme Working Paper no. 148, University of Bielefeld, Faculty of Sociology, Bielefeld.

Schrader, H. (1992) The socio-economic function of moneylenders in expanding economies: the case of the Chettiars, *Savings and Development*, vol. XVI, no. 1, pp. 68-81.

Schrieder G.R. and C.E. Cuevas (1992) Informal financial groups in Cameroon, In: D.W. Adams and D.A. Fitchett (eds), *Informal finance in low-income countries*. Boulder/San Francisco/Oxford: Westview Press.

Scoggins, A. (1996) From savings and credit groups to community-based financial institutions: the issue of institutionalization. Paper for the workshop on organizational options for savings and credit groups wishing to formalize and expand their operations. 26-27 March, Cochin (India).

Scott, J.C. (1976) *The moral economy of the peasant: rebellion and subsistence in Southeast Asia*. New Haven/London: Yale University Press.

Scott, J.C. (1993) *Every day forms of resistance*. Occasional papers series no. 15. Yokohama: Prime.

Seibel, H.D. (1997) *Upgrading, downgrading, linking, innovating: microfinance development strategies – A System Perspective*. Economic and sociology occasional paper no. 2371. Columbus: Ohio State University.

Seibel H.D. and B.P. Shrestha (1988) Dhikuti: the small businessman's informal self help bank in Nepal, *Savings and Development*, vol. XII, no.2, pp. 183-198.

Seligman, A.B. (1997) *The problem of trust*. Princeton/New Jersey: Princeton University Press.

Sen, A. (1983) Economics and the family, *Asian Development Review*, vol. 1, no. 2, pp. 14-26.

Shah, K. (1990) *Community participation in the Hyderabad Urban Community Development Project*. World Bank: Economic Development Institute.

Shaghil, M. (1989) *Islamic economics: a global perspective*. New Delhi: Ashish.

Siembieda, W.J. and E.L. Moreno (1999) From commercial banking systems to non-commercial banking systems in Mexico. In: K. Datta and G.A. Jones (eds), *Housing and finance in developing countries*. London: Routledge.

Singh, A.M. (1978) Women and the family: coping with poverty in the bastis of Delhi. In: A. de Souza (ed.), *The Indian city: poverty, ecology and urban development*. Columbia: South Asia Books/ New Delhi: Manohar.

Singh, K. (1983) Structure of interest rates on consumption loans in an Indian village. In: J.D. Von Pischke, D.W. Adams and G. Donald (eds), *Rural financial markets in developing countries: their use and abuse*. Baltimore/London: John Hopkins University Press.

Singh, Prem Prakash (1994) *A review of the role of housing development finance corporation in promoting housing development in India*. MP thesis. New Delhi: School of Planning and Architecture.

Sivasubrahmanyam, K. and D.V.L.N.V. Prasada Rao (1992) *Problems and prospects of housing the rural poor: a study of WSHP of Andhra Pradesh.* Hyderabad: National Institute of Rural Development.

Smets, P. (1992) *My stomach is my bishi: savings and credit associations in Sangli, India.* Urban research working papers, no. 30. Amsterdam: Vrije Universiteit.

Smets, P. (1995) Poor and in need for a house in the city! The government is there to help, but who is really helping who?, *Nagarlok,* vol. XXVIII, no. 4, pp. 78-92.

Smets, P. (1996a) *Informal housing finance in Hyderabad, India.* Urban research working papers, no. 40. Amsterdam: Vrije Universiteit.

Smets, P. (1996b) Community-based finance systems and their potential for urban self-help in a new South Africa, *Development Southern Africa,* vol. 13, no. 2, pp. 173-187.

Smets, P. (1996c) Groepskredieten: bank voor de armen succesvol, *India Nu,* juli-augustus, pp. 19-21.

Smets, P. (1997a) Private housing finance in India: reaching down-market? *Habitat International,* vol. 21, no. 1, pp.1-15.

Smets, P. (1997b) From lending towards marketing: toilet schemes in Andhra Pradesh, India. In: Report of conference proceedings *'Global and local development: new agendas, new partnerships'.* Edinburgh: Centre for Environment and Human Settlements. pp. 56-66.

Smets, P. (1998) Money-go-rounds for women: finance as instrument or as ultimate goal in lottery ROSCAs, *Anthropos,* vol. 93, no.1/3, pp. 209-215.

Smets, P. (1999) Housing finance trapped in a dilemma of perceptions: affordability criteria for the urban poor questioned, *Housing Studies,* vol. 14, no. 6, pp. 821-838.

Smets, P. (2000) ROSCAs as a source of housing finance for the urban poor: an analysis of self-help practices from Hyderabad, India, *Community Development Journal,* vol. 35, no. 1, pp. 16-30.

Smets, P. (2001) Self-help housing finance in Hyderabad: exploitation or hope for the improvement of slum housing. In: R.S. Sandhu, S.S. Minhas & J. Sandhu (eds), *Sustainable Human Settlements: The Asian Experience.* Jaipur, New Delhi: Rawat.

Smets, P. and E. Bähre (2001) ROSCA, ASCRA and SAVA: beyond the models. Paper presented at the international conference 'Livelihood, savings and debt in a changing world' Wageningen, 14-16 May.

Smets, P. and A. Broekman (1996) Turkse vrouwen en hun güns in Amsterdam. In: M. van der Linden and J. Sluijs (eds), *Onderlinge hulpfondsen: historische en etnografische essays.* Amsterdam: IISG.

Smets, P. and E. Hanssen (1996) The dynamics of patronage in the development of illegal settlements, *Urban India,* vol. xvi, no. 1, pp. 91-106

Smets, P. and A. Sivaramakrishnan (1997) Can money help urban community development? The case of Hyderabad. In: R.S. Melkote and S. Prasad (eds), *The Third World City: Emerging Contours*. Hyderabad: Delta.

Smets, P., H. Wels and J. van Loon (1999) *Trust & co-operation: symbolic exchange and moral economies in an age of cultural differentiation*. Amsterdam: Het Spinhuis.

Soen D. and P. de Comarmond (1972) Savings associations among the Bamilèkè: traditional and modern cooperation in Southwest Cameroon, *American Anthropologist*, vol. 74, no. 5, pp. 1170- 1179.

South Commission (1990) *The challenge to the South: the report of the South Commission*. Oxford, etc.: Oxford University Press.

SPARC (1996) Construction finance related experiences of SPARC, NSDF and Mahila Milan. Paper presented at the workshop 'Women and shelter finance', 22-24 January, Ahmedabad.

SPARC (1999) Another mela for housing in Hyderabad, 29th 30th 31st May 99. Available: sparc.ilbom.ernet.in!sheela@ilbom.ernet.in May 24 at 3:57:39 pm.

Srinivas, H. (1996) Development of a housing finance triangle linking people's organizations, NGOs, and commercial banks in developing countries (draft). At: The Virtual Library on Microcredit. Available: www.soc.titech.ac.jp/icm/phd-abstract.html May 29 at 20:45.

Steinberg, F. (1994) Non-governmental organizations (NGOs) and community based organizations (CBOs) in India's Habitat sector: Coming to the forefront? Paper presented at the high level policy seminar on Integrated Human Settlement Strategy. Society for Development Studies, New Delhi.

Stokes, C. (1962) A theory of slums, *Land Economics*, vol. 38, no. 3, pp 187-197.

Streefland, P.H. (1996) Armoede en onderlinge hulp in Zuid-Azië. In: M. van der Linden and J. Sluijs (eds), *Onderlinge hulpfondsen: historische en etnografische essays*. Amsterdam: IISG.

Struyk, R.J. and R.M. Ravicz (1992) *Housing finance in LDCs: India's National Housing Bank as a model*? Urban Institute Report 92-2. Washington D.C: The Urban Institute.

Sundaram, P.S.A. (1988) An institutional framework for housing finance in India, *Habitat International*, vol. 12, no. 4, pp. 21-27.

Taub, R.P. (1998) Making the adaptation across cultures and societies: a report on an attempt to clone the Grameen Bank in Southern Arkansas, *Journal of Developmental Entrepreneurship*, vol. 3, no. 1, pp. 53-69.

Taylor, P. (1999) Democratizing cities: Habitat's global campaign on urban governance, *Habitat Debate*, vol. 5, no. 4, pp. 1, 4-5.

Timberg, T.A. and C.V. Aiyar (1984) Informal credit markets in India, *Economic Development and Cultural Change*, vol. 33, no. 1, pp. 43-59.

Todd, H. (1996) *Cloning Grameen Bank: replicating a poverty reduction model in India, Nepal and Vietnam.* London: Intermediate Technology Publications.

Trialog (1995) Special issue on 'Community Based Housing Finance, no. 47.

Turner, J.F.C. (1968) Housing priorities, settlement patterns and urban development in modernizing countries, *American Institute of Planners' Journal,* vol. XXXIV, no. 6, pp. 354-363.

Turner, J.F.C. (1972) The reeducation of a professional In: J.F.C. Turner and R. Richter (eds), *Freedom to build.* London: McMillan.

Turner, J.F.C. (1976) *Housing by people: towards autonomy in building environments.* London: Marion.

Turner, J.F.C. (1988) An introductory perspective. In: B. Turner (ed.), *Building community: a Third World case book.* London: Community Books.

Umashankar, P.K. and G.K. Misra (1993) *Public-private responsibilities in urban housing.* New Delhi: Reliance/Indian Institute of Public Administration.

UN (United Nations) (1978) *Non-conventional financing of housing for low-income groups.* New York: Department of International Economic and Social Affairs.

UNCHS (Habitat) (1984a) *The promotion of non-conventional approaches to housing finance for low-income groups.* Nairobi: UNCHS.

UNCHS (Habitat) (1984b) *Community-based finance institutions.* Nairobi: UNCHS.

UNCHS (Habitat) (1989) *Mobilization of financial resources for low-income groups.* Nairobi: UNCHS.

UNCHS (Habitat) (1990) *Finance for shelter and services as a component of the global strategy for shelter to the year 2000.* Nairobi: UNCHS.

UNCHS (Habitat) (1991) *Integrating housing finance into the national finance systems of developing countries: exploring the potentials and the problems.* Nairobi: UNCHS.

UNCHS (Habitat) (1996) *An urbanizing world: global report on human settlements.* Oxford, etc.: Oxford University Press.

Van Bastelaer, T. (n.d.) Imperfect information, social capital and the poor's access to credit: a review of the literature. (mimeo)

Van der Harst, J. (1974) *Financing of housing by low-income groups.* Joint Research Project IV for Urban Development and Slum Improvement. Karachi: University of Karachi.

Van der Linden, J. (1983) The squatter's house as a source of security. In: J.W. Schoorl, J.J. van der Linden and K.S. Yap (eds), *Between basti dwellers and bureaucrats: lessons in squatter settlement upgrading in Karachi.* Oxford: Pergamon Press.

Van der Linden, J. (1996) On popular participation in a culture of patronage: patrons and grassroots organization in a sites and services project in Hyderabad, Pakistan, *Environment and Urbanization,* vol. 9, no. 1, pp. 81-90.

Van Lindert, P. (1997) Housing strategies of the urban poor in Latin America. In: T. van Naerssen, M. Rutten and A. Zoomers (eds), *The diversity of development: essays in honour of Jan Kleinpenning*. Assen: Van Gorcum.

Verhagen, K. (1987) *Self-help promotion: a challenge to the NGO community*. Amsterdam/Oegstgeest: Royal Tropical Institute/Cebemo.

Von Benda-Beckmann, F. and K. Von Benda-Beckmann (1994) Coping with insecurity, *Focaal*, no. 22/23, pp. 7-31.

Von Pischke J.D. (1992) ROSCAs: state-of-the-art financial intermediation. In: D.W. Adams and D.A. Fitchett (eds), *Informal finance in low-income countries*. Boulder/San Francisco/Oxford: Westview Press.

Von Pischke, J.D., D.W. Adams and G. Donald (1983) *Rural financial markets in developing countries: their use and abuse*. Baltimore/London: John Hopkins University Press.

Vora, P.P. (1999) Indian housing finance system. Paper presented at the 23rd World Congress of Housing Finance. Rio de Janeiro, Brazil, 5 October 1999.

Ward, P.M. and G.C. Macolo (1992) Articulation theory and self-help housing practice in the 1990s, *International Journal of Urban and Regional Research*, vol. 16, no. 1, pp. 60-80.

Wegener, R.H. (1982) Low-income housing finance: an integrated approach, *Habitat International*, vol. 6, no. 4, pp. 425-439.

Wels, H. (2000) *Fighting over fences: organisational co-operation and reciprocal exchange between the Save Valley Conservancy and its neighbouring communities*. PhD thesis. Amsterdam: Vrije Universiteit.

Wesselink B. (1992) Armoedebestrijding in de nota 'Kleinschalige Bedrijvigheid', *Derde Wereld*, no. 4, pp. 9-13.

Wils, F. (1990) *Income and employment generating activities of NGDOs: an overview*. Working paper series no. 88. The Hague: Institute of Social Studies.

Wilson, G. (1991) Thoughts on the cooperative conflict model of the household in relation to economic method, *IDS Bulletin*, vol. 22, no. 1, pp. 31-36.

Wilson, P.A (1997) Building social capital: a learning agenda for the twenty-first century, *Urban Studies*, vol. 34, no. 6, pp. 745-760.

Woolcock, M. (1998) Social capital and economic development: toward a theoretical synthesis and policy framework, *Theory and Society*, vol. 27, pp. 151-208.

World Bank (1980) *Shelter*. Washington, D.C.: World Bank

World Bank (1991) *Urban policy and economic development: an agenda for the 1990s*. Washington D.C: World Bank.

World Bank (1993a) *Housing: enabling markets to work. A World Bank policy paper*. Washington D.C.: World Bank.

World Bank (1993b) *The Housing Indicators Programme: preliminary results*. Washington, D.C.: World Bank and UNCHS.

Wratten, E. (1995) Conceptualizing urban poverty, *Environment and Urbanization*, vol. 7, no. 1, pp. 11-36.

Wright, G.A.N. (2000) *Microfinance systems: designing quality financial services for the poor*. London/New York: Zed Books/Dhaka: The University Press.

Appendix 1
Map of the surveyed slums and EWS housing schemes

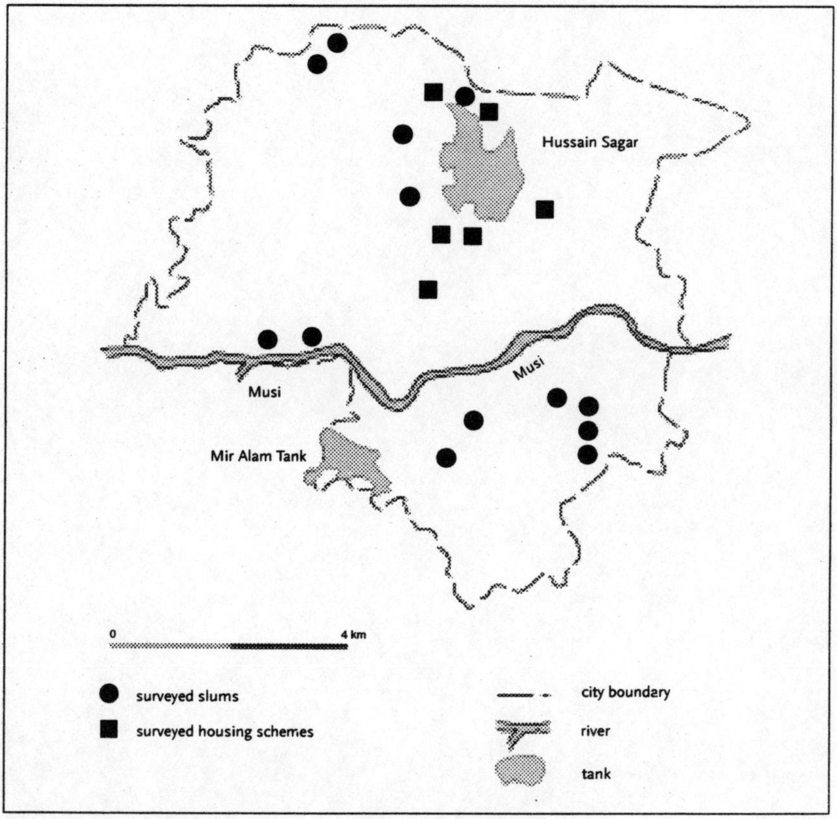

Figure 8 Location of surveyed areas in Hyderabad city

Appendix 2
Sources of housing finance used by interviewed slum dwellers in Hyderabad

Table 43 Two sources of housing finance used for incremental building by interviewed slum dweller households in Hyderabad

Financial sources	Step 1		Step 2		Step 3-5		Total	
	abs.	%	abs.	%	abs.	%	abs.	%
Moneylender/savings	12	20.7	4	22.2	0	0	16	18.6
Chit fund/savings	7	12.1	1	5.6	4	40	12	14
Relative/savings	8	13.8	1	5.6	0	0	9	10.5
Chit fund/relatives	4	6.9	3	16.7	0	0	7	8.1
Employer/savings	4	6.9	1	5.6	2	20	7	8.1
Friend/savings	3	5.2	1	5.6	1	10	5	5.8
Chit fund/employer	2	3.4	1	5.6	0	0	3	3.5
Buying building materials on credit/ savings	2	3.4	1	5.6	0	0	3	3.5
Neighbour/savings	2	3.4	0	0	0	0	2	2.3
Chit fund/pawnbroker	2	3.4	0	0	0	0	2	2.3
Moneylender/relative	2	3.4	0	0	0	0	2	2.3
Colleague/savings	1	1.7	0	0	0	0	1	1.2
Chit fund/moneylender	0	0	1	5.6	0	0	1	1.2
Chit fund/provident fund	0	0	1	5.6	0	0	1	1.2
Chit fund/friend	1	1.7	0	0	0	0	1	1.2
Colleague/employer	1	1.7	0	0	0	0	1	1.2
Colleague/relative	1	1.7	0	0	0	0	1	1.2
Colleague/provident fund	0	0	0	0	1	10	1	1.2
Colleague/credit co-operative	0	0	1	5.6	0	0	1	1.2
Chit fund/credit co-operative	0	0	1	5.6	0	0	1	1.2

Financial sources	Step 1		Step 2		Step 3-5		Total	
	abs.	%	abs.	%	abs.	%	abs.	%
Employer/credit co-operative	0	0	1	5.6	0	0	1	1.2
Employer/pawnbroker	1	1.7	0	0	0	0	1	1.2
Relative/friend	1	1.7	0	0	0	0	1	1.2
Moneylender/remittance	1	1.7	0	0	0	0	1	1.2
Moneylender/provident fund	1	1.7	0	0	0	0	1	1.2
Moneylender/pawnbroker	1	1.7	0	0	0	0	1	1.2
Customer/savings	1	1.7	0	0	0	0	1	1.2
Other	0	0	0	0	2	20	2	2.3
Total	58	100	18	100	10	100	86	100

Source: Own research (N = 86).

Table 44 Three sources of housing finance used for incremental building by interviewed slum dweller households in Hyderabad

Financial sources	Step 1		Step 2		Step 3-5		Total	
	abs.	%	abs.	%	abs.	%	abs.	%
Moneylender/relative/savings	3	10	1	14	0	0	4	10.8
Chit fund/moneylender/ relative	3	10	1	14	0	0	4	10.8
Chit fund/moneylender/savings	3	10	0	0	0	0	3	8.1
Chit fund/relative/savings	3	10	0	0	0	0	3	8.1
Employer/ relative/savings	1	3.5	1	14	0	0	2	5.4
Chit fund/pawnbroker/savings	1	3.5	0	0	1	100	2	5.4
Moneylender/employer/relative	1	3.5	1	14	0	0	2	5.4
Chit fund/moneylender/ pawnbroker	1	3.5	0	0	0	0	1	2.7
Chit fund/moneylender/ colleague	1	3.5	0	0	0	0	1	2.7
Chit fund/moneylender/ provident fund	1	3.5	0	0	0	0	1	2.7
Chit fund/moneylender/ employer	1	3.5	0	0	0	0	1	2.7
Chit fund/credit co-operative/ colleague	1	3.5	0	0	0	0	1	2.7
Chit fund/finance corporation/ savings	1	3.5	0	0	0	0	1	2.7
Chit fund/relative/ employer	1	3.5	0	0	0	0	1	2.7
Moneylender/relative/ credit co-operative	1	3.5	0	0	0	0	1	2.7
Moneylender/employer/savings	1	3.5	0	0	0	0	1	2.7
Employer/relative/savings	1	3.5	0	0	0	0	1	2.7
Relative/savings/ bank loan	1	3.5	0	0	0	0	1	2.7
Relative/ pawnbroker/savings	1	3.5	0	0	0		1	2.7
Relative/ employer/colleague	0	0	1	14	0	0	1	2.7
Relative/ friend/ savings	1	3.5	0	0	0	0	1	2.7
Other	1	3.5	2	29	0	0	3	8.1
Total	29	100	7	100	1	100	37	100

Source: Own research (N = 37).

Table 45 Four and more sources of housing finance used for incremental building by interviewed slum dweller households in Hyderabad

Financial sources	Step 1		Step 2		Step 3-5		Total	
	abs.	%	abs.	%	abs.	%	abs.	%
Chit fund/savings/ relative/employer	1	25	0	0	0	0	1	25
Chit fund/moneylender/ pawnbroker/savings	1	25	0	0	0	0	1	25
Employer/relative/ moneylender/savings	1	25	0	0	0	0	1	25
Chit fund/moneylender/ pawnbroker/friend/relative/ savings	1	25	0	0	0	0	1	25
Total	4	100	0	0	0	0	4	100

Source: Own research (N = 4).

Index